DIVIDED CITIES

Kevin Pogorzelski

DIVIDED
CITIES

The World's Most Passionate
Single City Derbies

First published by Pitch Publishing, 2023

Pitch Publishing
9 Donnington Park,
85 Birdham Road,
Chichester,
West Sussex,
PO20 7AJ
www.pitchpublishing.co.uk
info@pitchpublishing.co.uk

A CIP catalogue record is available for this book
from the British Library.

ISBN 978 1 80150 427 0

Typesetting and origination by Pitch Publishing
Printed and bound in Great Britain by TJ Books, Padstow

Contents

For my wife, Stacey. Without her encouragement and support this book would not have been possible, accepting without objection the rearranged holidays, lonely nights at home without me (which she secretly enjoys), and tolerating my obsession in pursuit of its completion.

Introduction

ALTHOUGH THE idea for this book came about on a late February night in 2014, while shielding from the bitter cold blowing through the port of Genoa, Italy, most of the journey was undertaken in 2018 and completed before the end of 2019. The global Covid-19 pandemic in March 2020 caused a minor delay, but also highlighted that football extends far beyond the 90-plus minutes when players take to the field. Matches returning to empty stadiums reminded me how important it is that we remember the wider influence outside of the matchday bubble, and seek deeper experiences to better our understanding of the world game. However, I did not fully share the view of writer Jonathan Wilson, expressed before the pandemic, that the sport is becoming overrated, suggesting that the modern fan just wants to find an atmosphere that they can post on social media to increase interaction and, for similar reasons, the bigger the controversy, the better. Otherwise, 'Did the fixture even take place?'[1]

There were times during the last 20 years that domestic football, and following Liverpool Football Club, had become

---

1   Fisher, J., 'Liverpool's run ends, Lampardball and El Clásico chaos' (*The Athletic*, 2019)

underwhelming, as I largely watched the same 14 teams visit Anfield each season while another six clubs yo-yo between top flight and second tier. Even European fixtures had an all too familiar feel, with the UEFA coefficient seedings making at least one group stage opponent predictable, and having experienced multiple Italian stadiums through my work with the website Forza Italian Football. Therefore, I started expanding my horizons and visiting weird and wonderful locations across mainland Europe such as Levski Sofia, RCD Mallorca and SM Caen.

With a childhood infatuation with Diego Maradona, there was something appealing about cities with one dominant team, like SCC Napoli, united behind a collective goal and where someone like the 1986 World Cup winner can become a god, and other less-gifted players gain a cult-like status if playing a vital role in securing rare silverware. The scenes when the Neapolitans captured the Serie A title in 1986/87 and 1989/90 were almost impossible to comprehend, and had me considering travelling to Naples to experience that when they got close again in 2018. Similarly, long periods of frustration and underachievement, like those seen in Newcastle and Sunderland, forge a collective spirit just as strong. In cities of comparable size hosting multiple clubs, like Prague, that sense of unity is missing and replaced with intense rivalries that increase every time one side watches the other triumph.

Therefore, as I sat in a restaurant a few days ahead of Genovese rivals Genoa and Sampdoria facing off, I became convinced that there was something unmatched about rivalries within the same city, where the people and place live the conflicts daily, which stems from a variety of diverse differences. Graeme Souness – who, as player or manager, experienced five of the matches selected – expressed his surprise to *The Players' Tribune* that 'football rivalries would take him to the forefront of religious and political debates in Scotland, or standing in the middle of a pitch staring down dozens of angry Turks ready to turn him into mince'.[2]

In nearly four decades supporting Liverpool, I had experienced the passion and ferocity of heated battles with rivals first-hand. However, although there were just 30 miles separating Liverpool and the city of Manchester, in recent years Liverpool had challenged both United and City for silverware. Closer local conflict with Everton always felt more emotionally charged and deeply engrained, regardless of the lack of trophy battles.

I decided to use existing listings of the 'biggest' or 'best' derbies or matches collated by popular publications, such as *The Mirror* or *FourFourTwo* to form an initial list of ten to 12 fixtures for consideration. Those chosen in no way act as any kind of definitive ranking or my own. How someone defines the finest or their own favourite is such a personal and subjective thing. If you were to survey 100 people, I am sure that they would propose additional games to these, and I have certainly had several suggested to me during my adventures or discussion with others. There are at least another ten that, if absent here, I wish to experience in the next few years.

We all have different perspectives and features we look for when we categorise our own 'greatest' list, such as importance (deciding a major championship), longevity (long and rich history) or high on controversy. The latter most often stems from much-publicised violence between warring supporter groups. I simply discounted matches without clubs from the same city competing and focused

---

2 Souness, G., *On Rivalries* (The Players' Tribune, 2017)

on the first ten most frequently identified at the top of the listings.

The fixtures all have similarities such as rich/poor narratives and long-standing feuds. Yet all are individual stories in their own right and can be read in any order, depending on your preference. What you will also notice are slight, if consistent, references to Liverpool throughout. This was never the intention, but it became so coincidental that it felt right to weave them into the tales of my visits, such was the connection between the Merseyside club and so many of the fixtures included, from former players and managers, like Souness, or historic encounters as in the cases of Glasgow Celtic, Genoa, Flamengo and AS Roma.

I had originally discounted the Merseyside derby, despite it sitting comfortably near the top of such rankings, due to my allegiance to Liverpool, and also assuming that English speakers would probably have already heard chapter and verse on the rivalry. However, fate conspired to include the conflict as an 11th and final fixture.

Some fixtures just missed the cut, such as the Tunis derby between Club Africain and Espérance, and Montevideo's clash pitting Nacional against Peñarol. One match proved elusive despite multiple attempts to travel.

I was desperate to witness Esteghlal versus Persepolis, played in front of over 100,000 spectators at the Azadi Stadium, Tehran. The arena creates an atmosphere that Jason McAteer once described as nothing like anything seen in his life and 'unable to prepare for' when walking out for the Republic of Ireland against Iran in November 2001. For reasons later explained, a trip that looked impossible proved just that.

You might also feel there are some notable omissions from Madrid and Milan. My process of selection excluded the Spanish capital, with the clash between Club Atlético de Madrid and Real Madrid never featuring high enough in the rankings. *El Clásico*, against Barcelona, is viewed as the 14-time European Cup winners' biggest rivalry, and other regional battles (one which is covered) are more prominent. The *Derby della Madonnina* between AC Milan and Inter just scraped into the fixtures for consideration, and I attended on 21 October 2018, but it would have resulted in three Italian matches being included, and the others were more regularly categorised as 'bigger'.

On- and off-pitch controversies, and regular incidents of crowd disturbances, have characterised many of these games, and they are touched upon. It was never the intention, though, to look for violence or hooligans, to write a Danny Dyer-style glorification of ultra groups. That provides a lot of the entertainment. The intention was to undertake these encounters as close to the average, or real, supporter experience, hopefully giving a truer reflection of the average fan experience, but also that of someone wanting to follow in my footsteps and experience these matches themselves.

Annual leave and budget restrictions made lots of the trips quick affairs (squeezed into long weekends), and the time pressures that brought resulted in discounting the possibility of interviewing playing or coaching staff. It was also never meant to be about a specific fixture or incident, such as the hostile scenes that ultimately resulted in the 2018 CONMEBOL Copa Libertadores Final being abandoned.

With rich, long-standing histories, I touch upon what made these derbies some of the most famous in the world and extend their standing in the game. I never intended the book to be a full historic account of the derbies or to give blow-by-blow accounts of the rivalry, but instead to add context to the stories you read. Other publications have gone into far greater detail and provided exceptional reference material before, during and after these journeys, so much so that I lost many an evening diving deeply into the past. Quickly becoming worried, I would end up writing a book, not a chapter, on each derby. However, they supplemented me with the knowledge to take to the games and quiz fans, even if I'm looking at notes I'll have taken with me.

Focusing on a particular game, especially if expecting the bigger the game to provide a better spectacle on the pitch, would put unrealistic expectations on the experience. As you will soon realise, goals are in short supply during such encounters, with increased competition reducing the numbers hitting the back of the net over the last 100 years, exacerbated when two bitter rivals or equally matched sides face off.

I agree with Chris Anderson and David Sally in *The Numbers Game: Why Everything You Know About Football is Wrong* that there is a misunderstanding about football fans attending just to see goals. We go to see matches in which every goal is essential and potentially decisive, something that feels less frequent now during Premier League matches and the final rounds of UEFA Champions League group stages.

Regardless of form, competition or significance, and with local bragging rights at stake, same-city derbies always provide an intriguing contest. The fixtures covered within this book further solidified that in my mind.

Acknowledgments

IT IS a much-used but very accurate cliché that we write no book in its entirety alone. Given this was my first attempt at something so vast, both in words and travel, this project was certainly one of those very such occasions. There are several people who I hope already realise the contribution they have made and how much I appreciate their help and support.

First on the list is colleague, friend and football fanatic Guy Townsin, who has accompanied me on many trips across Europe to feed our footballing cravings and listened to my many ramblings on the sport and fan culture. After first suggesting the idea, Guy has been a constant source of encouragement. He will be the first to complete the reading and give feedback.

With some locations seeing me venture into the unknown, whether a new country or region, the advice and guidance from the likes of Colin Millar, Onur Bilgiç and Suhayl Al-Sammari proved invaluable ahead of travel, and Behnam Jafarzadeh in Iran went out of his way without me even entering the country. Special mention also goes to Conor Clancy, who, with the help of Alan Feehely, put me in contact with Enrique Roldán of the Betis Bohemio group, whose guidance allowed me to finish my foreign encounters in memorable style, for which I will be forever grateful.

Tickets for such highly charged and historic fixtures were frequently difficult to come by, so I want to thank Pádraig Whelan for organising my entry into Glasgow Celtic. Dov Schiavone and Tom Nash went a long way to help me succeed in the near-impossible task of obtaining a ticket for the *Superclásico* between River Plate and Boca Juniors. However, had it not been for Martín Pérez Alonso, I may never have navigated the club offices to collect it. I cannot forget the hospitality of Kirsten Schlewitz and Uroš Popović in Belgrade, who also provided the unexpected vantage point of attending as a visiting supporter.

Then the many individuals that shared their own knowledge and experiences, usually over a beer or two, such as Simone Sanguineti, Federico Gusberti and friends in Genoa, and a trip supplemented by the wonderful food and late-night reminiscing with Michele Rifaldi. In Lisbon, Antonio and Jorge at my accommodation provided no end of stories, and Jérémy Charles Petitcolas, Manuel Carronha, Guilherme Anastácio Junior and Mariana Anacleto welcomed me with the open arms of the Directivo Ultras family. As did Dániel Karafiát and companion Robert, when a chance meeting in a Budapest bar resulted in access beyond my expectations. Then there are Alasdair Mackenzie (Rome) and Sam Kelly (Buenos Aires) who introduced me to two of my now favourite bars in the world!

Finally, completing this book, particularly during the last few months, would have resulted in many more sleepless nights had it not been for the support of colleague and writer Mark Hamilton Jackson, who acted as a sounding board, confidant, contract reviewer and several other now-forgotten roles.

They are all part of the success of this endeavour.

1

Derby della Lanterna – Genoa, Italy

IN 1992, Liverpool, after a six-year absence from the European stage – banned in the wake of the 1985 Heysel Stadium disaster – welcomed foreign opposition back to Anfield, creating the first continental occasions my young mind retained. The visits of Kuusysi Lahti, Auxerre and Swarovski Tirol gave supporters European nights to bask in once again, but two sides in particular during the 1991/92 campaign sparked an overwhelming interest in the Italian port city of Genoa.

With the Reds meeting Genoa Cricket and Football Club at the quarter-final stage of the UEFA Cup in March 1992, I witnessed the first leg on the peninsula through the filter of television. Undiluted, the electric atmosphere within the Stadio Luigi Ferraris that night saw a stunning long-range goal from Brazilian full-back Cláudio Ibrahim Vaz Leal, better known as Branco. Despite my team suffering a demoralising 2-0 loss (that became a humiliating 4-1 aggregate defeat), it had captured the heart of ten-year-old me. In the next round, *Il Grifone* (The Griffin) would exit the competition to eventual winners Ajax. But by then another side marching its way through continental competition had also caught my eye – city rivals Unione Calcio Sampdoria.

Parental indulgence on my birthday allowed me to stay up and watch the 1992 European Cup Final until its completion. Another wonderful free kick, by Ronald Koeman, secured Barcelona victory deep in extra time. Yet the enthralling technical display from the *Gemelli del Goal* (the Goal Twins), Roberto Mancini and Gianluca Vialli, had me spellbound. With both teams a huge part of my Italian football induction, there was no better place to start my journey across the biggest derbies.

World Cup-winning coach and former Genoa *libero*[3] Marcello Lippi was a fan, claiming, 'It is different to all the other derbies in Italy. The most special in Italy. The rivalry between the two sets of fans is based on mickey-taking, on pranks, like organising mock funerals for the opposition. It's the least nasty of all the derbies and I've rarely seen any violence.'[4] Not the best, nor the most important, but the most special.

It helped that the fixture did not exhibit the violent traits of many others I would visit. The encounter also differs from others around the world, where one team enjoys enormous support or is far more successful, like in Turin, where Torino's heyday is long-forgotten and Juventus are now a giant of European football.

This rivalry splits the city by purer allegiances, no doubt drawn from family ties or location, or, if free to choose, a case of selecting the club which offers the least heartache

---

3 Traditionally placed with the centre of a back three, a *libero* was versatile enough to sweep up the ball behind his centre-back partners and also progress upfield with the ball to initiate attacks

4 Dunne, F., 'Flags of our fathers: Why Genoa vs Sampdoria is more than a game' (*FourFourTwo*, 2009)

over the coming years. Genoa's last major honour of any note came nine years before the *Blucerchiati* (the Blue-circled) formed, the *Rossoblu* (the Red-and-blues) capturing the 1937 Coppa Italia. Sampdoria had a stranglehold on local bragging rights across the city as I entered my teenage years. They reached the 1995 European Cup Winners' Cup semi-final and England captain David Platt plied his trade with them, but I never developed an affiliation to either club.

Genoa is Italy's oldest club, having been in operation professionally since 1893. Rather than a rivalry built over a long and eventful history, though, this is a tale of a bygone master and a young upstart who sought to steal the crown from their more decorated neighbours. Sampdoria was born from a merger of Sampierdarenese and Andrea Doria in 1946. With those roots journeying back as far as the 1890s, they consider the *Derby della Lanterna*[5] the oldest and youngest derby in Italian football in equal measure. Since *Il Doria* formed, the fortunes of both sides have defined it as a clash between Genoa's history and Sampdoria's more recent success and it divides the city.

Il Grifone started as a cricket club to represent the English on foreign soil, achieving limited success until adding football to their sporting repertoire and securing an incredible six consecutive Scudetti[6] under Englishman James Richardson Spensley between 1897 and 1904. Compatriot William Garbutt took the coaching reins in 1912 at just 29 years old and extended the Anglo-Italian connection, leading the *Rossoblu* to a further three Serie A titles. National

---

5 The fixtures label is derived from the ancient Torre della Lanterna (Lantern) landmark and lighthouse

6 Scudetto or Scudetti means 'little shield(s)' in Italian and the domestic championship Serie A is often referred to as this due to the winner wearing a shield emblem with the Italian national flag on their shirts the following season and was first presented to Genoa in 1924

dominance was short-lived, though, with the last triumph, in 1923/24, their most recent to date.

Despite regular trips to the footballing hotbed of northern Italy, visits to one of my favourite Italian cities appeared cursed. The worldwide Covid-19 outbreak condemned an attempt to watch the 100th encounter between the pair in May 2020, and my first trip was no different. Doomed before we had set off, I almost researched whether the phrase 'if you didn't laugh, you'd cry' had originated from the peninsula.

It was not the first time the authorities had attempted to ruin my best-laid plans to enjoy some Serie A action. In October 2013, Udinese were due to travel to face AC Milan when the Italian Football Federation (FIGC) decided they must play the match behind closed doors for territorial-based insults hurled at Napoli the week before. While there is value in treating chants towards southern Italians the same as racial abuse, it was farcical, given the latter's significance. Go to any stadium, anywhere in the world, and you will hear derogatory songs based on the opposition's hometown. Same-city derbies may be the exception, but even then chants are aimed at certain areas of that city. Common sense prevailed and a ban on supporters was lifted, meaning I got to enjoy a lacklustre game settled by a solitary Valter Birsa goal.

Five months on it was the Genoa government, not FIGC, causing more anxiety for my companions and I, changing the original 12.30pm Sunday kick-off. Both sets of supporters threatened to boycott the match and protest outside due to the unpopular start time, which forced the FIGC to switch the game to Monday night, at just 48 hours' notice.

To mask fans' contempt at being used to satisfy overseas television markets, the head of the Genoa Municipal Police, Giacomo Tinella, claimed that the hosting of the Ligurian region's biggest market close by that day was the reason for the outrage. Sampdoria's Tito Cucchiaroni ultras, though, confirmed that the threats had nothing to do with shopping plans. Their statement read, 'It is a day and a time slot, which is disrespectful to the fans who go to the stadium. If they think they are going to get a spectacle to fill their television cameras with, then they've got it all wrong.'[7]

* * *

You often find a variety of fan groups at Italian clubs, unlike at Liverpool, for example, where the Spirit of Shankly dominates. At Samp there are the San Fruttuoso 1987, Valsecca Group 1991, Fieri Fossato and many, many more, including the oldest Fedelissimi 1961. Along with Tito Cucchiaroni, the Fedelissimi are their most famous ultras and self-proclaimed first, after Beppe Andreotti, one of the most charismatic figures in the Gradinata Sud, created them on 27 November 1961. In recent years, however, they have taken a back seat to the younger generation. While retaining a prominent role creating an intimidating atmosphere for opponents, they moved within the Gradinata Sud during battles for political power.

Tito Cucchiaroni, named after former Argentine winger Ernesto Cucchiaroni,[8] now dominate the Gradinata Sud, and are recognisable from their *A Clockwork Orange*-inspired banner depicting the famous image used to promote the long-banned movie's release in 1973, four years after their formation in 1969. If you keep your eyes peeled wandering the city, you may also see the words *Uniti Legneremo Tutti*

---

7 Gladwell, B., 'Genoa-Sampdoria set for Monday' (ESPN, 2014)

8 Ernesto 'Tito' Cucchiaroni played for the club between 1959 and 1963, and became an instant favourite of the Sampdoria supporters after scoring twice in his first *Derby della Lanterna* and playing a crucial role when they finished fourth in the 1960/61 season

I Rossoblu A Sangue (United, we will beat the red and blues until they bleed) on graffiti-marked walls, often associated with the group.

Regardless of allegiances, Sampdoria fans refer to Genoa supporters as *Bibini* (turkey, in the local dialect), as a griffin adorns the *Rossoblu* crest, while their cross-city rivals know them as the *Ciclisti* (Cyclists). The name pokes fun at their colourful shirt combination of blue, white, black and red, which resembles a traditional cycling uniform. Both are signs of the good-natured rivalry referenced by Lippi.

* * *

Broadcasters would agree which Serie A fixtures they would televise until Christmas, giving confidence to overseas visitors making travel arrangements. Unable to attend the first encounter, we booked flights, confident that the fixture was often a weekend game, but we were then due to return home while the match was taking place. Therefore, FIGC had to take some responsibility for confirming the original start time mid-January and allowing the ultras just two weeks to voice their disapproval, and deciding to rearrange the match just over 72 hours before kick-off, one day before we would depart. It would have been a simple decision if I was going alone, but not all of those travelling shared my passion.

Two years earlier, colleague Guy Townsin had invited me to join him and others on a 'football weekend' taking in Borussia Dortmund against Bayer Leverkusen. This was the third trip together as a group, and it was becoming an annual event.

Twenty years my senior and with three young daughters, Guy's world is as saturated with football as mine, albeit directed more towards the English pyramid than European football. An avid supporter of childhood team Peterborough

United, and Portsmouth, where he now lives, Guy has more 'favourite teams' than I have pairs of shoes. On arriving at each new stadium or city, Guy is hard to contain. A built-up anticipation transforms him into a childlike ball of excitement, bounding yards in front of you like a puppy exploring unknown territory. Convincing him to stay one extra night in Genoa was not an issue.

Somerset-based Ed Coupe, and Dan Massey from Norwich, though, took more convincing. I had yet to gauge whether Ed had a deep, burning passion for the sport, let alone a particular team. However, his well-defined role in the group was fundamental to its success. Quick-witted, with a dry sense of humour and a mischievous smirk that puts you at ease, Ed provided plenty of controversy and humour, and took care of a lot of the drinking. Dan, while just as witty, is harder to read, whether in person, by text or phone. If he were to scoop the jackpot on the lottery in front of you, I doubt his mood or demeanour would change. Only on rare occasions, when completely at ease, or a little tipsy, would you see a full smile. As a Norwich City season ticket holder, the trip was as much about experiencing one of the magnificent spectacles of Italian football as enjoying the wonderful food the Ligurian capital has on offer.

Everyone agreed that it would be a shame not to see the event. Then we had to persuade British Airways to rearrange our flights at a reasonable cost, but we should not have bothered!

Our original flights had cost around £80 each, so I hoped that, with single tickets just £76, there would only be a slight price difference and administration fee to pay, as a few months earlier they had changed our departure time from 7am to 9.55am for no apparent reason, but no. They demanded £120 per person to switch us to a return flight 24 hours later than intended. Attempting to charge us almost double the price of a single ticket meant there was no further discussion needed, and we booked new return flights. The Best Western Metropoli were far more accommodating and extended our stay for just €35.

The taxi journey towards the city centre was unremarkable. After touching down at Cristoforo Colombo Airport around 2pm, a thick blanket of grey cloud and unrelenting drizzle combined to suppress any scenery en route, and arriving at our destination we had the strangest of altercations with our driver, who refused to accept €20 for a journey that only registered €18 on his fare meter. It was the first time I had encountered a driver refusing a tip, but assumed it was an old Genovese custom we failed to understand. We headed straight out in search of alcohol. With only fleeting memories of a DJ, complete with disco lights, spinning tracks in one of the city's smallest bars as I entertained the few locals scattered around with dance moves better left at home, the video footage that existed is now long-destroyed.

With an extra day to fill, the others had earmarked a trip down the coastline to Camogli, a small fishing village 30 minutes east of Genoa by train and famed for its seafood restaurants. Despite growing up near the coast, I did not share the others' love of seafood. With the country still gripped by winter, most local businesses were closed. We missed the sun warming our faces and illuminating the pastel-coloured buildings, but benefited from fewer tourists cramming the cobbled streets and eateries. A day that began peacefully ended in less pleasant circumstances, though. With my tendency to get frustrated at breakneck speed by indecision, I called a premature end to my night, although I also blame a seasonal cold or flu that had taken hold on arrival in Italy.

As the evening drew to a close back in Genoa, we sought somewhere for dinner.

Walking round emptying streets as the temperature dropped and growing colder, I attempted to pull up the zip on my coat higher than was possible while displaying feverish symptoms, as Guy deliberated where he wanted to eat. After surveying the fifth or sixth restaurant menu, I dragged them into the next available eatery on the harbour. As we sat down at our table, the waiting staff set the table for dinner, unsurprising given the time of night, and Guy launched into a painful conversation, explaining we might eat once we'd had a drink. Although it was clear they preferred the dining option, I snapped, uttered some expletives, and exited the restaurant in a diva-like fashion back into the icy Italian night with only one destination in mind: bed. Within minutes I was wrapped in my duvet, with the spare included for good measure, attempting to sweat out whatever it was I was suffering from and comforted by the *Derby d'Italia* between Juventus and Inter[9] on the TV, which I had been eager to watch as we circled Genoa for the tenth time and that added to my disappearing act.

The night before the derby in 2022 was much quieter and more informative, if finishing just as late. During a traditional Genovese meal, at the delightful Trattoria Da Genio on Salita San Leonardo, I received an entertaining journey through the rich history of Sampdoria by the owner, Michele Rifaldi. After we had finished our meal, delaying Stacey's desire to get to sleep, Michele's eyes lit up after we explained our reason for visiting Genoa and he ushered us into a back room of the restaurant.

---

9 Although commonly known as Inter Milan in English-speaking countries, Football Club Internazionale Milano are referred to in this book simply as Inter, with that becoming the custom in recent years

The walls were filled with framed pictures, some signed, of historic *Blucerchiati* players, and he started going through each one with an individual tale. I could join in the reminiscing when he reached the 1980s and British players such as Trevor Francis, Graeme Souness, Liam Brady, Des Walker and David Platt appeared. I think I even saw a picture of ex-Manchester United starlet Lee Sharpe.[10] An hour had passed by the time we left, while Stacey took great pleasure filming us conversing on her smartphone and found amusement in my broken Italian and our energetic gesticulations.

With our falling-out forgotten and the others more concerned with my health, we headed out on the morning of the match to sense the pre-derby mood across the city. However, I maybe expected too much, despite its position as *the* derby in Italy. Over the past three decades I had become accustomed to the Merseyside derby, where Liverpool is full of supporters in club colours. With football tourists descending UK towns and cities to sample Premier League action, the globalisation and commercialisation of British football might have contaminated my expectations, yet there was no sense of anticipation building in Genoa.

Most supporters in the Marassi would be match-going regulars who, like me, spend their disposable income watching their team, rather than on countless new kits offered by clubs. It was also a regular working day. School children, often keen to don their colours even on non-matchdays, were studying and businesses going about daily life. Fashion-conscious Italians are often more concerned with how they appear in public, unlike many of the British tourists seen wandering

---

10 Sharpe spent the first half of the 1998/99 season on loan at Sampdoria from English club Leeds United and made three Serie A appearances

the streets of a European city with replica shirts stretching across expanding waistlines.

With the weather having improved, we got to see Genoa in its full glory, walking along the historic palatial residences of Via Garibaldi and heading to Spianata Castelletto for a wonderful panoramic view of the city. Without needing to turn my head, the historic port and Ligurian Sea dominated the view in front of me, the historic lighthouse from which they have dubbed the fixture visible above the many apartment blocks in between. It was clear to see why the Genovese people call the city *La Superba* (The Superb), although friends have disagreed with my assessment.

I like somewhere with a bit of grit and humility. As the capital of Liguria, with a population of around 600,000 in the metropolitan area, Genoa has a prime position in the centre of the Italian Riviera. The connection that the harbour brought to the rest of Europe ultimately gave birth to the first sports society on the peninsula and changed the culture of an entire country, in a similar way as the birthplace of Italian football, that spread like wildfire across Italy. Like both Genoa and Sampdoria, though, the city has struggled for several years and shows little sign of turning around its fortunes.

Out of sight, though, was the Stadio Luigi Ferraris, still some 1.5 miles east of where we stood gazing.

The Marassi, built in 1911, is one of the country's oldest stadiums, and takes its official name from a *Grifone* legend who died during the First World War, and was used only by Genoa during their dominant early years in Italian football. It is that history and emotional attachment to one side of the city that makes it difficult to comprehend allowing Sampdoria to call it their home straight after their formation in 1946 and is the only venue to host fixtures between the pair.

While there were much bigger concerns for the country towards the end of that decade, you wonder whether Genoa even considered the new club as a legitimate threat to their city supremacy, but the first match between the teams should have served as a warning. A long-range Giuseppe Baldini strike went down in history as part of a 3-0 victory for *La Samp*.

Two seasons later, the *Blucerchiati* recorded a 5-1 triumph over their housemates, which remains the largest winning margin of any top-flight Italian derby. Then, in April 1951, Sampdoria dealt the *Rossoblu* the ultimate humiliation. *Il Doria* led through goals from Vittorio Bergamo and Adriano Bassetto. Genoa thought a late Bror Mellberg equaliser had saved them demotion to Serie B only for an 88th-minute winner from Mario Sabbatella to relegate them.

For lots of fans, travelling away to support your team adds an element of exhilaration, such as the prospect of overcoming home advantage, which is increased when a local derby comes around. The widespread ground sharing across Italy, though, always made me wonder whether fans in the likes of Genoa, Milan or Rome get the same thrill of victory at what is their own home.

On the third weekend of the 2013/14 campaign, Sampdoria were the hosts and well beaten 3-0 by Genoa. That proved a high point for *Il Grifone*, who sacked coach Fabio Liverani after six games. Improvement under replacement Gianpiero Gasperini had lifted Genoa into the top half, though, and Sampdoria were just as unlikely to be threatened by relegation, sitting in 13th place and only looking to avenge their early season capitulation. When I returned on 1 May 2022 the situation was very different. With four games left to play, the *Rossoblu* were second from bottom and four points from safety. Sampdoria were just five points better off than their city neighbours. Victory for *Il Doria* would all but guarantee their Serie A survival and almost certainly relegate *Il Grifone*. The stakes could not have been higher.

With just one Serie A title between them in the last 60 years, the fixture is now renowned for determining the rivals' fates at the opposite end of the table. In 1977, Genoa returned the favour from 26 years earlier, aiding Sampdoria's descent towards Serie B by inflicting a 2-1 defeat then losing at home to fellow strugglers Bologna and Foggia to condemn the *Blucerchiati*. A quarter of a century later, the executioner's axe was back in *Il Doria* hands, this time in Serie B. Goals from Bratislav Živković and Mirko Conte helped send *Il Grifone* sprawling into the third tier and the result was made sweeter when Sampdoria then secured promotion to the top flight.

Back across town, the pendulum swung again in 2011 when, in the penultimate match of the season, an injury-time winner from Mauro Boselli all but relegated *La Samp*. At *Il Grifone*'s last match of the season against Cesena, supporters revelled in their relegation. Genoa fans held a five-minute silence during the game to mourn their passing before a 30,000-strong funeral procession later that afternoon carried a coffin draped in *Blucerchiati* colours through the city. With the amount of suffering inflicted upon each other since 1946, it is unsurprising that this is unlike many of the derbies in Italy which are characterised by violence and deep animosity. This fixture, despite its ferocity and passionate support, has a humorous side.

Ahead of the game in February 2014, the weather took a significant turn for the worse. From our rooms we listened to the torrential rain growing in intensity as it hammered at the windows. Although the stadium was within walking distance, it forced us to seek a taxi. At first they refused attempts outside our accommodation to hail a lift for 'traffic reasons'. After reception secured us transportation, the taxi driver sped through the flooded streets with no consideration for the conditions, and then only dropped us at Brignole Station, a 20-minute walk from the Luigi Ferraris.

Joining the increasing numbers heading along Via Canevari wading through puddles that almost consumed your entire footwear, within minutes (if not seconds) our jackets were soaked beyond having any waterproof capabilities anymore, with us all wishing we had dressed more appropriately. As we hurried north, there was a brief respite from the weather, taking shelter under one of Genoa's many bridges, the short tunnel illuminated with the red glow of brake lights and congested traffic creeping forward at a ridiculously slow pace. The chance to end the rainfall streaming down our faces reduced our own forward momentum and just as we reached the end of our refuge, a loud firecracker exploded. Enhanced by the tunnel, I felt it pulsating through me, filling me with anticipation that the colour and passion of the *Derby della Lanterna* was nearby. First, though, was more rain.

Out of the corner of my eye (or maybe Guy's), we spotted an elderly woman ushering us to enter the doorway in which she was standing. Assuming that food and water would be on offer, we darted into the most welcome sanctuary. Until we raised our sodden heads, we did not realise that we were in someone's lounge and found ourselves seated on a sofa and assorted chairs. In the room's corner, other guests sat by a homemade bar. That convinced me they had not tricked us into some kind of captive-style scenario like you often see in horror movies, and we removed as many of our drenched layers as was appropriate with our hosts providing some small towels to help us get dry and took our order. Although there was just over an hour until kick-off, the opportunity to enjoy a freshly made warm panini and a couple of large beers was unlikely to present itself again. Therefore, we sat listening to the growing number of explosions outside and watching the shadows of those passing a small window at the front of the property before we confronted the cold, wet February night once more.

As we did, another blast welcomed us and reignited my expectancy, just as the rowdy chants from a pocket of Genoa supporters that my mediocre Italian could not translate also did. Turning right on to Via James Richardson Spensley, we caught our first glimpse of the stadium, so far hidden by housing running adjacent. It was hard not to see the English influence in its design, with the red-brick façade and more rectangular style compared with many of the oval Italian arenas. With a jet-black sky, the floodlights provided the Marassi with an angelic glow, and the rain continued to fall almost horizontally to the ground. Inside, spectators are closer to the playing surface than any of those spoiled by including an athletic track. It was too wet for Guy to enjoy his customary lap of the stadium, while the steely glare Dan gave through a small gap in his well-fastened hood suggested that adding more steps to his sodden journey was not an option. We had also stumbled upon the very point at which we had to enter, so it was foolish to delay, but I had a sense that conditions had lessened the visual spectacle.

When I returned in 2022, though, the weather allowed Stacey and I to witness the full colour of the derby, with the sun on our backs as we walked from the centre along Corso Carlo Armellini. When we reached the Piazza Manin, we found a huge orange smoke plume rising beside bar Maninvino, as multiple firecrackers being detonated were accompanied by enthusiastic singing.

Without hesitation, we went to investigate and found a couple of hundred Genoa fans had congregated outside. After purchasing a couple of beers, we entered the crowd and spotted a couple of empty chairs and a table, asking whether they were free. They invited us to sit, our accents bringing the usual questions from a group of men in their early 20s. Despite Genoa's predicament, they were in high spirits and, once I explained the reason for our visit, Simone Sanguineti's interest in us increased, even setting an alarm on his smartphone for the potential release of this book, and he introduced us to friend Federico Gusberti. Both were Genoa-born. Federico now worked in Milan and, Stacey thought, bore a resemblance to comedian Bob Mortimer.

The obvious discussion point was Serie A survival and, having expected to meet Sampdoria fans, I proclaimed, 'You could relegate them today, no?' The look on Simone's face drew attention to my mistake, and he responded, 'You mean us.' With just five points between the pair, I told them I thought a Genoa win had the potential to save them and drag Sampdoria into the relegation battle. I assume my quick thinking worked as they furnished us with more beers from their own supply, before another member of the group, Valerio Biolzi, interrupted, keen to show us they drink a 7.7 per cent strength ale called Ceres and departed from view with a call of 'Forza Genoa!'

Simone believed that even victory was unlikely to save Genoa from relegation as Juventus were next up, yet they were hopeful of a quick return to Serie A and had won a bigger battle already that season. In September 2021, long-serving president Enrico Preziosi had sold the club to US investors 777 Partners and, despite significant debt, hoped it signalled a revival of *Il Grifone*'s fortunes. At the very least, Federico expected more engagement than Preziosi had shown during his last few seasons at the helm.

To our right, Genoa supporters had gathered en masse on another stairway that was essential to navigate the hilly landscape, under a homemade banner reading 'DRAGHE ZENA'.[11] That was soon invisible behind another, expressing that 'A GENOVA IL GENOA' (Genoa is Genoa), which works much better using the local spelling of the city. I could hear the joyous atmosphere in the upbeat sound of their singing and hilarity breaking out of the surrounding conversations. The amusement peaked with a fan climbing halfway up a lamppost, and using the end of a flagpole to attach a Genoa sticker over the glass, a sticker Simone would then hand me as a memento. By then, general madness had broken out on the stairs, crammed with bodies jumping up and down, waving flags with vigour and holding smoke canisters aloft. While someone was sending fireworks into the sky, that had minimal visual impact. I leant towards Stacey and, just as I uttered 'we need some more firecrackers', an enormous explosion went off alongside her and made her jump, which made the entire table break out into laughter. We had to leave Simone and friends, though, as we wanted to sample the opposite side of the divide, grabbing a quick picture together and moving back downhill towards the Marassi.

All the pre-game excitement had me wondering whether I could have got tickets with the Genoa supporters. I had gone straight to the Sampdoria website when the start time was confirmed. In 2014, the Gradinata Nord (where the Genoa fans are located, whether home or away) was only available to members, at least when facing Sampdoria, so

---

11 Zena is the word for Genoa in Ligurian dialect

we decided on modestly priced €27 tickets in the Tribuna Inferiore, holding away fans for regular fixtures, which was close enough to enjoy their exuberant displays. However, given the proximity of the two sections, as we passed through our gate with relative ease we found ourselves squeezed into a small corridor heading into the Nord. We moved with the crowd unnoticed on to the terrace with less than 30 minutes to go. The noise pitchside was so loud it felt like the stadium foundations were shaking. The chants within the confined space reached a level that ignited my childlike excitement. At one point, though, we heard the rather unnerving roar of supporters, as if celebrating a goal. Unable to check the time, my mood switched to a fear that we were missing the action. After ten minutes attempting to gain access, the pressure of bodies within the hallway was becoming ever more uncomfortable. Then a few heads, maybe 15 rows in front, turned to the crowd and announced the stand was now full (and some!). A heavy steel door closed behind them to confirm that it was time to head towards our assigned seating.

On both occasions, Genoa ultra groups, such as the Fossa dei Griffoni (the Pit of Griffins), Via Armenia 5r (5r Armenia Street), Ottavio Barbieri[12] and Vecchi Orsi (Old Bears), packed the terrace, attempting to create a visceral wall of noise of intimidation for opposition players and fans. The Fossa dei Grifoni are accepted as their first ultra group and the catalysts of the ferocious support Genoa receive today. Formed in 1973 from the supporters' club, Ottavio Barbieri, during one of the darkest periods of the club's history with *Il Grifone* struggling in Serie C, was the main Genoa ultra

---

12 Midfielder Ottavio Barbieri was born in Genoa on 30 April 1899 and spent his entire playing career with the club between 1919 and 1932, appearing over 300 times and winning two Serie A titles, eventually coaching the side twice between 1939 and 1946

group until folding in the summer of 1993. Battles with then-president Aldo Spinelli, the police and local press resulted in some members leaving to join or form a growing number of ultra movements.

What I found interesting was how few clashes there have been between Genoa and Sampdoria fans. Violent incidents with other ultra groups have resulted in off-the-pitch incidents Genoa would like to forget. On 29 January 1995, a Genoa supporter fatally stabbed AC Milan fan Vincenzo Claudio Spagnolo and, with the game abandoned at half-time, riots ensued all around the stadium. Such was the rarity of such events that a monument to Spagnolo exists outside the Marassi, bringing together the city as they mourned at the 24-year-old's funeral, just as they had in October 1993 when Sampdoria lost president Paolo Mantovani – who oversaw their transformation into a Serie A powerhouse during his tenure.

After establishment, *Il Doria* seemed determined to set off at pace to match the trophy haul the *Rossoblu* had amassed during a 53-year head start. It wasn't until the mid-1980s that Sampdoria had their own set of major trophies to hold aloft. During a decade of often stunning football, mostly under legendary coach Vujadin Boškov, the *Blucerchiati* won four Coppa Italias (two before the Serbian's arrival), a European Cup Winners' Cup in 1990 and, most crucially, the 1990/91 Scudetto, something so craved by Genoa since 1924, to put a star above the crest on their shirts to signify ten titles. *Il Grifone* had to live off victories over their neighbours.

With Sampdoria flying high in November 1990 and heading towards title success, the *Rossoblu* were winless against them for 13 years. Against the odds and with *Il Doria* having home advantage, coach Osvaldo Bagnoli's men pulled off a victory that is still fresh in fans' memories.

A questionable penalty, converted by *Blucerchiati* striker Gianluca Vialli just after half-time, seemed to end any hope of a win, after bringing the sides level following an earlier goal from Genoa captain Stefano Eranio. Up stepped Branco, though, to send a 25-yard free kick arrowing past the Samp goalkeeper. The moment was immortalised on Christmas cards gleefully distributed to *Il Doria* following friends and family over the next month. Sampdoria would soon be Italian champions, but victory allowed *Rossoblu* to briefly rule the city.

The fixture is not without its unsavoury moments, though. During a clash in the 1980s, infamously known as the *derby delle scimmie* (monkey derby), Sampdoria ultra Claudio Bosotin took a monkey into the stadium wearing a Genoa shirt and paraded it in front of his fellow supporters. The intention was to mock Genoa's Brazilian attacker, Elói, for his perceived lack of quality, and that his walk was not dissimilar to the animal. Whatever the origins of the joke, there were obvious and unsavoury racial undertones. Bosotin played a similar trick with a donkey outside the ground on another occasion. It was very much the aim to poke fun at your rivals, with the occasional insults hurled across the Luigi Ferraris pitch.

Genoa soured relations in 1989 when Barcelona beat Sampdoria in the European Cup Winners' Cup Final in Bern, Switzerland. The supporters ran amok around the city, celebrating and spraying walls with fun-loving slurs, but *Il Doria* fans did not see it that way, expecting fellow Genovese and Italians to at least not want them to lose a first continental final.

It is in moments of tragedy, though, that you see a better reflection of the rivals' relationship. On 14 August 2018 the collapse of the Morandi Bridge killed 43 people and left hundreds homeless, bringing into focus how ultra groups in Italy are a social network before mere supporters. Those on both sides joined forces to create the Genoa Together charity, which worked on several initiatives to help fund education programmes for orphaned children, and the first *Derby della Lanterna* of the campaign was an outpouring of collective emotion. A show of solidarity across ultra groups up and down the country saw them mobilise to deliver aid parcels during their visits throughout the 2018/19 season.

When Stacey and I reached Via Tortosa, the Luigi Ferraris was in view, as were thousands of Sampdoria fans packing the 200m stretch of street running towards Corso Alessandro De Stefanis, which also runs alongside the stadium and is filled with fans on matchdays. With the sun shining, conditions were perfect for most of the fans to be sporting the traditional royal-blue home shirts, with a mixture of modern versions and retro offerings that have become popular, but very little else.

As I squeezed past towards Bar Kafesito, I could feel the crunch of plastic cups underfoot and the occasional chink of a beer bottle or two. Rather than the rhythmic singing of the *Rossoblu* fans earlier, there were momentary, if repeated, shouts of 'Genoa merda!' (Genoa shit), extending to 'Bastardo Genoa' and something unrecognisable as I walked up to the bar and ordered four beers – expecting to choose but being handed eight per cent Tennent's Super. Outside, the crowd was thinning out. With just 30 minutes until kick-off, I could hear many supporters singing their hearts out in expectation that their team would send Genoa down. Already a little tipsy from the earlier beers and downing two of the super-strength beers in hand, we made polite conversation with a handful of Sampdoria fans who realised we were not local, but I soon made my way into the stadium after pointing Stacey in the direction of our hotel.

With Italian clubs investing in automated turnstiles back in 2014, they had seemed to have reduced their in-house stewarding, allowing the crowd to police themselves regarding seating, and the rightful occupant would never arrive to turf you out. A 29,868 attendance was just short of capacity, though, meaning it was unlikely to happen.

Watching and waiting for the pre-game choreography from the front row of the upper tier, it was clear that the Gradinata Nord was slightly over capacity, although the driving rain left the first few rows empty, as their fellow supporters created every inch of additional space to help shield them from the terrible conditions.

Just before the players emerged from the belly of the Distini stand opposite the dugouts, another curious component of the fixture. The Genoa supporters unfurled their tifo,[13] depicting two medieval knights in chain mail armour on either side of a castle, complete with a golden griffin hanging from the roof of the stand and floating above them. At the bottom of the terrace, directly behind the goal, a handful of fans held a banner reading 'A TUA DIFESA' (In Your Defence), completing the call to arms theme.

What caught my attention, though, was a huge Saint George's Cross flag emblazoned with 'F.C. GENOA 1893' pinned to the furthest inside wall. In the early 1980s Sampdoria fans would fly British flags, sometimes adorned with 'TREVOR' in homage to English striker Trevor

---

13 Tifo is the phenomenon whereby fans of a sports team make a visual display of any choreographed flags, signs or banners in the stands of a stadium, with its roots in Italy and southern Europe, most commonly seen in important matches, local derbies and rivalries, primarily arranged by ultras or a supporters' club to show their love to the club, but sometimes sponsored or arranged by the club itself

Francis.[14] But after the Heysel disaster, many ultra groups in Italy started disassociating themselves with the British, yet both clubs kept links to the English emblem within their club crests. To my surprise, the Distini, along the side of the pitch, was getting involved in the choreography, 'LA LEGGENDA HA IL VOLTO DEGLI EROI E IL CUORE DEL SUO POPOLO' (The legend has the face of the heroes and the heart of his people) spread across two-thirds of the middle tier, although the top tier soon unrolled flags all the way to ground level covering the banner. It started with bland red and navy-blue stripes at either end, before two more with ZE and NA appeared above pictures of historic Genoa players and coaches in a traditional pre-match pose. I made out the faces of Branco and Eranio, who were part of that famous 1992 victory over Liverpool, but only striker Diego Milito on the opposite side. With several of the 22 men pictured in black and white, I congratulated myself for recognising three.

There was now an enormous gaping hole in the middle of the four banners, timed to descend as the current players entered the arena. It turned out that this was the work of the I Figgi do Zena (Sons of Genoa) ultras who, since their formation, have always preferred a more subdued viewing position. In the Gradinata Sud, the Sampdoria fans were taking aim at local officials, with their own statement stretching across the supporters reading 'NON DI SONO GIORNI E ORARI AL VOSTRO SISTEMA SEMPRE CONTRARI LIBERI DI ESSERE SAMPDORIA', loosely translated to 'there are no days or hours in your system always', referring to the intention to hold the fixture at 12.30pm, and something about Sampdoria being the

---

14 Francis spent four years with Sampdoria after being signed from Manchester City for £700,000 and helped Sampdoria win their first Coppa Italia, in 1985

opposite and free from any imposed rule upon them. Front and centre of this protest, and the only other banner in sight, was the name 'FEDELISSIMA', highlighting the group's involvement in the rearrangement or wanting those around them to know who created it.

At the opposite end of the Marassi, the Genoa fans were adding the final touches to their display. Two huge Saint George's flags filled each corner of the top tier and remaining fans held shimmering blue sheets of material and let off the odd blue smoke bomb. Below them, even more reflective material covered the top two-thirds of the stand, creating a dozen or so rows of blue and white stripes. A sudden roar from all four sides of the Luigi Ferraris signalled the players' arrival, and the Distini completed their tifo by dropping a fifth and final flag, displaying a proud golden griffin in the Genoa kit, puffing out its chest and looking towards the sky, and the famous Lanterna visible in the background.

As they crossed the pitch, the players arched their necks to inspect the spectacle. The fans to our right had now finished their protest and were waving hundreds of large Sampdoria flags – not those small handheld pieces of plastic rubbish often distributed by clubs enforcing a spectacle, but unique homemade offerings. The top tier had ignited red smoke flares that were covering the playing surface in a thick fog during an energetic rendition of anthem 'Ma il cielo e sempre piu blu' (But the sky gets bluer and bluer) by singer-songwriter Rino Gaetano, penetrating the Genoa efforts.

The visitors' pre-match routine had taken less to organise, but took the spoils for best Gradinata on the night. With the smoke clearing and tifos packed away, the players awaited the referee's whistle and the Genoa supporters now displayed their own homemade flags and banners. Attempting to pick out the various ultra groups, I spotted a 'BRIGATA

SPELONCIA' flag hanging from a TV camera station and then realised that throughout the tifos they had hidden the huge 'YOU'LL NEVER WALK ALONE' banner, which hangs from the top tier by the Via Armenia 5r ultras during every fixture in tribute to Anfield's famous terrace, the Kop. This had afforded them a respectful round of applause on defeating Liverpool at home. It surprised me that, unlike Borussia Dortmund, who also adopted the famous anthem, there was no quick rendition from the home crowd.

Arriving much later in 2022, there was no crammed corridor to squeeze along, and it left me to skip up the interior stairs towards the terrace just in time for the fan choreographies. With the players still going through some pre-game training routines, Genoa's fans had already started. A huge flag, half red and half blue covered the entire Nord, with a club crest in the centre surrounded by their nine Scudetto shields. One side read 'UN GRANDE' and the other 'CUORE COSI' (such a big heart). In response, the Sampdoria fans held a blue banner across the Sud with 'PASSIONE E ORGOGLIO DI QUESTA CITTA' (passion and pride of this city) in white lettering, while the tier from above unfurled an equally large flag covering the terrace mirroring their classic shirt, with front hoops and shield, and 'La' and 'Sud' written in each corner. This time the Sampdoria fans were making use of the Distini, but with a much less impressive version of the flag rippling over the fans behind the goal.

Il Grifone's fans held aloft their flag for so long that you almost forgot it was still flying as the home supporters started whistling the Genoa team announcement, which only stopped to welcome their own side on to the pitch and then provided an impressive rendition of the classic master of ceremonies routine of calling the forename of a player and allowing the supporters to complete the surname formalities. The Genoa ultras unrolled their flag to reveal another display across the Nord, made up of individual placards, replicating the red and blue halves, but with Genoa in joined-up font emblazoned in white cardboard. Above it was a white banner, stand-wide, with 'questa lunga leggenda e rossa e blu' (this long legend is red and blue). At the other end of the stadium, though, the Sampdoria fans were holding their scarves high and belting out an emotive version of 'Ma il cielo e sempre piu blu'. Multiple pyrotechnics exploding from within the Genoa ultras could not spoil the sound. These seemed to spark the discharging of several around us, while a middle-aged man next to me lit a huge cigar and I wondered if he had gone too early celebrating Genoa's demotion.

Within the opening minute of the first encounter, Matuzalém had a goalbound effort blocked, and it was clear that Genoa were after the lead their supporters demanded, but Sampdoria rallied, Manolo Gabbiadini having a similar attempt thwarted. Angelo Palombo also saw a free kick fly just wide and Roberto Soriano headed over, all within ten minutes. It was surprising that any attacking took place inside the first quarter of the match, with an astonishing 13 of the 34 fouls that would take place committed. Rather than the referee's decision to penalise players bringing a sense of calm, it was a Sampdoria goal that had such an effect. On 24 minutes, Shkodran Mustafi played a ball from halfway into the feet of the debuting (although returning on loan from Catania) Maxi López. He quickly offloaded to Éder, who played a one-touch lofted ball over López and his marker. The Argentine striker reacted first and fired a low, first-time shot that deflected off an outstretched Nicolás Burdisso and bobbled over helpless Genoa goalkeeper Mattia Perin.

The whole Samp bench, except for coach Siniša Mihajlović, created a wave of shiny black, knee-length coats as they sprinted the length of the pitch to celebrate with the players and fans. Gabbiadini looked full of enthusiasm despite the drab weather and, with Genoa struggling to restrict his contributions, Andrea Bertolacci was cautioned for a robust challenge on the youngster. With feelings impaired by trailing, the Genoa supporters around us were incensed that the challenge would even warrant a yellow card. Just as it appeared the first period would peter out through a series of needless fouls, the Genoa attack came to life. Captain Alberto Gilardino with a tame header and Bertolacci with a long-range drive had efforts saved by Angelo da Costa, and then they believed they had equalised. Bertolacci scuffed a right-footed shot which defender Luca Antonelli stabbed home from four yards. Before he could raise his arm in full to salute the Genoa supporters going wild, he was waving it furiously at the assistant referee, who had signalled for offside.

The first half of the match in 2022 was eerily similar to eight years earlier. The home side went close when Antonio Candreva whipped over a low cross from the right flank, which Stefano Sensi side-footed wide, and the visitors responded. Nadiem Amiri sent a dipping effort at goal that Emil Audero could only palm into the ground, allowing striker Mattia Destro to head a fraction over the crossbar. The surrounding supporters were expressing their displeasure with the referee soon afterwards, as he halted play to warn Candreva about persistent fouling. Something had pumped the veteran winger up for the game and he played a part in *Il Doria* taking the lead on 25 minutes, just as they had in 2014. The Italian sent over a high ball that the *Rossoblu* defence failed to deal with and, when left-back Tommaso Augello returned a low high-speed cross, loanee Abdelhamid Sabiri burst through two Genoa players unnoticed and volleyed home from ground level just two yards from goal.

Those around me soared almost synchronised in celebration as a tremendous roar rolled around the Luigi Ferraris and, as the ecstasy relented, I noticed a woman in front of me embracing her companion as tears ran from her eyes. I would have loved to know whether they were in the hope that the goal would send Genoa down or that *La Samp* were closer to survival, especially with three quarters of the match remaining. Sampdoria stood their ground as Genoa continued to dominate possession before a scrappy period of head tennis in the home box exposed the quality on offer, as did a wayward shot from the edge of the box by Milan Badelj that ended the attack and also brought hostile cries of 'Genoa, Genoa, vaffanculo!' Neither side could build any momentum, such was the amount of misplaced passes and fouls in midfield, although only Audero was cautioned during the opening period. The half ended with a little excitement when another Candreva cross found Sabiri at the back post, but Genoa custodian Salvatore Sirigu made a terrific save. Next, Caleb Ekuban and Destro both fired efforts into the side netting in injury time.

Desperate for the toilet but also dehydrated from standing all day in the Genoa sunshine, I raced into the darkness of the Marassi bowels, also keen to find a fresh vantage point for the second half. On the way back towards the pitch, though, I got sidetracked by refreshments signs and unnecessarily went searching for another beer. I was quickly wedged into a narrow corridor with several others, not sure where I was heading and looking over the shoulders of a couple of fans watching the first-half highlights on their smartphone. When I reached the end of the hallway, what

I found was a shock. The stadium refreshment kiosk was a shoebox-sized hole carved out of a brick wall. A handful of young men were pouring bottle after bottle of beer into plastic cups and little else, so I requested two and handed over €10, holding out a hand to receive some change and only meeting a shake of the head.

* * *

Taking advantage of the 9pm start back in 2014, the supporters had made the most of nightfall with multiple pyrotechnic displays at the break, which delayed the start of the second half for a moment. When the smoke had cleared, Sampdoria forced Perin into another save from Roberto Soriano, convincing coach Gasperini to place no further confidence in the starting 11. On came winger Giannis Fetfatzidis for defender Sebastien De Maio in an obvious change of formation. The diminutive Greek had not arrived to add defensive physicality to their efforts and was noticeably the smallest player on the pitch at 5ft 6in. Yet few more attacks were created until the 65th minute when Bertolacci played a clever pass through the Sampdoria defensive lines to Moussa Konaté. The Senegal international controlled the ball instantly with his right foot and drilled low past Da Costa with his left. This time it took both players and supporters longer to realise that Konaté had strayed offside, leaving the *Rossoblu* fans to endure the taunting from the *Il Doria* following.

A second disallowed goal had Sampdoria fans believing that they would avenge that early season defeat, while Genoa's players took their growing frustrations out on their opponents. Matuzalém, Giuseppe Sculli and Paolo De Ceglie were all booked for needless fouls during the final attritional ten minutes. When the whistle blew, the Sud erupted and flags were waved frantically as the players' arms interlocked celebrating with them. Sampdoria moved into 13th, two points behind Genoa, in the only race either were still interested in.

At the end of the match it was great to see most of the Gradinata Nord still present displaying their unwavering support, defying the celebrations at the opposite end, which were impressive. Some local rivalries I have witnessed have seen fans of the losing side often exiting long before the clock reaches 80 minutes. Even if the waves in their direction from the players looked half-hearted, Genoa had technically won the league clashes 3-1 on aggregate. We, well maybe not Dan, felt compelled to watch the drama play out and were some of the last to leave despite two sides of the stadium having emptied, but Genoa fans were still letting off smoke flares.

In May 2022 there was much more drama as the match reached its conclusion. Other than a shot over the crossbar by goalscorer Sabiri straight after the restart, Sampdoria struggled to threaten the Genoa goal, maybe realising that their rivals had not kept a clean sheet in eight games. I had now moved to the upper tier expecting a better view of the Samp attacks, but most of the action remained at the far end of the ground. However, all *Il Grifone* could muster was a deflected strike from club captain Domenico Criscito and another wasted effort from Badelj, slicing the ball well wide from the edge of the box again on 80 minutes.

Ageing Sampdoria hero Fabio Quagliarella arriving seven minutes later appeared to prompt the Genoa fans to toss several flares on to the pitch. That brought a significant delay to proceedings, as they first had to be removed and then there was a wait for the pitch-level smoke to clear. The *Blucerchiati* supporters around the stadium booed the actions of their city cousins, before the Gradinata Sud broke into furious screams of 'Doria, Doria, Doria'. As the fourth official raised the electronic board to signal a minimum of six minutes of added time, the Gradinata Sud came alive, sensing the three points and that their hated neighbours were teetering on the brink of relegation. The songs and chants coming from the terrace were louder and more purposeful, firecrackers got lost among the commotion, and flags were waved with more vigour.

Then, halfway through the additional time, Destro contested a cross with defender Alex Ferrari and the ball rolled out for a corner kick. As we awaited the delivery, a Sampdoria player fell to the ground, delaying the set piece further, and whistles rang out from both sets of supporters. When referee Fabio Maresca then signalled for a VAR (Video Assistant Referee) review, it could only mean one thing and the Genoa screeches turned into cheers. A brief look at the video monitor and the official awarded a penalty for the ball brushing Ferrari's forearm, although there was also a high foot during the earlier collision. What was laughable was the yellow card for the 28-year-old Ferrari as it was an accidental handball. The Sampdoria fans fell almost silent for a moment as the experienced 35-year-old Criscito waited patiently for the opportunity to secure another vital point.

There was no one else the *Grifone* supporters wanted standing over the ball, having converted five penalties from five already that season. When Maresca put the whistle to his lips, 97 minutes were showing on the advertising hoarding clock. Criscito took a few steps forward but placed a tame left-footed attempt at the perfect height for Audero to push away. The Sud celebrated louder than any goal scored that campaign, as I watched the defender drop to his knees and pull his shirt over his head.

There was still time for one last attack, but it came to nothing and left the Genoa players staring at the sky in disbelief as the final whistle sounded. The noise coming from the animated Sampdoria fans was incredible and parties that would last long into the night began. The Genoa supporters were once again remaining behind to cheer their players off the pitch, preoccupied by comforting skipper Criscito, who was sobbing uncontrollably among team-mates near the halfway line.

Much like 2014, as I headed back towards my accommodation via a route under several bridges, there was the familiar sight of brake lights trickling away from the stadium and singing from within the Luigi Ferraris echoing in the background, although this time at a much higher volume, given that two-thirds of the supporters were inside celebrating. Several waiting in the traffic responded to the horns of overloaded mopeds speeding past, either in cheering for *Il Doria* or trying to provoke distraught *Rossoblu* fans.

You might think that I would feel shortchanged, with just two goals across 180-plus minutes of football, although it was a significant accomplishment getting to witness the first encounter. Yet both fixtures delivered, even with dreadful weather first time around. Had the football matched the quality of entertainment off the pitch, they would have been quite something. With both sides' glory days long gone and struggling in mid-table or worse, the football was, like most derbies, a little low on quality, but excellent nevertheless.

2

Derby della Capitale – Rome, Italy

CONSIDERING THE impact of the Roman Empire, I find it surprising that the Italian capital's football clubs, Società Sportiva Lazio and Associazione Sportiva Roma, do not command the same authority. They have failed to dominate, even domestically, when compared most recently to Juventus or the great AC Milan side of the late 1980s and early 1990s.

As a fresh faced nine-year-old, my interest in European, if not world, football began watching Italia '90 and listening to Luciano Pavarotti providing the perfect soundtrack for a tournament high on drama but low on quality. The Italian league, Serie A, was at its strongest. Even Napoli, under the mesmerising magic of Diego Maradona, had a significant presence outside the peninsula.

When the *Biancocelesti* (the White and Sky Blues) announced a multimillion-pound deal for England international Paul Gascoigne, and Bari and Sampdoria signed fellow World Cup stars David Platt and Des Walker respectively, Italy was more important to focus on.

Despite being founded in 1900, with two major trophies, you understood Lazio's lack of recognition across Europe and why I had to research just who Gascoigne was joining. It turned out that, concerned by a lack of trophies won in the capital, former Italian prime minister Benito Mussolini had a role in founding AS Roma. The fascist dictator intervened in 1927 to influence Roma's formation. Trio Foot Ball Club di Roma, SS Alba-Audace and Fortitudo-Pro Roma SGS merged, not to increase exposure, but to challenge and dominate northern clubs. At the start of the 20th century the sheer number of clubs in existence in Rome was becoming restrictive.

Had army general Giorgio Vaccaro not supported *Le Aquile*'s (The Eagles) fight to remain independent and made an almost conscious effort to ignore city colours and symbols, there would be no rivalry to celebrate. That early display of defiance helped to fuel the ill feeling that remains today, whereas the creating of the *Giallorossi* (the Yellow and Reds) somewhat saw Lazio relegated to second-class citizens in a city they once dominated.

Based 40 miles outside Rome, south-east of Lago Albano, it was a label many would struggle to shake off. Their proximity to the countryside has them referred to as *Burini* (Peasants) by the *Romanisti*.[15] Lazio reclaiming city supremacy is another fascinating aspect of the ongoing hostility between the pair.

With a limited budget and Liverpool facing Bournemouth at Anfield, my first journey to the *Derby della Capitale* started with a restless five hours of sleeping on the floor of Gatwick Airport. Friends took a slight detour on their way back to Portsmouth.

I first slept rough as a 15-year-old in November 1996 after a rearranged Merseyside derby, somehow unaware that

---

15 AS Roma followers are collectively referred to as *Romanisti*

trains did not run 24 hours a day. Although I expected my grandfather to know. He had a certain laissez-faire attitude towards planning, though, and knew of a spot the homeless used at London Waterloo that would 'see us all right until morning'.

After drowsily passing through departures, I awoke from the jolt of aircraft wheels hitting the runway and was brought back to life by the chaos of Rome-Fiumicino International Airport. One half of the crowd was awaiting the return of loved ones and the other was offering taxi services. The Leonardo Express train delivered me to Roma Termini station, just as my stomach reminded me that the last thing I ate was pre-match pie and chips the previous day.

After pausing at Toast Amore, I had my first interaction with the Roman locals. Exhausted from travel, I looked up from my brunch to see a burly, unshaven man in his late 30s who had already approached my table and with a determined handshake insisted we had met the night before in a bar, which would have been preferable to sleeping on a cold concrete floor. He gripped my hand ever tighter and stared intensely into my eyes. Although it was almost 11am, I think he'd had less sleep than I and more alcohol. Expecting me to wilt under pressure, the silence became too much and he left me to eat. The incident was a reminder that Italian cities I have visited further south, like Naples or Catania, can have an entertaining edginess.

With ten million visitors from outside of Italy each year and many customs and cultures dating back to when it controlled most of the continent, Rome differs so much to capital cities like London, Paris and Madrid. Those are the economic strongholds of their nations and more identifiably metropolitan. However, the superior weather lends a certain holiday feel to the Italian capital, despite being home to three million locals. Stumbling across so many important monuments, from Ancient Rome to classical or Imperial Roman-style buildings, plays a huge role in making it seem so different and provides a distinctive charm. Lazio and Roma have struggled on the pitch because of the capital's dependence on tourism, an economy characterised by a lack of heavy industry that could not compete with Turin, Milan, and even Genoa.

Things started positively for Roma. Within 15 years of their formation they became the first of the capital pair to win a Serie A title, in 1941/42, despite the *Biancocelesti* having a near three-decade head start. That body blow almost sparked a Lazio fightback and five years later they almost clinched the Scudetto themselves only to end the season as runners-up to Bologna. *Le Aquile* secured a Coppa Italia in 1958, but were soon surpassed again when *Il Lupi* (The Wolves) lifted the trophy in 1964 and 1969, Roma having already added a European crown to their honours board with the 1961 Inter-Cities Fairs Cup – the forerunner to the UEFA Cup.

* * *

People often question me travelling alone, unless assuming business, and Marco, who greeted me at the accommodation, was no different, although quicker than most to proclaim his allegiance to Roma and insisting on knowing who I favour. I attempted to remain neutral, but with Roma being drawn against Liverpool in the Champions League just before departing, I joked that I should want a Lazio win. He suggested light-heartedly that I should hide my club allegiance from any Roma ultras I meet. A look in his eyes implied an element of truth. With Lazio the assigned home team, though, I had little intention of straying into enemy territory.

I disembarked at Flaminio station four hours before kick-off in search of the tram to take towards Ponte Milvio bridge, an area known for congregating *Laziali* and close to the Stadio Olimpico's Curva Nord terrace. It's the regular home of their hardcore support and beyond the restrictions of the capital's metro system, and off limits to *Romanisti*.

The Lazio ultras have made more headlines than the team in recent years: paying tribute to Mussolini in Milan in April 2019; in October 2017 displaying an antisemitic message and distributing stickers of Anne Frank in a Roma shirt; spending the first game of the 2019/20 campaign paying tribute to murdered *Irriducibili* (Irreducible) leader Fabrizio Piscitelli. The 53-year-old, known more widely as 'Diabolik', was shot in the back of the neck, execution-style, while sitting on a park bench in broad daylight, most likely because of his criminal connections.

It was the 1960s when ultra movements across the peninsula became more prominent, and the Tifoseria Laziale were no different; half a dozen small groups filling the Curva Sud (not Nord as now) terraces on matchdays, until 1971, when a more united collection of fans formed the Commandos Monteverde Lazio (CML), and later the Gruppi Associati Bianco Azzurri (GABA). They then merged to become the Eagle Supporters. The British influence in the creation of many groups resulted in the Anglicisation of their name.

The move to the Curva Nord came about when a group called VIKING Lazio formed, and the Eagles flew north and made it the stronghold it is today. It is unclear whether VIKING disbanded, but they are known not to have migrated. A decade later, the *Irriducibili*, formed by Antonio Grinta, arrived and wrestled power away from the Eagles, changing how the ultras supported their team, yielding power over the terraced masses and how they profited from their obsession as the side triumphed on the pitch.

In 1992, entrepreneur Sergio Cragnotti took control of the *Biancocelesti* and, just as the new millennium approached, he was constructing a squad envied across Europe, albeit at a huge financial cost, as the likes of Siniša Mihajlović, Marcelo Salas, Hernán Crespo and Pavel Nedvěd arrived in Rome during one of the largest spending sprees witnessed in world football. In irrational protest, they believe Roma supporters refused to purchase Cragnotti-branded milk Cirio, convinced that a three cent rise per litre was because of their rivals' lavish spending. When Lazio defeated the *Giallorossi* four times during the 1997/98 season and won the Coppa Italia, I could have forgiven the *Laziali* for thinking life had peaked. Yet their wildest dreams were soon to be fulfilled.

As Roma watched on, *Le Aquile* matched their European success by lifting the 1999 European Cup Winners' Cup. Lazio then capped their centenary celebrations in perfect style, winning a historic league and cup double. An amazing late run under coach Sven-Göran Eriksson enabled them to catch Juventus on the last day. A reported 200,000 *Biancocelesti* fans took over the capital to hail the most important of seven trophies won over three campaigns. However, within two years, the dream became a nightmare. Cirio, ultimately Cragnotti, defaulted on private bonds worth €1bn during a major economic crisis, which saw his empire come crashing down and the squad dismantled.

After navigating my way through a sea of market traders selling counterfeit football shirts, sunglasses and trainers, and table after table of €1 magnets and key rings, the sight of the few sky-blue scarves convinced me of my trajectory and then the tram station finally emerged. A mass of bodies had gathered and, when the first tram arrived, the crowd converged upon the carriages, squeezing against each other until beyond normal capacity and those of us inside tried not to make eye contact with disappointed faces at almost every stop we passed, heading northwards.

With the bridge in view, I disembarked and headed towards a group of Lazio followers surrounding Cornetto Imperiale, watching another Serie A match playing on a large widescreen TV in the bar's corner. After lifting two bottles of Peroni from the fridge, it felt like an unreasonable number of supporters were agonising over a routine Juventus victory over Sampdoria. What was missing was the bravado, sometimes misplaced, often found ahead of fixtures regardless of form or opposition.

Earlier in that 2017/18 season, Roma had defeated Lazio 2-1 in a hard-fought encounter memorable for a laughable attempt by midfielder Kevin Strootman to win a penalty despite a swinging *Biancocelesti* leg missing the Dutchman by some distance. The VAR avoided widespread outrage, though, which would have had Roman conspiracy theorists debating for years. For the rest of the season the duo vied for a UEFA Champions League qualification place, *Le Aquile* holding a slim advantage. Roma had a major European semi-final to look forward to against Liverpool, though, whereas Lazio went out of the UEFA Europa League quarter-finals three days before the Serie A fixture.

The sound of helicopters hovering just overhead interrupted the tranquillity generated by the regulars' concentration on events in Turin, monitoring the increasing numbers marching towards the stadium. A mixture of those around the bar were tilting their heads skyward or scanning passing groups for anything more sinister than vociferous chanting. Juventus grabbed a second goal through Benedikt Höwedes and a man looking in from the doorway lets out a booming cry of 'Ciao Napoli'. The Old Lady of Italian football has no obvious connection with Lazio, but it was clear the locals preferred they win the title ahead of southern rivals Napoli.

I decided to follow the increasing numbers crossing the River Tibor, squeezing between tightly parked cars and scooters, being abandoned anywhere and everywhere. Two tiny Fiat 500s had even mounted a concrete traffic island in the middle of the road. Ticket inspectors must not work when the derby is scheduled, a bit like taxi drivers in Genoa. Halfway across the Ponte Milvio, miserable-looking armed police examined supporters passing through the bridge's narrow arches. With the sun setting and flashing blue lights behind them, they resembled your average nightclub bouncer – had it not been for the significant number of automatic weapons on show. There were some boisterous teenagers but there was a minimal threat from our direction of travel.

There appeared more need for their presence at the handful of bars behind them, where hundreds of singing Lazio fans had congregated. The closer you got the louder the matchday sounded and the scent of pyrotechnics became more prominent. Just as I considered where my next refreshment break would be, a large group of strutting *Biancocelesti* fans emerged from the Piazzale di Ponte Milvio and caught my eye with the energetic waving of a Scottish flag. Their ferocious singing and chance crossing were too good an opportunity to miss and I joined the parade, trying not to look out of place.

As we advanced, a couple of fans ignited a smoke flare that got thrown ahead of us, before they tossed a firecracker to our right. Although following its trajectory and final destination, the explosion still startled me. A few members of the group stopped for beers at Il Punto Caldo. A mobile panini truck boomed out Lazio anthems from two of the biggest speakers possible, but not loud enough to resist the delicious-looking sandwiches.

As I tore my way through a prosciutto-filled version. A pair in their early 20s asked whether I wanted firecrackers, although it was just a conversation starter before offering me some cocaine, 'just for later'. Which I declined. Noise from inside the Stadio Olimpico was so loud that I could hear it across the surrounding area. Supplemented by the Roma fans at the other end of the oval-shaped arena, you could feel the atmosphere crackling in the air – a quick reminder that it was the biggest fixture left in a Lazio season fading into insignificance and envy, if *Il Lupi* were to capture Europe's biggest crown.

With 35 minutes until kick-off, I rushed past the Ministry of Foreign Affairs, where thousands of fans gathered at the entry gates. However, I realised that, in my efforts to seek the *Laziali*, my entry point was the other side of a tall steel barrier. After turning around, I took a sharp left turn and climbed the ever-inclining Viale dello Stadio Olimpico running along the west of the ground until reaching a poorly lit service road closed off to vehicles.

The opening between the Olimpico roof and walls allowed the floodlights to provide some illumination of the pathway. When entrance 8S appeared, my pace quickened. Security guards at both checkpoints rushed me through, checking my passport against the ticket, so I would not miss the start. Before I knew it I was soon standing in wonder at the colours and sounds of the Stadio Olimpico in full flow.

As I took my place, the supporters released *Biancocelesti*'s famous mascot, eagle Olimpia, from somewhere upon high and she soared down towards her handler. Music accompanied her arrival, but it was difficult to hear in the din reverberating around the stadium. I could feel the hairs on the back of my neck prickle. Having missed the team announcements, I was forced to watch the big screen nearby to know who would appear for Roma.

Such was the volume of whistles and jeers ringing around the stadium that two-thirds of the ground became covered in booming roars. Accompanied by consistent heavy drumming, the Olimpico foundations almost shook as if a giant was approaching and crushing all in their path. The crowd were being whipped into a frenzy as they announced the home team, ahead of an emotional rendition of the club anthem 'Vola Lazio Vola' (Fly Lazio Fly).

With the two captains and officials having completed the pre-match formalities, the teams began defending their respective curva and, as with Genoa, I reflected upon the masses of opposition fans enhancing the spectacle. A sea of red and yellow flags swayed and pockets of flares were among the troops, generating enough support for it to feel like an even split of spectators filling the vast bowl.

As the action got under way, the players struggled to hear the referee's whistle. An opening ten minutes lacking incident soon dampened the mood, until ex-Liverpool midfielder Lucas Leiva misplaced a pass and smashed into a Roma player in his attempt to rectify the mistake, collecting a needless yellow card. The act brought an element of familiarity to proceedings as the home supporters whistled their unhappiness at the referee's lack of sympathy.

In the hospitality section below, a handful of security guards dressed in immaculate three-piece suits looked disinterested with either the match or their employers, as they chain-smoked their way through a packet of cigarettes. The Lazio fans became the first to raise the volume on 30 minutes, urging their players to continue their advance on the opposition goal, despite a *Giallorossi* man lying prone. Then they bemoaned the eventual act of sportsmanship from winger Felipe Anderson, a deed that could have backfired moments later when Roma full-back Bruno Peres rifled a low shot against the foot of *Le Aquile*'s goalpost. What followed was a collective gasp as loud as some goals I have experienced.

At half-time, I scanned the Curva Nord in greater detail and spotted a flag missed earlier, adorned with Gascoigne in Lazio kit and holding a pint of Guinness. It brought back memories of his arrival when the ultras welcomed him with a banner reading 'GAZZA'S BOYS are here … SHAG women … DRINK beer!' Strong, if not poetic.

A hero before he had kicked a ball, Gascoigne cemented that status with his contribution to this fixture on 29 November 1992. Ahead of the game he had told *Football Italia*, 'Sunday is like life or death for me and, I hope, come Sunday, I'm still alive.' It is often wrongly remembered that the midfielder won the game with an 86th-minute header, when in fact it was an equalising goal as important as a winner.

This instalment would have no such excitement. Edin Džeko of Roma and Lazio's Ciro Immobile wasted opportunities, which both sets of supporters reacted to as if near-misses, but more out of desperation than reality. The histrionics of midweek Champions League hero Kostas Manolas[16] earned a bigger reaction. The *Laziali* became enraged at the defender frequently.

On 75 minutes, Lazio attacker Luis Alberto went close with a drilled effort, but two gigantic explosions in the Curva

---

16 On 10 April 2018, four days before the *Derby della Capitale*, Manolas scored an 82nd-minute header against Barcelona to win their Champions League quarter-final second leg 3-0, which meant that Roma won the tie 5-4 on away goals

Sud caused an abrupt halt to the groans of supporters. With Lazio defender Ștefan Radu sent off for a second bookable offence five minutes later, not losing became as important as taking three points. In injury time, though, Džeko sent a powerful header against the crossbar and a looping effort from the halfway line by Lazio's Sergej Milinković-Savić almost delivered an unexpected moment of ecstasy.

With the flanks of the Olimpico having departed, the Curva Sud stood proud. The Lazio fans sung along to the club anthem blasting out from the stadium loudspeakers. A man in his mid-30s to my left, balancing on a thin wall, arms outstretched, was pleased that Lazio had kept their slender advantage. There will have been worse goalless draws in these clashes.

On 15 May 2005, with three games left to play and neither side safe from relegation, a lifeless stalemate saved them both, suspected to have resulted from a gentleman's agreement between captains Paolo Di Canio and Antonio Cassano ahead of the game.

I took my chances heading south past the *Romanisti* leaving the stadium, with little choice but to walk back to my accommodation. And they appeared anything but satisfied with this result. By delaying my departure, I had missed the swell of fans leaving and walked among the few small groups heading into the darkness. But some sets of individuals were choosing to kick over rubbish bins or smash items against buildings and cars for no real reason. These mindless idiots, who you come across in day-to-day life, were setting a handful of bins on fire with unused flares.

Once clear of the disturbance being caused by these morons, the humid night air provided perfect conditions for a moonlit walk along the Tibor and back into the city centre, in direct contrast to the atmosphere three hours earlier.

My next visit to Rome and the *Derby della Capitale*, in January 2020, would be more relaxed. It produced much more on-field action and was witnessed from the less sterile Curva Sud. In addition, I had the company of journalist Alasdair Mackenzie, after meeting two days before the match and having a very enjoyable evening at the delightful Be.Re. bar.

A graduate of the University of Edinburgh in his homeland, Alasdair moved to the Italian capital around a decade earlier and started following Lazio. A veteran of seven derbies, Alasdair's first experience was as a student in 2011 and, given the difficulties of getting a ticket, it had cost him €120, which made my paying €90 in 2018 easier to accept. Now watching on from the comfort of the press box, Alasdair had a healthier euro-to-derby investment, although it sounded like there was a trade-off with the added anxiety he suffered – unable to watch on with fellow *Laziali*, and the only fixture in which it became difficult to maintain neutrality.

While stopping at Ristorante Giulio Cesare to ensure that Stacey ate before I left, I received a message from Alasdair asking if we could meet at Bar Metro, just outside the Ottaviano metro, where he was catching up on the early Serie A fixture between Inter and Fiorentina. By pure chance, there was one solitary Mini Mart between the two venues.

He had also suggested that, given the walk north along Viale Angelico would take around 30 minutes, we could travel by Uber bicycle and save some time. However, I had assumed that Alasdair had used one before, but the fact that he hadn't resulted in us spending around 15 minutes looking for which one was ours and thinking the transaction code on the app was the registration number of our bike.

We flew, with electronic assistance, along the cycle path leading all the way to the stadium, passing hundreds of Roma fans en route, and much of the graffiti that appears around the city ahead of a derby, which is usually signed by the specific fan group, as Alasdair explained.

Despite his allegiance to Lazio, knowing I had secured a €30 ticket with the Roma hardcore and with the *Giallorossi* at home, Alasdair headed for *Romanisti* hotspot Bar della Musica. Convenient in its placement by the Ponte della Musica bridge nearby, a well-known site of altercations between the two sets of fans, it was the last official Uber drop-off area.

* * *

Without doubt the best-supported club in Rome, it never takes long to have a *Romanisti* telling you they are the only side that truly represents the capital. Lazio's agricultural origins on the city borders are used as evidence they were never Roman or too uneducated to appreciate being the representative of a city of such stature. It all fuels a mutual hatred for each other that sometimes spills into tragedy. *Biancocelesti* fan Vincenzo Paparelli was killed when struck in the eye by a flare hurled from the Roma section in 1979, an incident that reinforced the view that the fixtures were synonymous with violent acts, although it was the first fatality in an Italian stadium resulting from crowd violence.

More common over the next four decades were inflammatory tifos, with the distasteful unfurling of a 50m-long banner by Lazio ultras reading 'Auschwitz is your town, the ovens [are] your houses' during the 1998/99 season. That gave the media another opportunity to label all Lazio fans as racist. Di Canio gave further reason to attach this tag, which Alasdair feels is unwarranted for an entire fanbase, by celebrating victory over Roma in 2005 with a fascist salute.

Instead, Lazio and Roma fans are as known for clashes with other supporters and the police. In 1989, fighting with Milan supporters outside of the San Siro ended with the death of young ultra Antonio De Falchi.

Individuals claiming to be *Aquile* fans undertook an orchestrated attack on Tottenham Hotspur supporters in 2012, with one Spurs follower having his head hacked open with a machete.

March 2004 appeared to have been the last time that violence marred the derby. The fans came together to battle with police after they had forced referee Roberto Rosetti to abandon the match four minutes into the second half. Riots broke out around the Stadio Olimpico because of false reports of a boy being killed outside the stadium by police.

Roma legend Francesco Totti understood the severity of the situation and was first to plead with the officials to end the contest. It did little to quell the fan unrest, and a lengthy war between supporters and police saw streets ablaze. Some 170 police officers needed medical treatment when the fighting eventually ended and 13 arrests made.

On 11 November 2007, the bitter rivals came together once more amid widespread chaos across the country. This time there had been a fatality, with 26-year-old *Biancocelesti* fan Gabriele Sandri killed by a stray police bullet while sitting in his car at a service station. The shot was intended to distract Lazio and Juventus fans fighting – who were not even facing each other – but struck Sandri in the neck.

The authorities postponed Inter v Lazio and Roma v Cagliari, but Atalanta v Milan was only halted when ultras began tearing down protective barriers to get on the pitch. In Rome, hundreds of armed ultras from both sides attacked police guarding the Italian Olympic National Committee headquarters, with scenes similar to those seen in 2004.

* * *

Surrounded by *Giallorossi* fans kitted out in club colours, Bar della Musica resembled a mobile snack bar supplemented by an enormous television screen on one side and a 20m-long covered extension bustling with tables full of people, adding an element of permanency. After joining the queue, there was a sudden outpouring of cheering and applause. The people in the road with us were clearing for the Roma coach.

Moments later we were standing among them with beers in hand, feeding off the positive energy of the expectant crowd. I then realised that Alasdair was a little uncomfortable behind enemy lines and, maybe, also sensing that the *Romanisti* believed that the day was an opportunity to disrupt the high-flying *Biancocelesti*, lessening his own optimism.

Despite suffering a surprise defeat to Napoli in the Coppa Italia quarter-final the previous Tuesday night, free-scoring Lazio were arriving on the back of 11 straight league wins. With a game in hand, they had overtaken Inter as the most likely team to stop reigning champions Juventus clinching a ninth title in a row. Immobile had bagged 23 Serie A goals and looked unstoppable.

The *Giallorossi* had stuttered all campaign, with winning runs in short supply. Victory over Genoa the previous weekend boosted morale but they had suffered back-to-back defeats before that, to Torino and Juventus. Unable to call upon a striker in the same form as Immobile, Roma's ability to keep pace with the top-scoring sides in Serie A had allowed them to cling on to the last Champions League qualification place. Therefore, both sets of players had plenty to fight for at the Stadio Olimpico.

Just across the road from Bar della Musica was a disused petrol station that, during the last 30 minutes, had received an increasing number of visitors both young and old who used it as a parking spot for mopeds, looking unconcerned that anything would happen to them while at the match. And there was no one offering to 'watch' the vehicles for a small fee.

Alasdair left for the press area just over an hour before kick-off, so I grabbed another beer and sheepishly ventured inside to a vacated stool and joined everyone in watching the last moments of Parma v Udinese. As I watched those filtering out, I noticed several of the older generation following their beers with espressos. Not a tradition I had plans to replicate soon.

Then I brought attention to myself with a few strange looks in my direction when getting overexcited finding a forgotten Twix chocolate bar stuffed in my jacket pocket. My delight led a man in his 60s on an adjacent table to approach me and ask me something in Italian, to which I could only reply – in Italian – with, 'Sorry, I'm English.' It's a phrase I have used plenty over the years. In broken English, he introduced himself as Giuseppe and enquired why I was attending.

Giuseppe was a long-standing *Romanisti*, who started following Roma during something of a resurgence in the early 1980s, although, once again, it was cup success rather than championship dominance. *Il Lupi* won four Coppa Italias, and they did capture the Serie A crown in 1983 under coach Nils Liedholm.

Lazio fans, in contrast, were suffering. In 1979/80, a points deduction for illegal betting activity on matches saw the *Biancocelesti* relegated. They would return to the top flight and just avoid relegation in 1984, when they saw their joy multiplied after Roma lost that season's European Cup Final at the Stadio Olimpico to Liverpool. Giuseppe insisted that *Romanisti* had the last laugh, though, as a year later Lazio finished bottom of the table with a mere 15 points.

Without revealing my allegiances, I told him I was more familiar with the title-winning side of 2000/01, Liverpool having knocked Roma out of the UEFA Cup that season. Former AC Milan coach Fabio Capello built a wonderful side that secured a third Scudetto for the *Giallorossi*, but Giuseppe again focused on local rivalries, like a derby victory that campaign secured through Paolo Negro's own goal, from which Roma fans taunted the defender for the rest of his playing days. As I listed off names from that famous side to appear somewhat knowledgeable, the mention of Vincenzo Montella stirred another derby recollection from Giuseppe. In March 2002, the striker became the first player to score four times in the encounter, when Roma won 5-1.

Giuseppe was a little too old to be captivated by Lazio's brief popularity during the early 1970s. Demoted to Serie B in 1971, the *Biancocelesti* turned to coach Tommaso Maestrelli, who somehow assembled a squad of misfits from the lower reaches of Italian football and led them to the top of the domestic pyramid.

* * *

Thanks to the performances of striker Giorgio Chinaglia, Lazio were back among the elite within 12 months of relegation and surprised many by narrowly missing out on the 1972/73 title. Juventus clinched the Scudetto amid conspiracy theories that the *Giallorossi* succumbed to the Old Lady with little resistance to ensure their city cousins missed out. Maybe that was because, during their brief spell in the second tier, Lazio defeated Roma 1-0 in the first round of the Coppa Italia when Chinaglia – named the greatest player in their history during the club's centenary celebrations – netted the only goal.

Not content with his match-winning contribution, though, as *Le Aquile* players were leaving the Olimpico pitch under a shower of coins and other projectiles, the Italian international ran down to the Roma fans with a middle finger held aloft. Chinaglia became a symbol of newfound optimism, was loved by the *Laziali*, and, with a raise of his arm, was a hate figure for *Romanisti*. Not until Paolo Di Canio's salute toward the *Giallorossi* supporters in 2005 was such an act of direct provocation witnessed in the *Derby della Capitale*.

Before the game, some reported, Chinaglia had walked into the Roma dressing room and announced that he would fight their entire team. However, it was their notoriety as a team that would fight their way to victory, that saw them unable to challenge Europe's elite after clinching the Serie A crown in 1973/74.

In the November of that campaign, the *Biancocelesti* faced Ipswich Town in the second leg of the UEFA Cup second round and, after exiting the competition 6-4 on aggregate, all hell broke loose in the capital, forcing the visitors to shelter in the changing room, while Lazio players and fans expressed their frustrations and alleged injustices.

Roma supporters had called in on the visitors' hotel the evening before, to make the travelling team honorary *Romanisti* and added to the discontent within the stadium that night. The eventual outcome was a three-year ban from European competition and missing the rare chance to compete for the European Cup.

That short-lived period of success fell apart in somewhat strange and tragic circumstances. Maestrelli stepped down as coach before succumbing to terminal cancer in

December 1976, while a jewellery shop owner shot and killed midfielder Luciano Re Cecconi when a prank went tragically wrong. *Laziali* favourite Chinaglia became so disconnected with the ownership that he fled to New York Cosmos, having to be smuggled out of Rome for fear that supporters would riot.

* * *

The final whistle in Emilia-Romagna, and recalling my late arrival in 2018, was my sign to head inside and gave another reminder of that previous visit. The local supporters consumed Caffè Borghetti[17] in enormous volumes, which was maybe a modern twist on post-beer espressos. They left you kicking the small black plastic containers out of your path, whichever side were hosting at the Stadio Olimpico. As I joined others shuffling along, Lazio's recent form seemed to have resulted in a subdued atmosphere around me. A gentle hum of conversation filled the air as we eased through the first checkpoint.

When the imposing arena was in view, though, that unbelievable noise from within escalated. Once beyond the perimeter fencing I headed straight towards the turnstiles, ignoring a temporary AS Roma stall and small festival-style stage, with the entertainment inside far more appealing. As I joined those gathering at the gate, people were less courteous and became squeezed against the person in front. Several men in their late 20s trying to barge their way through the crowd.

It was quite satisfying standing my ground and seeing the frustration on their faces, and some metal railings assisted

---

17 Caffè Borghetti is a liquor with a strong coffee flavour, around 30 per cent alcohol and considerable amount of caffeine

my one-man roadblock. Surprised that beer was €1 cheaper inside the stadium and with 30 minutes until the start, I headed towards the refreshments window before spending a while mingling on the congested concourse. However, such was the stench of urine filling my nostrils that I soon departed for the terraces.

Although taking Marco's advice not to expose myself as a Liverpool supporter in April 2018, I had also shrugged off the suggestion that there was anything to fear. I believe that if you are looking for trouble, you will find it, and being a football tourist is a relatively risk-free hobby. Ten days after that trip there was a powerful reminder that, no matter how little interest you may have in finding trouble, it sometimes finds you.

Ahead of the Champions League semi-final first leg at Anfield, as I stood outside The Park Pub full of expectation, around 60 masked Roma ultras armed with weapons attacked a group of Liverpool fans, leaving Sean Cox in a coma and fighting for his life. Three Romans would appear in court 11 months later charged with assault, with 30-year-old Simone Mastrelli sentenced to four years in prison after pleading guilty. UEFA fined Roma €50,000 for crowd disturbance, but it changed Cox's life forever. Also, remembering the angry scenes post-game last time, I was at least slightly wary of being in with this set of fans.

While the Curva Sud is today still awash with a variety of ultra groups, often identifying with a particular neighbourhood within the city, in the late 1970s multiple groups merged to create the Commando Ultra Curva Sud (CUCS), who remain the prominent ultra movement. Police had identified one of those merging, the Fedayn, as Cox's attackers. Highlighting that they still referred to them as single entities.

A collective ideology helped the CUCS become one of the strongest and notorious ultra movements across the peninsula, but it sometimes led to those outside of Italy judging *Romanisti* as one rather than separate groups. The hardcore elements of the Roma support are often associated with left-wing politics, yet the Fedayn and leader Roberto Rulli were communist in their views and, as the next decade began, right-wing groups were present on the Curva Sud through the likes of the Boys of AS Roma.

Alasdair highlighted that it was impossible to associate Lazio or Roma supporters with a specific political belief, believing many outlets made ill-informed attempts to, when commenting on violent acts, which was a source of great frustration for fans.

As I crept up the concrete steps, my eyes became transfixed on the beautiful purple-coloured sky created by the setting sun. Then the floodlights along the rim of the stadium roof came into focus above the Lazio fans filling the Curva Nord opposite. I reached for my smartphone to capture the moment but was shaken by a firecracker that felt like it had detonated alongside me, the serenity of the moment broken and reminding me that this was still a ferocious Rome derby. Often in Italian stadia, Juventus excluded, they leave you to sit wherever you like, but with the Curva Sud almost full already I chose the seat assigned to me only to find two young ladies standing in my place.

I shuffled past them, double-checked the seat number and turned my gaze to the Olimpico crowd. They shuffled to their left and the older gentleman in a deerstalker next to me appeared relieved that he was no longer being disrupted by them constantly taking selfies. It was almost as if this had lifted his entire mood, and it encouraged me to join them in a rendition of 'Lazio, Lazio vaffanculo!' That was interrupted by most of the crowd exclaiming 'Ole' each time another Roma goal against Lazio appeared on the screens above us, with much louder cries arriving when any of the 11 goals legend Francesco Totti netted against their rivals appeared.

* * *

The attacker retired at the end of the 2016/17 campaign after remaining loyal to Roma for his entire career, but he had at least captained them to the Scudetto in 2001.

Being unable to break the recent domestic stranglehold on Serie A from northern powerhouses had left Lazio and Roma with just the Coppa Italia to satisfy their trophy cravings. It was Totti and co who finished the first all-Roman final in 2013 disappointed, the *Biancocelesti* winning through a 71st-minute Senad Lulić goal. In January 2015 Totti wrote another chapter in the fixture's history, becoming its all-time leading scorer on his 40th appearance. Totti rescued a 2-2 draw with a beautifully executed acrobatic volley and famously celebrated with a selfie in front of the Curva Sud.

The fixture meant a lot to Totti. When his career began, players were more accessible. Fans would gather on the walls around the training ground to watch, sometimes singing in support, but also overlooking events with menace to transmit just how important victory was. On 6 March 1994, when Totti emerged from the substitutes' bench to help win a penalty against Lazio, his hero and captain Giuseppe Giannini failed to convert and Roma were beaten 1-0. Fans attacked Giannini as he drove away from training the next day. Two years later, after 15 years with the *Giallorossi*, fans had not forgiven him and Giannini's farewell match turned into a riot. Totti would later comment, 'Losing a derby [back then] would mean six months of ball busting, but still, I loved those days'.[18]

* * *

As I surveyed the small section of empty blue seats in the distance separating the two sets of supporters, another roar from the crowd greeted a suited individual walking along the running track in front of us, fist-pumping and energetically swinging a Roma scarf in our direction. I did not know who he was, despite images from his playing days projected on to the big screens. Alasdair later identified him as former striker Ruggiero Rizzitelli. The club seemed short on legends, but the Italian scored 29 times in 154 Serie A appearances and was crucial when winning the 1991 Coppa Italia.

The anticipation and excitement were clear across both sets of fans, matching each other for the energy and noise on display from their curva. The fans surrounding me started belting out their anthem 'Roma, Roma' by Antonello Venditti, being played out from loudspeakers.

The girls next to me got moved on by a man of a similar age, who soon joined the others singing, making up for the verses that he had missed with his own furious version. With those around me either holding aloft their scarves or shining the lights from mobiles, the floodlights dipped ahead of announcing the starting line-ups. You could see that the Lazio fans were attempting to display 'FORZA LAZIO' in smartphone lights across the Curva Nord. However, confusion among some supporters left the final three characters little more than a random collection of torches.

---

18 Gianani, M., Mieli, L., *Mi chiamo Francesco Totti* (Italy: The Apartment, 2020)

The whistles from the Roma fans grew so loud that the Lazio team remained unknown.

A fan over my right shoulder started a violent cry of 'Lazio Merda, Lazio Merda!' until his voice crackled with anger. Losing this game was beyond comprehension for those around me. As the Curva Sud embarked upon another song, the second part of the Lazio tifo was far more successful, lifting individual cards to form a mosaic displaying two grey forearms with outstretched fingers touching amid a sky blue background as seen on Michelangelo's famous *Creation of Adam* painting adorning the Sistine Chapel's ceiling in Vatican City.

The sheer number of Lazio fans in attendance resulted in their whistles being able to disrupt the Roma singing. A trio of firecrackers exploding throughout our terrace seemed to signal it was time to wave the red and yellow plastic flags left on our seats. I had to wrestle mine from under the foot of the supporter behind me.

The Roma effort looked quite poor in comparison, although from my position I could not see a Roma crest the height of the stand held front and centre of the curva. It was hard enough making out the playing surface. Until the waving stopped six minutes into the match, I wondered whether I would get to see any of the action. When the pitch came into view, the Lazio display changed to a banner stretching across the fans reading 'LA LAZIO NON PROVIENE DA, LA LAZIO E!' (Lazio does not come from [Rome] ... Lazio is [Rome]!).

Just like in many other Italian cities, Alasdair had reflected upon how they would place spies within the camps of their rivals ahead of these fixtures, desperate to win the visual battle between the two, but I found myself disappointed.

At the *Derby della Madonnina* between AC Milan and Inter the previous season, Inter had unfurled an impressive snake tifo only for the *Rossoneri* to respond with a serpent being torn in half. Maybe that spoiled me.

Back in 2000, as Roma charged towards the Scudetto, the Curva Sud unveiled a terrace-sized mosaic that declared 'above us only sky'. Lazio's ultras knew what was coming, though, and unfurled a pre-planned response of 'yes, and it's blue and white'.

Both sides showed more urgency than two years earlier. Although surprising how dominant Roma were over that in-form Lazio side during the first 15 minutes and rewarded on 26 minutes.

While Roma deserved to be ahead, it was down to a huge mistake by Lazio goalkeeper Thomas Strakosha after Bryan Cristante lofted a high ball towards Džeko on the edge of the box. Despite being unlikely to reach the ball, the Greek came rushing out. Džeko beat his marker to the ball and it looped up into the air, landing at the foot of the goalpost and bobbling over the line.

With the action taking place at the goal furthest away, you could feel the brief intake of breath from the *Giallorossi* fans as they awaited confirmation the ball had crossed the line. Then the Curva Sud erupted in celebration. I received congratulatory slaps on my shoulders from behind me as if I had headed it in myself. The older gentleman to my right was standing with hands clasped, thanking a higher power for whatever he had prayed for earlier that morning.

However, within a minute of taking the lead, the celebrations paused. Roma had dispossessed Lazio straight from kick-off and Džeko was driving towards a hesitant *Biancocelesti* defence with the ball. After it was released to

Cengiz Ünder, the young Turkish attacker had a low shot saved by the legs of Strakosha. The loose ball fell to Džeko, but the desperate lunge of a Lazio player deflected his shot away, denying a certain goal. The Curva Sud exploded in celebration with more looking inevitable.

Lazio would regain their composure, and *Romanisti* cheers switched to whistles at each touch by the opposition. Every second they kept possession appeared to increase the volume. When Luis Alberto readied himself to take a corner on 35 minutes, the terrace was aiming so much vitriolic abuse in his direction that I reached to make a note.

As I raised my head back towards the action, disaster struck for Roma in somewhat comic fashion. The ex-Liverpool midfielder swung a curling delivery towards the back post that was sent into the air by the head of Davide Santon. As the ball dropped just outside the goalpost, goalkeeper Pau López punched the ball, sending it spinning backwards towards the goal with his poor connection. He then challenged team-mate Chris Smalling for the dropping ball, which resulted in it falling at the feet of Lazio defender Francesco Acerbi who poked home.

As the *Laziali* went wild, I could hear lots of the Curva Sud muttering things among themselves, accepting that this was inevitable. Just a few pockets of supporters directed their anger towards their often-reliable custodian. The ridiculousness of the goal was the sole reason there was brief hope they would disallow it. VAR looked for something illegitimate, but soon confirmed that the game was 1-1 and balanced on a knife edge.

The first half had produced enough excitement, with thoughts of those around me turning to their usual half-time rituals. With seconds to go, though, Lorenzo Pellegrini struck the post with a curling right-footed shot from range.

A gasp from the Sud preceded a surge of bodies towards the concourses.

I debated trying for a beer, but the sheer number of people shuffling in and out the nearest entrance decided for me. Then I spotted someone selling refreshments on the terrace, which grabbed my attention.

A young man tried to wrestle a beer away from a vendor without paying, giving them the 'do you know who I am' look. The urge to get involved was interrupted by the fans booing an announcement made regarding the activities within both curvas.

Nothing sinister had taken place, to my knowledge. From what I could gather it was nothing more than a standard announcement warning of disrupting the viewing pleasure of others with persistent standing or the use of smoke bombs. Yet there seemed an unreasonable level of animosity towards the broadcast.

The man behind, screaming in my ear earlier, was full of rage again. He needed a win to lift his mood. And then, before you knew it, the players were returning to the pitch to a chorus of high-pitched whistles I was still struggling to cope with, as Lazio entered first. So I was relieved when replaced with cheers of encouragement for the emerging Roma players.

The second period, like the first, began with *Giallorossi* dominance, and Jordan Veretout's low effort from the centre of the box went just wide, helping raise the atmosphere to the pre-break levels.

A minute later, Ünder skilfully made his way towards the Lazio penalty area and delivered a clever pass towards the penalty spot. The onrushing Justin Kluivert appeared to be tripped and the referee awarded a penalty. It felt like they had scored a goal as everyone around me celebrated.

Two girls in front dropped to their seats, though, and were holding hands, praying, unaware that the decision was being reviewed by VAR. While this was going on, there was minor outrage within the curva as Džeko handed spot-kick duties to Pellegrini, but VAR overruled the decision. Fans turned their outrage towards the video officials, wherever they were based on the peninsula.

Despite taking place just ten minutes into the second half, the lengthy delay and lack of penalty had a strange effect on the atmosphere within the Curva Sud, almost bringing an acceptance that that was their last chance to win the game.

For the next ten minutes there was a noticeable tension surrounding each move. When another Strakosha mistake fell to Džeko in the box 15 minutes from time and he hit his effort straight at the goalkeeper, there was no belief that it would spark an assault on the *Biancocelesti* goal.

They instead spent the closing stages displaying their displeasure at various things, like Marco Parolo replacing Alberto given the whistling during the substitution, or widespread abuse of their own players such as Kluivert, after wasting a splendid opportunity when failing to release the ball.

The referee eventually became the focus of complaints and something thrown from the crowd. Considering the distance required to get anywhere near the official, you question why anyone would even attempt this, regardless of how mindless the act was.

On-loan defender Smalling appeared the only player deserving of any praise. However, even I could admit that the Manchester United centre-back looked imperious and the love he received was understandable.

As we awaited the full-time whistle, 'Lazio Merda' was being chanted throughout the curva and you could hear the

Lazio fans opposite whistling to drown out the Roma fans. When the final whistle did sound, the fans around me went into overdrive during renditions of the team anthems and I headed to the exit.

I decided I would walk back to our accommodation when watching a few locals trying to navigate their bicycles through the crowd of bodies heading south.

One of my last memories was the army of hundreds and hundreds of mopeds just past the bar I had sat drinking at earlier being held back by traffic police. I was navigating my way through the brake lights while they were using their horns to display their impatience. Once most of the crowd had passed, the police released them. A few minutes later, wave after wave came humming past me.

Unlike 2018, the Roma supporters walking alongside me seemed content with a point, helped by a significant portion of the season still to be played, and there was no setting light to dustbins or smashing windows. It may also have been a slight sign that the derby was changing, just as modern football was becoming more commercialised and sanitised.

In February 2020, the *Irriducibili* would even disband after 33 years. The group stated that there had been 'too much blood, too many banning orders, too many arrests'.[19] The Curva Nord would now unite under the 'Ultras Lazio' name. However, while the violence may become a distant memory, the passion and competitiveness of the fixture will no doubt endure.

---

19 Campanale, S., 'Lazio "Irriducibili" Ultras Disband' (Football Italia, 2020)

3

Dérbi da Segunda Circular –
Lisbon, Portugal

IN 2004 Portugal came within 90 minutes of claiming a first major honour on the international stage, only for Greece to end their European Championship dreams. The underdogs overcame the odds to defeat the Golden Generation on their own turf, containing the likes of Real Madrid's Luís Figo, Rui Costa of AC Milan and the soon-to-be worldwide phenomenon Cristiano Ronaldo. It was a squad packed with stars that entertained crowds all across the continent. Bringing joy from Manchester to Madrid was the city of Lisbon, which laid claim to some of the best players to grace European football during the previous two decades. Six of the players who took the field originated from the youth ranks of Sport Lisboa e Benfica and Sporting Clube de Portugal.

When Portugal were eventually crowned European champions, Sporting CP would have an even bigger influence, with their academy providing ten of the 14 players who appeared for Portugal in the final at the Stade de France, Paris, 12 years after that fateful day at the Estádio da Luz, home to Benfica. Even considering FC Porto's domestic domination and brief European success of the early 2000s, the two clubs' contribution to Portuguese football ensures that their clashes remain a significant date on the football calendar. It is Lisbon that is the true heartbeat of Portuguese football.

The oldest and most western capital city in Europe, Lisbon is at the mouth of the Tagus River and gained its fame and importance while flourishing in the 15th and 16th centuries as the centre of Portuguese exploration. The Kingdom of Portugal's vast empire gained great wealth and influence as it colonised parts of Africa, Asia and South America. The city may not hold such power and authority anymore but the landscape still reflects the period, many dominating centuries-old buildings still standing, despite much of the centre being destroyed by a huge earthquake in 1755. Almost 150 years later, the first steps that would lead to European supremacy on a sporting level were taken.

Founded at the start of the 1900s, the *Dérbi da Segunda Circular* – stadiums separated by a 2km stretch of highway of the same name – is now entering its second century of competition, first taking place back in 1907, a year after Sporting CP formed in 1906. Eight Benfica players headed across town in search of better playing conditions than they were receiving at *Los Águias* (The Eagles), despite having only been operating since 1904 themselves. Even then, players wanted their value determined by what clubs would offer for their talents. Bankrolled by the wealth of the grandfather of co-founder José Alvalade, Sporting CP had plenty to entice them with.

From a Sporting CP perspective, the famous eight departed under their own free will. Staunch followers of Benfica will say they were 'stolen' from the club with the riches – playing facilities and conditions – on offer. That is the view held by the club, stating in their museum, 'Sporting deprived them of their eight best players, harassing them in exchange for privileged conditions.' A century on, a sour taste remains in Benfica mouths. Immediately, the defectors' decision to leave appeared vindicated with a 2-1 win over their old bosses after convert Cândido Rodrigues netted the opener and Benfica co-founder Cosme Damião ensured the spoils eluded his team, scoring an own goal.

With the sudden lack of players, it forced Benfica president Marcolino Bragança to promote most of the B team up a level just to ensure they could continue to operate. That meeting in late December also saw the club appear as Sport Lisboa – the name given by the group of students who launched the club. Merging with Sport Clube de Benfica, though, they reverted to the name the club is now known as throughout the world.

As with many great same-city rivalries, Lisbon's relates to the social background of the club's fanbases. The supporters of Benfica had dug into their pockets to help provide the funds for the original Estádio da Luz construction, becoming the club of the working class, whereas the viscount title handed to Alvalade's grandfather by King Carlos I of Portugal saw Los Leões (the Lions) associated with the social elite.

With that air of superiority existing in some of Sporting CP's players, it helped fuel the vitriol that exists to this day. They refused to welcome their Benfica counterparts ahead of a fixture in 1911, believing that their opponents were not worthy of such treatment even though it was a common courtesy a century ago. Benfica should not have concerned themselves with the snub from their socially conscious city neighbours and instead waited for their quality on the pitch to speak for itself when the Portuguese league began in 1933. Porto may have pipped the Lisbon duo to that maiden title, but Benfica claimed the next three from 1935 to 1938, continuing to add to their collection throughout the next decade at a rate that Sporting CP could not contend with. It was the first *Tricampeao* (triple championships) of many in their history and only bettered recently when securing a fourth consecutive title in 2016.

Although Benfica's 1-0 defeat to Porto on 15 April 2018 had all but handed that season's league title to the *Dragoes* (the Dragons), I headed to Lisbon, hopeful that there would still be plenty at stake when Benfica visited the Estádio José Alvalade on the penultimate weekend of the season. Points are rarely dropped except during clashes with each other or Porto, given the competitive level of the Primeira Liga. Therefore, campaigns drawing to a close increases fixture importance and battles often become more highly charged than at the start of a season.

This encounter was no different, with Sporting CP pushing their cross-city rivals all the way in the race for a place in the third qualifying round of the Champions League. The two sides were neck and neck on 77 points each. However, while Benfica were used to dining at European football's top table, *Los Leões* had appeared just twice in the competition in the last decade. Their attempts to return to the UEFA Champions League were also being threatened by off-field complications. President Bruno de Carvalho had suspended 19 first-team players in the wake of a social media squabble, the players having taken collective offence to online criticism from him after they exited the Europa League to Atlético Madrid.

That my journey started in Rome was almost as unexpected as Liverpool's run to the Champions League semi-finals. Taking me to the Italian capital just days before Sporting CP v Benfica meant that, just like the *Derby della*

Capitale, travel began straight afterwards, although I was spared camping out on the floor of Gatwick Airport. Flying from Ciampino Airport to Portugal saved me around £200 as it was the start of the May bank holiday weekend and school half-term. After landing, I joined the metro towards the city centre and was reminded of how strange public transport can be in large and diverse cities, even when the sun has barely risen. Sitting, contemplating how or when I may secure a ticket to the match, on stepped a 20-something pale young man sporting large dark shades, despite us being deep in the lower reaches of the underground, sleeveless t-shirt and basketball shorts, with a schoolboyish face that would look more comfortable in a private school uniform. He had accessorised his outfit with a smartphone armband around his bicep, booming out Aerosmith at full volume. To the rest of the carriage's surprise and amusement, he followed that up with 'X Gon' Give It To Ya' by DMX and was playing Green Day as I exited at Baixa Chiado metro.

Heading straight to my hostel, Surf In Chiado, Jorge, one of the reception staff, greeted me like an old friend who, on hearing that I was there to witness the famous Lisbon derby, took great pleasure in telling me how big a Sporting fan he was while bad-mouthing Benfica at any opportunity during my stay.

* * *

It was midway through the 1940s, with Europe recovering from the Second World War, that Sporting CP embarked upon a period of prolonged success, starting with the championship in 1946/47. They won seven of eight national titles through the talents of the 'Five Violins' – Manuel Vasques, Albano Pereira, José Travassos, Jesus Correia and Fernando Peyroteo. Considered a *Los Leões* legend, with an astonishing 544 goals in all competitions, Peyroteo was also one of Portugal's first greats, and is still held in high esteem. The last of Sporting's league triumphs also brought the novelty of participating in the inaugural European Cup fixture, drawing 3-3 with Partizan Belgrade in September 1955, but Benfica would make the first impact in Europe. Under the tutelage of legendary coach Béla Guttmann, the Eagles secured the 1961 and 1962 instalments of the competition, overcoming Spanish giants Barcelona and Real Madrid, respectively, and although Sporting CP captured the European Cup Winners' Cup in 1964 it was a new Portugal legend emerging, Eusébio da Silva Ferreira, who thrust Benfica further ahead of them into the international spotlight.

Los Leões may have been the club of the royal elite but it was Eusébio, after scoring two crucial goals against *Los Blancos* in the 1962 European Cup Final when just 20 years old, whom Benfica fans nicknamed *O Rei* (The King). If Benfica fans still felt aggrieved at the 'theft' of their players half a decade earlier, Sporting CP could claim they were, at the very least, outmanoeuvred in securing the signature of possibly the greatest Portugal player of all time, appearing for their feeder club, Sporting Clube de Lourenço Marques, in his homeland of Mozambique. They believe that when Sporting CP were struggling to secure the services of the formidable youngster, Guttmann swooped in after being tipped off regarding the apparent breakdown in contract negotiations. That moment, in 1960, could be called a turning point for the clubs, but probably discredits the efforts of many unheralded contributors. The trajectory of the teams took different paths during that period, though.

Level with ten titles each on his arrival, when Eusébio departed in 1975 Benfica had amassed another 11 championships and appeared in five European Cup finals, albeit losing the last three and believing that Guttmann had cursed them when quitting during a pay dispute. Considering Benfica only opened their doors to non-Portuguese players as late as 1979, you wonder what would have come of them had they not colonised the attacker's homeland to grant him citizenship.

These crucial four decades in both clubs' histories had allowed both to claim to support the 'original superpower of Portuguese football', but also portray the poorer relation.

* * *

With a smile that was as wide as it was bright, despite the thick dark beard he wore, Jorge confirmed what the Sporting website had told me for weeks: that tickets were only available for *Los Leões* members. Realising this could be my opportunity to secure a ticket, I enquired whether Jorge would attend and, when he admitted that he could rarely find the time, I felt my hopes rising a little. He brought the hammer down on my optimism almost immediately, no doubt sensing where my line of enquiry was heading. He said that, as he had not paid his monthly €5 members' fee for some time, the club would want to recover those absent payments before he could purchase. Not wanting any further time wasted pondering when or where I would get a ticket, I jumped back on to the metro to the stadium. It was the best place to try with 36 hours before kick-off.

At the club ticket office, they ignored my pleading and telling them I was writing this book (which only helped on one occasion, but when most needed). However, when I turned around, two young men were waiting for me. A classic little and large combo; one 6ft 4in tall or more and the other barely 5ft 6in and offering to sell me a ticket they had purchased as members. If it hadn't been for the larger of the pair's welcoming demeanour, contradicting a huge muscular frame and hands that consumed mine when greeting me, I may have walked away. His accomplice, diminutive and scruffy, had a Gollum-like skeletal appearance and seemed less trustworthy. The pair gave no sales spiel regarding how the tickets were the best in the stadium, although they started the bidding at €90. With no price on the tickets, it was useful that I'd spent weeks monitoring the official sales. Knowing that tickets in the area I was being offered were just €30, I was also aware that if tickets became available to non-members, then the starting price was €60, the price we would settle on. It was the highest markup I had ever paid to a tout, but content I was no worse financially than had I bought through official channels.

Returning to my quirky hostel, relieved and pleased that I had secured a ticket, the reception desk had changed hands and football allegiance, with Benfica fan Antonio taking the reins for the night shift. Antonio had the attributes of a young Iberian heartthrob, stealing the heart of a young heroine as the sun goes down in some coming-of-age drama – tall, tanned, athletic and with the black sweeping hair of a young Jamie Redknapp, or the early Real Madrid years of Francisco Román Alarcón Suárez, better known as Isco. He knew it as well. With an unrelenting series of young travellers passing through the hostel, there was always one button too many undone on his shirts, providing me much entertainment watching several lusting after him as they requested dining or tour suggestions.

Planting myself in the communal area for my first night with a large bottle of Sagres, Antonio provided splendid company and, like Jorge, was very willing to discuss his passion for his club. His claim to fame was the proximity in which he lived to former Benfica stars Bernardo Silva and Renato Sanches. Antonio's home was situated perfectly on the border between the more affluent neighbourhood Silva grew up in and the working-class estate that gave Sanches his footballing education. Keen to tell me what had gone wrong with the career of teenage prodigy Sanches, at that point on loan at Premier League strugglers Swansea City, Antonio suggested the talented youngster lacked the dedication and was often seen back socialising and driving a lavish white Ford Mustang on the tough streets of Amadora, hinting that the 2016 European champion was allegedly partial to a late night with friends. That fate, he insisted, would not befall a 16-year-old by the name of João Félix, who was destined for future stardom.[20] Never in the same room together, Jorge and Antonio were perfect examples of the cross-city divide, with neither saying a good word about the other club and belittling the other at every opportunity.

While almost certainly too young to remember first-hand, Antonio spoke of Benfica's success during the 1980s. Watching them secure a clean sweep of trophies in 1981 left *Los Leões* supporters having to celebrate the failures of their neighbours rather than their own triumphs, such as the Eagles losing the 1983 UEFA Cup Final to Anderlecht. It is fitting that while Sporting's most memorable win over their rivals was a 7-1 mauling on 14 December 1986, Benfica still clinched the title that year. However, a few months later, a Portuguese Super Cup victory would be Benfica's last trophy for almost a decade, which Antonio seemed to gloss over.

---

20 On 3 July 2019, a 19-year-old Félix joined Spanish club Atlético Madrid for a club record fee of €126m, the fifth-biggest transfer fee in football and the second-highest for a teenager. Renato Sanches would have something of a resurgence at LOSC Lille, where he won a league and cup double in 2020/21, and signed for Paris Saint-Germain in the summer of 2022

The league championship took even longer to return to the Estádio José Alvalade, though, and even when Sporting CP came close to ending their championship drought, Benfica had the last laugh. A squad containing Luís Figo, Emílio Peixe and Paulo Sousa looked on course to secure the title in May 1994, but Benfica pulled off an unexpected 6-3 victory at the Alvalade, inflicting one of *Los Leões'* biggest disappointments in their history. It was a triumph made all the sweeter for the Benfica fans as former starlet Sousa had joined their hated rivals at the start of the campaign, becoming an instant target for their rage.

Whether the midfielder's transfer increased the rivalry and resentment between the sides is open to debate, but Antonio suggested it contributed to hostility being at its most intense when tragedy struck during the 1996 Portuguese Cup Final. After Benfica netted the first goal of a 3-1 win, a member of the No Name Boys group tossed a firecracker into the opposition section, which struck a fan, Rui Mendes, in the chest and killed him instantly. That remained the most significant act of violence between the two sets of supporters until Sporting CP supporters set fire to a stand at the Estádio da Luz in 2011 after yet another defeat.

Players continue crossing the divide, though, with striker João Pinto one of the most famous to appear in both famous colours, while ex-Benfica full-back Fábio Coentrão was plying his trade in green and white hoops. We then recalled when Benfica, suffering their own title drought, turned, unexpectedly, to Graeme Souness in 1997 in an attempt to turn around their fortunes.

Although, I suspected I remembered more of Souness's spell in Portugal than Antonio. He may have blocked it out of his mind as, despite a famous 4-1 win over their neighbours helping them qualify for the 1998/99 Champions League, the Scot lasted for around 18 months. Souness told *The Independent*, after leaving, 'Benfica have the most demanding group of fans I've ever come across, far, far more than at Rangers or Liverpool. They think Benfica have a God-given right to be the best in Europe.'[21] The supporters showed their displeasure with failed British imports like Steve Harkness – who made the interesting decision to wear his forename instead of surname on the back of his shirt – in the most visible way possible, 80,000 in the Estádio da Luz waving Souness off with white handkerchiefs. However, while the ex-Liverpool midfielder had a fractious relationship with supporters, that is par for the course at both Benfica and Sporting CP. Coaches are often the scapegoat when fans feel let down by the club hierarchy.

Much was made of Sporting CP ending an 18-year wait for the league title on the last day of the 1999/2000 campaign, but less is said about also claiming a league and cup double two years later. Instead, both sets of fans, particularly Antonio, appeared drawn to *Los Leões'* stupendous collapse at the end of the 2004/05 season. What should have been the fitting end to a wonderful campaign in the UEFA Cup Final at their own stadium ended with Sporting CP being defeated 3-1 by CSKA Moscow, already having relinquished the Portuguese title with two games left to Benfica.

I reminded Antonio, though, that in May 2013 Sporting must have enjoyed their own opportunity to make fun of their rivals' misfortune. Benfica had gone one better and lost three competitions in a matter of weeks. A 90th-minute goal handed Porto the league title, then Chelsea beat them in injury time to secure the UEFA Europa League, before two goals in two minutes from Vitória de Guimarães ensured a

---

21 Stafford, I., 'Souness unmoved at mock farewell' (*The Independent*, 1999)

mentally deflated squad almost inevitably lost the Portuguese Cup Final. While those late capitulations no doubt pleased the Sporting faithful, they could not hide the fact that for too long they had barely challenged their city neighbours – later finishing 36 points behind them in 2011 and 57 off champions Porto – until controversial president de Carvalho arrived in March 2013.

Sporting CP finally mounted a significant title charge but lost admirers at the same time. To my surprise, Antonio admitted he would sometimes watch *Los Leões* with friends. But de Carvalho, the man nicknamed King Jong-il of Lisbon – once banning all but in-house media from reporting on club affairs – had turned most neutrals against them through his antics. After the sale of Marcos Rojo to Manchester United in 2014, de Carvalho withheld 80 per cent of the fee shareholders Doan Sport Management were due, out of sheer bloody-mindedness. Not agreeing with the terms at which the club had secured several of their South American imports. That he did so for three years, during which he was involved in bitter legal wrangling and at huge financial cost personally when losing, suggests that it was a moral position that harmed his own club more than it benefited them.

A man no stranger to riling opponents then stoked the fire between the two clubs in 2017 when he convinced Benfica's most decorated coach, Jorge Jesus, to switch sides and take on the significant challenge of bringing glory back to his boyhood club, adding spice to a fixture that, in the last 100 years, Antonio commented, had witnessed a reversal of the financial superiority of the clubs and the social background of their fanbases.

Even though he could take the moral high ground given Benfica's success, Antonio insisted on diminishing Jorge's credentials as a genuine fan because of the frequency at which he watched Sporting CP. Jorge later hit back by lamenting his colleague's advice on where to head pre-game, questioning how a Benfica supporter would know the best place to gather when it was *Los Leões* hosting the encounter.

With kick-off at 9pm local time, groundhoppers[22] can imagine my joy at being able to see fellow Primeira Liga side – and Lisbon residents – Belenenses entertain Portimonense, and quickly catch a taxi across town at full time.

After I was dropped at the top of Rua Fernando Namora, the trickle of Sporting CP fans increased as I meandered down the street with the fading sunshine warming the back of my neck and the faint sound of police sirens ringing in the distance. A group of supporters carrying an unknown amber substance, in what looked to be a five-litre container, captured my interest. That, I assumed, was beer or cider, and I quickened my pace to catch up with them. To my good fortune it turned out that the group, in their late teens and early 20s, were Directivo Ultras who had made the 40-minute journey along the Lisbon coast from Caxias and were heading straight to the Directivo bar, housed in the stadium's belly; here, they informed me, the approaching 'happy hours' meant that beers were as little as 50 cents. Although in reality the servings in a small plastic cup were at most 250ml.

Unwisely wearing a pastel pink polo shirt, but not too close to Benfica's famous red shirts, Jérémy Charles Petitcolas, who had taken me under his wing since we met, decided it would be a bit too risky to enter alone and potentially be refused entry. He also told me that, at the previous encounter between the sides in January, ultras had forced a supporter wearing a red t-shirt to remove it and watch the rest of the

---

22 Groundhoppers are individuals who take part in the hobby of groundhopping, which involves attending matches at as many different stadiums as possible and is particularly popular with football supporters

match shivering. I headed inside to grab a few drinks for us both and Jérémy enlightened me on the history of the ultra groups in operation. At that moment the Brigada gathered over our shoulders, letting off a huge firecracker that even made Jérémy flinch. As they 'preferred to party, the group were members of Directivo rather than the more crazy antics of Juve Leo Ultras', Jérémy explained, pointing towards hundreds of supporters bouncing in unison some 200m away for what I considered the benefit of television cameras filming each leap.

* * *

Like most mainland European clubs, the hardcore elements of both Benfica and Sporting CP fan groups often refer to themselves as 'ultras' and their activities can reflect those seen in Italian football, such as singing full voice before, during and after the game and creating vibrant and witty choreographies. However, while you might expect this to succeed through a collective undertaking, four separate Sporting fan groups operate around the Estádio José Alvalade: Juventude Leonina, Directivo, Brigada and Torcida. Although Jérémy confirmed that in recent years a truce between the four supporter factions had improved internal relations, the two prominent Benfica ultras groups still clashed regularly.

Leonina, known as Juve Leo, are by far the most famous and, reportedly, the oldest set of ultras in Portugal – rival groups thought to have arisen from their establishment in 1976, like The Blue Dragons of FC Porto or the Diabos Vermelhos (Red Devils) of Benfica. Juve Leo's previous willingness to engage in acts of violence instigated groups with similar tendencies. They simply created Directivo to sing and encourage their team to victory. After Benfica's

Diabos Vermelhos formed in 1982 and saw an estimated increase in numbers to around 5,000 members, they too saw internal politics split loyalties. However, while Sporting CP's ultras fractured into four separate entities, the breakaway group, No Name Boys, left the Red Devils with all but a dozen supporters among their ranks.

They were far more than willing to incite their opponents' fury and unfurled banners in relation to the death of *Los Leões* fan Rui Mendes, killed by a flare thrown by the No Name Boys in 1996. In 2015, Sporting fans followed suit after the death of Benfica legend Eusébio, unveiling an enormous sign inscribed with 'Sigam O King' (Follow The King). Trouble now, particularly outside the stadiums, is extremely rare. For some time the police have marched the away fans en masse from their respective stadiums, to limit individual clashes. This made me question why Antonio was giving me tips on where to go when possessing a Sporting ticket. This approach did not stop a Fiorentina supporter from getting caught up in skirmishes 12 months earlier.

Attempting to escape charging Benfica ultras the day before the fixture, Marco Ficini ran into traffic and was killed when struck by an oncoming van. Unable to see eye to eye even in such tragic circumstances, the Directivo Ultras insisted the Italian got pushed into the road by the rioting fans, while Benfica supporters take the view that it was cowardice that saw him step into the road amid their light-hearted chasing.

* * *

An obvious language barrier, given Jérémy's near-perfect English, had slightly alienated us from the rest congregating behind a parked car a few yards away, so we went to join them. Jérémy soon introduced me to designated driver Manuel

Carronha, Guilherme Anastácio Junior, and his girlfriend Mariana Anacleto. Despite being the youngest at 19 years old, Guilherme's extroverted personality positioned him as the leader of the quartet. He was outwardly welcoming with a strong, formal-like handshake, and standing about 5ft 10in but with the stocky build of a rugby player. The warmth of his reception made me feel comfortable joining their close-knit unit. I broached the subject of the huge amount of amber substance they had now distributed, as beers from the Directivo Ultra bar were so cheap.

It turned out that my new associates shared my money-saving tendencies and had concocted a beverage of their own containing not a drop of beer or cider, not wanting to waste their leftovers from a party the night before and deciding (not for the first time) to pour everything into the container for later use. A mixture of white wine, vodka, tonic, gin, and the Monster energy drink was swilling around inside. They thrust a small plastic cup into my hand and, with no hesitation, I began knocking them back with more enthusiasm than my companions had expected. It wasn't as bad, although warm, as I had feared, but it gave a sharp kick with each mouthful, which led me to suggest that I get everyone a few beers to wash it down, even with happy hour over. At €1 a serving, it was the cheapest round I had bought for some time and I was desperate to try my luck at seeing the inside of the Directivo inner sanctum. Plus, it was clear by the look on their faces that they needed some relief from the tangy aftertaste of their moonshine.

Guilherme tossed me his Sporting scarf to help me gain entry, but also insisted that I keep it as a gift, on one proviso: that I would tell everyone I met of the Directivo Ultras' hospitality and take the scarf with me to the Champions League Final in Kiev a few weeks later. Although Jérémy followed me in, Guilherme was right. I breezed past the burly security guards with not so much as a glare in my direction. A couple of Scottish youngsters were being turned away because of non-Directivo affiliation. Inhaling a huge, if unexpected, mouthful of marijuana smoke as I squeezed through the narrow doorway, the sheer amount of people shocked me, crammed into a space of similar size and appearance of a domestic garage. Stationed in a corner was a DJ providing a steady flow of dance tracks. As they played Sporting anthems through loudspeakers and a drummer was hammering away a steady beat, everyone was singing with energetic enthusiasm. While chaotic, it created a brilliant atmosphere.

We made our way over to a temporary table. In a celebratory mood, they distributed small plastic cups at an alarming rate from barrels behind them. Accompanied by an impromptu light-show, the room's electrical circuits struggled to cope. Prompted by Jérémy, and lost among the euphoria, I was shouting random words I thought were being yelled, not wanting to look out of place. Extending the Directivo welcome, they then insisted that they treat me to their customary pre-match delicacy, but with 45 minutes until kick-off we had to hurry as it was a short walk from where we were. Despite his scarf hanging around my neck and at least a litre of the bootleg alcohol sloshing about inside me, Guilherme insisted on them buying me dinner. Even though it was less than a sausage dinner outside Anfield at just €3, I had been watching them pooling their resources throughout the evening, but my offer to pay was once more ignored. What arrived was the perfect answer to the volume of alcohol consumed: A *bifana*[23] packed as densely as

---

23 A *bifana* – pork sandwich – is a cheap and tasty meal on its own of bread soaked in a pork marinade or sauce with beer instead of wine, the meat having been marinated overnight in a spicy, salty, garlic sauce

possible, inside a crusty yet fresh bread roll, and more pork than you should consume in a week, let alone one meal. As soon as I sank my teeth into the delicious offering, I got a not unpleasant burst of salt across my tongue from the heavily cured meat. Washing it down with the remaining home brew, more enthusiastically than the others, we headed towards the Alvalade.

As luck would have it, we were entering through the same gate, albeit likely to be separated shortly after joining the mass of bodies shuffling forwards, until the space between us was consumed by the pressure from behind. Hardly able to move, I turned my head. Sensing how uncomfortable our fellow traveller Mariana was, with her chest pressed firmly into my back, I tried to convey, using facial expressions, an understanding that pushing was coming from further down the crowd. I was becoming equally embarrassed by how the surge had thrust me into a similar possession against a girl of comparable age ahead. Attempting to lighten the mood, I started joking with Jérémy about the awkwardness of the situation.

With that, a fellow Sporting CP fan recognised my British accent and wanted to offer a warm, if drunken, welcome to Lisbon, when the mood suddenly changed on our approach to the line of police officers. Without warning or reason, they aggressively attempted to push the crowd backwards, sending the girl in front of me stumbling and treading on my toes, my inability to retreat ensuring that she remained upright. I checked to see if I had knocked Mariana over. Guilherme's considerable frame had, as expected, kept her upright. He then told me to raise my arms aloft, ticket in hand, signalling to the police that we were legitimately trying to gain access. That seemed to see us past the security cordon only for the automated barrier to reject my ticket, and a wave of anxiety consumed me briefly. Earlier allaying fears my ticket was fraudulent, Jérémy could not understand why it would not work. I looked blankly at the female steward hurrying me along. Then in swept the drunken fan who greeted me mid-queue, explaining that the crowd surge had sucked us toward the wrong entry point, and dragged us through a gap in the barriers. We were in.

Taking my first glimpse of the playing turf, the noise was already deafening and, after making my way to my seat, I found a German stationed there. He attempted to convince me to swap seats so he could remain with his friends alongside him. I had already worked out that he had a ticket nearer the ultras section, and was soon pacing towards them.

Despite my unfamiliar face, the fans on either side of me welcomed me with open arms. We conducted some hasty pleasantries as the supporters were bursting into song with an emotional rendition of 'O mundo sabe que' (The world knows that) to the tune of Frank Sinatra's 'My Way'. I could not help but think of the 1980s Dulux advert as I stared out at the sea of green and white, the hairs on the back of my neck rising. I spotted a solitary Fiorentina flag flying among the crowd, representing the newly formed friendship between the clubs. According to Jérémy, my salmon polo shirt made me easy to locate, and he was frantically waving, but I could see little among the flags and plumes of smoke rising around me. The flashing pyrotechnics delivered a spectacle unlike any I had so far experienced in England. Such displays were apparently permitted if distributed by one of the official fan groups.

However, when hundreds of sparkling white flares came flying on to the pitch in unison from the ultras behind the goal, play had to be halted. Sporting CP goalkeeper Rui

Patrício was barely visible, and he certainly could not see the other 21 players on the pitch. At that point I noticed a lack of animation from the 3,000-plus Benfica supporters housed in the corner opposite. The hostility of the home crowd, though, drowned out their rivals.

There was little reduction in the home fans' thunderous support when midway through the first half Bruno Varela made a wonderful save from Coentrão and, although arriving as a neutral, I began craving a Sporting CP goal just to witness emotions erupt, as I was getting drawn in by the underdog mindset with them second best for so long. Things I would usually brush off as a marketing gimmick, like leaving the number 12 shirt free for the fans and giving anyone ordering in the club shop a €10 discount, sounded admirable.

Amid the noise, I could hear a drum setting the pace of the *Los Leões* carnival. Guilherme had found it strange when I explained that, while not banned from British stadiums, some supporters frown at the use of drums, or maybe it was just Liverpool who despised attempts to manufacture an atmosphere. The lack of visual spectacle at your average Premier League game would disappoint him and Jérémy.

Despite the feelgood factor filling the Alvalade, on 30 minutes a fan two rows in front of me loudly shouted something to his left. That appeared relatively harmless but a fellow supporter leant across and punched him straight in the face. Both started attempting to land further blows until being dragged away by security and never being seen again. That was as exciting as the opening period got and the supporters' energy diminished ahead of the second half, almost resigned to their fate. Benfica's players seemed content with the point likely to guarantee second place, with just struggling Moreirense to face at home.

After a drone briefly stopped play, ex-Liverpool centre-back Sebastián Coates scythed down an opponent. The fans were raging at the injustice that he was penalised for the foul. Ten minutes later, a tussle broke out between opposing players, stirring the anger further among the home fans fighting back the increasing apathy that the game, and potential Champions League riches, were slipping from their grasp.

As the match neared its conclusion, the party-like atmosphere had disappeared. However, with most of the 49,335 crowd a simmering rage and as the fourth official displayed seven additional minutes, the Benfica fans sparked into life when a solitary red flare shined brightly from the away section in what looked like a pre-planned act.

Three more flares were lit but from within the home section at the other end, it seemed. Had some Benfica fans infiltrated the Sporting section? The flares were extinguished soon afterwards. Some home fans started making their way home and I could see pockets of vacated seats, while those who remained just about managed a rendition of 'Ate Morrer Sporting Allez' (Until Death, Up Sporting).

Despite being assured I would be 'partying late into the night' with Directivo Ultras, the others were already waiting for me in our pre-agreed location but not ready to celebrate one point too wildly. Manuel also had an hour-long drive to undertake. However, as I got closer, he had his arm supported by a homemade sling made from a scarf. I was told that he had dislocated his shoulder during the pre-match excitement. It wasn't through punching the air in jubilation, I was sure. I shook the lads' hands and we wished each other goodbye. Mariana silently leaned in awkwardly for a hug out of politeness, and I followed the other supporters towards the metro.

Maybe my new friends were putting on a brave face, or the light-hearted nature of their departure hid the true feelings of the fans, because a week later a group of around 50 individuals (let's not call them supporters) broke into the club's training ground and assaulted Sporting CP players and staff, not even sparing striker Bas Dost, who had netted 34 times during the campaign. He suffered cuts and bruises to his head. Star players, such as goalkeeper Rui Patrício and midfielder William Carvalho, used the incident to facilitate their exit from the club.

I saw the obvious disappointment on the faces of the Sporting faithful as I travelled back on the metro. The atmosphere as I disembarked at Baixa Chiado around midnight was the polar opposite, with groups of revellers heading towards the many bars and clubs on offer, unaware that one of the world's biggest fixtures had taken place less than an hour earlier and was a mere five miles away. The city was hosting the Eurovision Song Contest, increasing the party atmosphere when I had ventured into Lisbon at night. Exhausted from an emotionally charged evening of football, though, I grabbed a bottle of water from a local mini-market, hopefully lessening the expected hangover from Manuel's homemade concoction – which was already showing signs of ruining my morning – and headed back to my accommodation.

Settling down for the night on the top floor, I draped Guilherme's scarf over the end of the bed and reflected on a wonderful evening. The faint sound of cheers interrupted my reminiscing before they faded into the distance, a lot like Sporting's chances of overturning Benfica's slender advantage in the Primera Liga.

4

The Old Firm Derby – Glasgow, Scotland

FOR A long time, I did not comprehend in full how deep the animosity, hatred even, ran between supporters in one of the oldest rivalries in British football. It wasn't on the streets of Glasgow or the terraces where a 22-year-old me first witnessed the tensions created by an Old Firm derby between Celtic and Rangers, but a factory floor, 450 miles away in Hampshire.

Arriving for another uneventful day working for Creative Fires UK Limited, I was called to an escalating disturbance between staff, with David 'Davy' Jones threatening to slash two colleagues with a Stanley knife. With a look in his eyes suggesting he was dead serious, Glaswegian native Davy was not a cheerful individual after a life of struggle that few could comprehend. That included a couple of spells in prison. He was hardworking, approachable and honest, though, admitting that most weekends involved a television, 'slab of lager' and little else.

When Glasgow Rangers-supporting Jones returned to work that Monday, someone had spray-painted bright-green Celtic clovers or 'CELTIC' all over his workbench, just in case he had missed the defeat to their bitter rivals. It sent him into a flying rage. Two young agency workers with even less knowledge or experience of the deep-seated hatred between the clubs were the culprits, underestimating their prank. While I defused the incident, it came flooding back as I headed to Scotland 17 years later.

As Simon Kuper highlighted in *Football Against the Enemy*, and I tried to explain back then to two startled youngsters, the conflict is more than mere sporting rivalry. More than other city derbies, it extends beyond country borders and is linked to the Northern Ireland conflict because of a complicated series of complex disputes, religious divides (Catholic and Protestant), politics, social ideology and national identity. Religion appeared at the forefront when growing up in the 1980s, but with religious associations less pronounced in wider society it feels like faith no longer defines supporters and rather the team they support, linking fans with everything associated with their chosen club.

Scottish football is very much a duopoly. The pair have shared 103 top-flight league titles – Rangers leading 55 to Celtic's 52 – plus 74 Scottish Cups, 47 Scottish League Cups, and both have a solitary European triumph to their name, although Celtic supporters point out that their one European Cup does trump Rangers' European Cup Winners' Cup (a now dormant competition) trophy. Such has been their dominance that the longest sequence without a Glaswegian title was the three seasons between 1983 and 1985.

* * *

Originally formed (we'll get to this later!) in 1872, Glasgow Rangers Football Club gained support among the local Conservative-following inhabitants. Later, a poverty-stricken Roman Catholic population on the east side of the city began associating themselves with Glasgow Celtic Football Club after its establishment in 1887, to provide money and resources to that struggling community. The lines of political and religious associations were drawn deep in the sand early on. One unsubstantiated claim is that the term 'Old Firm' stemmed from an early reference to the clubs being 'firm friends', while it seems more likely to be because the pair were among the original 11 clubs forming the Scottish Football League in 1890.

I prefer the tale suggesting that it originated from a satirical magazine in 1904, with a sandwich board holder reading 'Patronise the Old Firm: Rangers Celtic Ltd'. The size and publicity of matches was a significant commercial advantage for even then.

One of many showpiece events between the pair started at Hampden Park in 1894. The frequency with which they contested fixtures at the national stadium resulted in the West and East terraces being allocated to Rangers and Celtic permanently for matches. The venue also hosted the highest attendance in Old Firm history, when 132,870 witnessed Celtic lift the 1969 Scottish Cup, although that's lower than the national record when facing Aberdeen in 1937, which attracted 147,365 spectators.

Unlike in other cities and compared to recent history, though, for the first six decades of their existence neither side embarked on a prolonged period of domination over their neighbours. A hat-trick of league titles was the most either club achieved before the other wrestled power back from their enemy, even if only for one campaign. That all changed in the 1960s. Although recently crowned champions Rangers lost the 1961 European Cup Winners' Cup Final to Fiorentina, they had looked set to extend their achievements both at home and abroad. As the decade progressed, though, it was the Hoops[24] who embarked upon a period of unprecedented success.

In 1966 Celtic won their first Scottish title for a decade, starting a run of nine consecutive triumphs and securing entry to the European Cup. They overcame Italian giants Inter in the final the following year in Lisbon to complete a historic treble and become the first British club crowned European champions. Six days later, Rangers had the chance to soften the blow of their neighbours beating them to continental success but lost another European Cup Winners' Cup Final, this time to Bayern Munich of Germany.

Amid the backdrop of an economic downturn, Dutch side Feyenoord saved Rangers fans from watching Celtic raise another European Cup in 1970 when defeating the Hoops in the final. A second European crown for their cross-city rivals would have been a footballing tragedy for Rangers followers, but then a human tragedy struck their Ibrox Stadium seven months later. When departing fans rushed back into the stadium to celebrate a late goal against Celtic, it sparked a catastrophe as 66 supporters died during a crush on an external stairway.

Rangers themselves would then secure continental silverware in May 1972 with a 3-2 European Cup Winners' Cup Final victory over Dynamo Moscow, but they failed to add a second trophy with Ajax defeating them in what was the first UEFA Super Cup Final.

* * *

Leaving straight after work on a Friday, my trip to Scotland almost didn't happen. After spending eight hours staring

---

24 Glasgow Celtic are also known as the Hoops due to the green and white rings on the traditional home shirt

at the crammed backpack beside my desk, I rushed out of the door at 5pm and raced towards the station only to find that they had cancelled my intended train, meaning that an already tight schedule was being squeezed further. The next available train was on time at least, but when I arrived at Southampton Airport a broken scanner was causing delays getting through security. The look on their faces at the departure gate suggested I was close to watching the plane rising from the tarmac from inside the terminal, and not onboard.

After a rare early night, my visit began early on Saturday morning, wandering 40 minutes to the east side of the city in miserable conditions to join the Glasgow Reds[25] at the Record Factory on Byres Road to watch Leicester City v Liverpool. Given the much-publicised animosity that exists between Celtic and Rangers, supporters had come together in their united support for Liverpool, showing little concern for what may take place 24 hours later. Over 50 people filled a small backroom, just big enough to fit a snooker table, which was essential to avoid interrupting a veteran brass band playing in the main function room. At full time, a few people stuck around to share tales of the Old Firm and what to expect when the clock struck midnight and the 'real fun' started.

Once most of the crowd had departed or moved into the main bar area, Irishman Ed Byrne – not the comedian – was last to remain discussing football and, a lot of time, failed relationships. Despite a long-standing affinity with Celtic, it was a whirlwind romance that left him forever connected to Glasgow, spending almost 20 years living in the city after having had a child with a former partner.

---

25 The Glasgow Reds were formed in 2004 and became a branch of the Official Liverpool Supporters' Club in February 2013

Deciding not to suffer more Scottish drizzle, we jumped on the metro back to the city centre where Ed promised a tour of the 'trendy bars' that had sprung up during the city's recent regeneration, before flying back to Dublin that night to witness the 2018 All-Ireland Senior Football Championship. When we agreed we should have one last drink, I glanced at my watch, and realised it was only 5pm. Bars were already filling with people dressed for a night of revelry, helping me mistake it for much later. A few couples sitting near us took over chaperone duties on Ed's departure, telling me how the mood in Glasgow 'turns bitter' when the fixture embarks upon the calendar.

Outside of Scotland, Glasgow is clearly the country's second city. The capital, Edinburgh, has a higher profile from events such as the annual Fringe Festival, and is maybe even considered more sophisticated, but that ignores the revival the country's biggest city has undergone. Once a small rural settlement along the River Clyde in the West Central Lowlands, the Glasgow seaport developed into a transatlantic trade hub that allowed it to thrive as centres for chemicals, textiles, shipbuilding and marine engineering sectors. Somewhere near 620,000 inhabitants live within the City of Glasgow boundaries and another 1.2 million in the Greater Glasgow urban area.

As touched upon, the changing composition of a population growing when the economy thrived is a contributing factor to the rivalry, with Rangers fans historically native Scots and Ulster Scots, from Protestant communities, and Celtic supporters Catholic Irish-Scots. This prompted confrontations to be labelled 'Sectarianism', but, as Kuper pointed out, the hostility also stemmed from immigrant tensions as the steelworks, coal mines and other heavy industries closed during the economic struggles of the 1970s and early 1980s. Despite some of the population leaving in search of work, those tensions remain.

Forty years on, I found a more vibrant Glasgow as we walked its streets and enjoyed many of the packed bars and restaurants. A riverbank left derelict as shipbuilding disappeared has become a centre for entertainment and luxury accommodation. While increased cultural events have improved its image, attracting more and more tourists, as well as major sporting events. They redeveloped the western side of the city into a new central business district, which is not always appreciated by those who grew up during a depressed period – local singer-songwriter Gerry Cinnamon appearing to criticise those profiting from the area's development, and turning their back on their humble beginnings and pretending to be something they are not, in the hit song 'Diamonds In The Mud'.

Within a couple more hours (as I kept delaying my exit to hear more Old Firm stories), I was feeling the effect of six or seven hours of Glaswegian hospitality getting the better of me. Excusing myself from the group, I headed back to my accommodation. I must have passed out attempting to watch Parma v Juventus while reading a newspaper and consuming a triple pack of Jaffa Cakes. I awoke several hours later to the unwelcome sound of my alarm, dry-mouthed and nursing a slight headache. With a midday kick-off there would never be a gentle awakening to matchday.

For two decades, Old Firm encounters had taken place around midday in the wake of a title-deciding clash back in May 1999, also at Celtic Park. With home fans fearing the start of another lengthy period of Rangers dominance, and unlikely to halt their title procession, the fixture descended into chaos with the goals of Neil McCann and Jörg Albertz and three red cards during a 3-0 Gers victory largely forgotten. My lasting image is of referee Hugh Dallas on his knees covered in blood, after being struck by one of the many objects thrown by Hoops fans, several of whom invaded the pitch to confront him, while another fell from the top tier of the stadium into those below.

With a three-mile walk ahead of me and the need to drop my bag at Buchanan Bus Station, I set off at 8am hoping the early start would not lessen the pre-game atmosphere, like many morning fixtures squeezed into the calendars of European leagues aimed at enticing overseas television revenue and often a contest between a traditional big club and an underdog. The city had a sense of calm with a mix of people heading to work or sheepishly making their way home from an overextended night out. Few were preparing for one of the historical clashes in European football. I doubted that it was what Ed and the others meant when they told me that Glasgow 'transforms' on derby day.

It didn't take long to reach the bus station, aided by the familiarity of its location from previous visits. After purchasing a £4 storage locker for my bag, essential when you have no alternatives on a whistlestop trip, the text message arrived I had dreaded. Delayed in Dublin, Forza Italian Football colleague Pádraig 'Paddy' Whelan had my ticket in his hand. A regular at Celtic Park, like so many other Ireland-based fans, it was Paddy who I turned to when getting a ticket myself appeared among the most difficult of my European trips. It was too early to panic or worry that this would become a wasted journey.

With both clubs having supporters' clubs throughout Scotland and Ireland, as well as several cities across the globe, they might have outgrown Scottish football. Fixtures between the pair have added importance and interest. Therefore, getting tickets through official channels has become difficult and played into the hands of those looking to turn a profit. When experts estimate that the Glasgow duo contribute more than £120m each year to the Scottish economy, it is unsurprising that unofficial partners spring up across the city. I was thankful to have befriended Paddy back in 2012.

The mid-1980s witnessed the first signs of their commercial power, as sponsorship became more widespread across the footballing industry. Fife glazing company CR Smith sponsored both clubs for fear that it would lose half its customers if seen to be siding with one or the other, such was the loathing between the fanbases. This continued for over two decades, with Glasgow-based brewery Tennent's, cable television company NTL and another brewery, Carling, among those following a similar marketing strategy.

Trying instead to enjoy the solitude of my morning stroll, it was almost an hour before the first sighting of a Celtic or Rangers shirt, which came when I turned on to Gallowgate Road for the second half of my journey. Through the doors of the Coronation Restaurant I spotted two supporters sporting the famous green and white hoops, somehow tucking into fish and chips. I would have understood a full English (or Scottish) breakfast. Most people would struggle to have dinner at 8.50am, but many fans are creatures of habit and the duo could not resist what looked like their regular pre-game ritual. With a powerful stench of urine rising from the pavement as the morning sun appeared, there was no risk of my thoughts turning to food at that juncture.

As one of the more deprived areas of Glasgow, there was an abandoned look about the mile-long stretch of road. Shutters were bolted down, making it difficult to know if many of the independent retailers were no longer in operation or just closed, as they would have been decades before

Sunday opening hours became the norm. When the large and imposing, but much-neglected, Barrowland Ballroom dance hall came into view, it was the perfect reminder of better times, adorned with multi-coloured neon lights that I thought had not been switched on in decades. However, after refurbishment in 1960, it acts as a popular live music venue in the city. Across the road was Bar 67, followed by Hoops Bar, the first visible signs that, despite being a mile from the stadium, I had entered a Celtic stronghold. Both venues also looked abandoned. Therefore, it was with some relief that Paddy had asked me to meet him at the Celtic Supporters' Social Club (CSSC) on London Road, nearer Celtic Park.

When the famous old stadium came into view, the surrounding area was also coming to life. The naked scaffold skeletons of street stalls were yet to be decorated with scarves, hats and shiny badges that cause passing children to tug on a parent's sleeve in the hope they will part with their hard-earned cash. The increasing scent of burgers emanated from the many food vans, reminding me that my breakfast comprised the remaining ten Jaffa Cakes. With 'Boys Republic IRA' graffiti scrawled along the concrete pathway catching my gaze, I raised my head to survey a stadium that looked under development or in need of expansion.

The lofty Jock Stein Stand – named after the manager of the 1967 European Cup-winning side – came to an abrupt end alongside the Main Stand, which remains untouched since renovation in 1971 but adds a touch of prestige to the ground. As with many British stadia, the once untarnished walls are now sought-after advertising space. I stared across an empty car park at the historic figures adorning a huge green poster and the word 'Paradise' stretched from left to right. It was the first time I heard the term used in relation to Celtic Park, but it wouldn't be the last. Making my way

around to the front of the Main Stand, image
players looked down at me and I tested my Scot
knowledge, trying to recall the faces on the w
doing too bad.

With just two hours until kick-off, I wall
statue of Billy McNeill, the captain of the famo
and who also defeated Rangers with ten men in
the league title in his first season as manager. S
myself fighting against a steady flow of people,
further east towards the CSSC I was growing co
Paddy was yet to confirm that he had touched a
appeared I could not steady my nerves with a stif
an alcohol ban being enforced across the metrop

I find moving fixtures to midday, to st
possibility of hoards of drunken fans, somewha
The police know that a large majority of support
start drinking earlier than usual, often much q
before. It doesn't take a lot to convince some
included, who may begin their matchday wit
midday for a standard 3pm kick-off, to start at
these circumstances. In the case of the Turnstile E
they found ways around the restrictions. As s
police officers were out of sight a doorman lifted t
shutters halfway up and a dozen men scuttled t
opening, almost on their knees. For a moment I
an Indiana Jones-style roll underneath to join
came clattering back down. Despite the bar ap
complete lockdown, the muffled hum of voic
clinking of bottles or glasses could be heard, all
and I got the feeling that the authorities cared
such self-policed establishments.

Reaching the CSSC there was a noticea
presence, which I assumed was standard because

ncidents, but it turned out that they were investigating an attack on the premises: the contents of multiple red and blue ins of paint, hurled under the cover of darkness the previous night, splashed across the façade of the imposing building. As the lone English voice among the Scottish and Irish tones surrounding me, the look I received from reception made me assume I was about to be denied entry. Once their surprise at an English accent had dissipated, they accepted my £2 fee (as a non-member) and I wandered into the bar area, shocked to find no queue for service.

However, unlike some of their local counterparts, they were unwilling to flout licensing regulations and were enforcing no alcohol until 11am so I ordered a can of Coca-Cola, while trying to hide my disappointment. After heading to a table in the corner and taking a seat alongside two older gentlemen, I realised almost everyone else in the room had selected Irn-Bru as their soft drink of choice, and chuckled inwardly at the thought I had singled myself out from the crowd again. A few seats away, I noticed a man was sipping a can of Stella lager carefree, but had little time to consider why others had not followed his lead. Someone waved a Blackout card under my nose and asked if I wanted to pick a team, transporting me back to the early 1990s when my grandfather would partake ahead of fixtures back home or give me £1 and play as my proxy.

While this was going on, a crowd was forming at the bar to prepare for the legal sale of alcohol and a man in his late 40s, also called Kev, joined me at my table. He took great pleasure in telling me that his friend Mick had lost some kind of bet en route and was waiting in the queue. My willingness to invite some company made Kev's job of securing seating far quicker and he enjoyed waving to Mick from our corner. Soon realising that I was not a local, the

discussion turned to my footballing allegiances, although Kev did not mean Liverpool. He expected me to favour one of the two Glasgow giants, then recommended that I 'best not say that [you support Liverpool] out loud in here', albeit with a mischievous grin. There has always been a strong connection between Liverpool and Celtic.[26] But Rangers coach Steven Gerrard's iconic status at the Merseyside club, he believed, had rendered the two clubs inseparable in the minds of many Celtic fans. 'If you support Liverpool, you'll be cheering him on today, then?' he reiterated.

Those comments were a little tongue-in-cheek, but his hatred of Rangers was deep-rooted, yet he was desperate to point out that the rivalry was almost no more. After raising an inquisitive eyebrow, Kev clarified his statement, 'There hasn't been an Old Firm game in six years. The match is no longer seen as a derby.'[27] He had taken particular offence with my earlier use of the term 'Old Firm'. 'They're just another *diddy*[28] team who we'll beat on our way to the title,' he snapped.

With the clock ticking ever closer to serving time, the crowd was growing more vocal, singing along to the Wolfe Tones album *Let the People Sing* before an even louder rendition of their 'Celtic Symphony'. The lyrics provided the second reference of the day to 'paradise' as Mick appeared with their drinks. Four pints of lager and two scotches, to drink within an hour! Asking whether I was there 'for the Old Firm game' prompted an even more aggressive reaction from

---

26 Celtic became the first opponents for Liverpool after the tragic events at Hillsborough during the FA Cup semi-final in April 1989, where 97 supporters lost their lives

27 Rangers' financial collapse in 2012 led to the liquidation of their commercial entity. They were allowed to continue in the lowest division of Scottish football after a new company acquired the sporting assets and their playing membership continued unbroken

28 A *diddy* is a spineless idiot in regional language

Kev, who growled, 'Even he forgets they died and, at most, it is just a Glasgow derby now.' For someone who proclaimed that the game, and opposition, no longer mattered, it still meant much more than he would admit.

In July 2012, a month after Rangers' liquidation, Celtic fans flew a banner at Celtic Park depicting the Gers as a zombie, rising from the grave and being shot by a sniper, leading to an increased use of the reference by Hoops supporters. The gunman's resemblance to a paramilitary during the Northern Ireland conflict was another reminder of the long-standing political differences that remain. A group of Celtic supporters also paid for a full-page advertisement in a local newspaper in January 2015, heralding their first match against 'New Rangers'.

With kick-off fast approaching, I headed to meet Paddy, who had assured me he was in a taxi just minutes away. I thought to myself that I could never leave it that late to arrive at a match of this importance, only to remember that I travel thousands of miles on the morning of European away fixtures to watch Liverpool. There was little time to catch up and, after handing me a membership card to gain entry, we set off at pace back along London Road, stopping to grab a programme and let his compatriot Liam purchase a scarf (not half and half!). We joined the waves of green and white sweeping towards the stadium, those around us belting out renditions of 'The Boys of the Old Brigade' and 'Ooh Ah Up the Ra'. A look of embarrassment rolled over Paddy's face before a wry smile broke out. 'You didn't hear that,' he joked. Old habits die hard, it seems, although I got the feeling that the younger members of the group were singing those songs more because of those that have gone before them than a deep-seated hatred, some having not lived through those countries' darkest periods of conflict.

* * *

There was a time in my lifetime when tensions between the two clubs appeared to escalate in the wake of Graeme Souness becoming player-manager at Rangers in 1986, establishing the side that would win nine titles in a row. During his five years at the club, Souness won three championships and four Scottish League Cups, and was still playing when Celtic defeated Rangers in the 1989 Scottish Cup Final. A man who has experienced the intensity of derbies in Istanbul, Lisbon, Merseyside and Turin admitted that these fixtures were the biggest he had experienced, 'Nothing prepared me for the passion and the enormity of the Rangers job. A lot of the enormity is in your own mind because you feed off the passion your supporters have for your football club. When you win it is a great feeling, but on the opposite side, losing was the biggest disappointment I have had in my professional career. There is an upside when you win. You are very much elated. But to lose it has the opposite effect. It is with you for a long time.'[29] It was the controversial signing of Maurice 'Mo' Johnston that was a powder keg for the religious and political tensions across the city.

The striker became the first high-profile Roman Catholic to sign for Rangers when arriving from French side Nantes in 1989. Celtic had always signed Protestants, but Rangers would never field a Catholic for fear of losing support or sponsorship. Johnston had also head-butted Rangers' Stuart Munro in the 1986 Scottish League Cup Final while playing for Celtic. Souness credited Johnston for making the move, suggesting that he 'admired his courage in taking it on because he was the one in the spotlight playing the games

---

29 McLaughlin, C., 'Rangers v Celtic: Nothing comes close to Old Firm derby – Souness' (BBC, 2019)

and taking the stick, sometimes from both sides'.[30] A last-minute winner at Ibrox against their bitter rivals lessened the animosity on the Rangers side, but incited the other, who petrol-bombed Johnston's Edinburgh home.

Few players have appeared for both clubs until more recent years, Kenny Miller and Steven Pressley running that gauntlet, although they didn't make the direct move across Glasgow. And almost ten years after Johnston there was the curious case of Italian Lorenzo Amoruso, who was thought to be Catholic yet became Rangers' captain. The lack of explicit publicity of his religion appeared to prevent outrage from the home support.

On several other occasions, the fixture had exploded among religious controversy. In 1998, Paul Gascoigne of Rangers mimicked playing a flute – a loyalist symbol – at Celtic Park in response to taunts from the home crowd. His club handed the midfielder a £20,000 fine. A decade later Celtic goalkeeper Artur Boruc angered the opposite side of the divide with a post-victory t-shirt reading 'God Bless the Pope' and a picture of countryman Pope John Paul II. The Pole was spared a financial penalty, but the incident was so inflammatory that Members of the Scottish Parliament (MSPs) debated the act in parliament.

* * *

After 30 minutes in each other's company, Paddy had to leave us for his regular spot closer to where the Green Brigade of Celtic stood and directed me and Liam towards our entrance gate at the opposite end of the stadium. We had to go through an imposing tunnel created by the underside of the

---

30 Souness, G., *Football: My Life, My Passion* (Headline Book Publishing, 2017)

North Stand overhead crammed with people. As soon as we entered, the joyful post-match singing softened, ground to a halt even, and was replaced by disgruntled murmurs from the sea of people surrounding us, gradually increasing in volume. Within seconds we were stuck a third of the way in, with no option of turning back given that stewards were operating something of a one-way system around the perimeter, and we were being crushed alongside those around us.

With kick-off fast approaching, the crowd's impatience grew, yelling at others to move forward, and some scaled the 12ft concrete walls and shuffled along while gripping the wire fence for support. My height allowed some relief from the squeeze, and I could see movement at the end of the passageway. Turning my head back towards ground level, there was a look of fear on some of the younger faces and as always, my thoughts turned to the horrific events at Hillsborough in 1989. This time, though, I also recalled that fateful day at Ibrox in 1971.

The level of anger and anxiety growing inside the increasing swell of bodies signalled that this was far from a regular occurrence, even when their bitter cross-city rivals are the opposition and ensure a sellout crowd. Of all the ways in which I imagined my sense of unease being broken, though, someone behind pinching my left buttock was not it. But it worked perfectly, if unorthodox. Turning my head to identify the culprit, I cannot say it disappointed me to see two young lasses (as the locals might say) in their early 20s accepting responsibility with a smirk rather than one of the sweat-drenched middle-aged men making up most of the throng.

Looking at some other surprised faces, it was an obvious tactic they had employed to advance their way through the crush, and it had indeed created a small gap that allowed them to pass us before reverting to a more traditional method of shouting 'dad' in a thick Scottish accent at, I suspected, a non-existent parent beyond the bottleneck. While the girls had brought a short-lived moment of amusement to the pocket of people nearby, the mood returned to the increasing aggression among the senior members of the crowd. As we reached the end of the underpass, several of them let the police officers, allegedly managing the crowd flow, know the level of their displeasure. Despite being eager to get into the stadium, I froze, anticipating one particular altercation. A man in his late 40s, face turning a red-pink with rage, unleashed a tirade of abuse just inches from one officer's face. It was as if the spittle propelling from his mouth every time he called the officer a 'cunt' was landing in slow motion.

Ignoring how they aired their grievances, their annoyance centred around redistributing supporters inside Celtic Park for this fixture, arguing that the authorities should have been better prepared and not blocked the usual pathways to gates. In 2011, a freedom of information request highlighted that the Strathclyde Police spent £2.4m on the seven derbies during the 2010/11 season. With that level of expenditure, it would be reasonable to assume they would regulate the crowds much better. You might also expect the two clubs to contribute over 12 per cent of those costs. It seemed a little strange that a stadium you can access from five or six different directions would operate a one-way system. In January 1994, Celtic supporters were banned from Ibrox after the club refused to contribute financially to repeated acts of vandalism claimed by Rangers during previous contests. Clearly aware of the commercial repercussions of the Old Firm without its unique atmosphere, though, the Scottish Premier League passed a law that would prevent a repeat of the lifeless fixture, which ended 1-1 with no away fans present.

Ahead of this campaign, after consultation with supporters, Rangers announced that Celtic's ticket allocation would be reduced from 7,000 to 800, driven by a need to increase revenues through season ticket sales, and Celtic responded in kind. According to Paddy, this required the displacement of the away supporters from their usual position to better place this mediocre amount.

One of the most significant Rangers supporters' groups is Club 1872, which holds a shareholding in the club since being formed in May 2016, in the recovery years following liquidation. This resulted in a merger of existing groups – Rangers First and the Rangers Supporters Trust – while two smaller entities dissolved to take an active role within Club 1872. However, the group more aligned to European ultras and looking to provide the atmosphere and spectacles on matchdays are the Union Bears. Founded in 2007, the group's name is likely to originate from the unionist background of the fanbase and the Teddy Bears nickname Rangers held. If you are visiting Glasgow, you are almost certain to find a Union Bears sticker glued to a bathroom wall or lamppost, or be offered one, as I was a 'Rangers Ultras Union Bears' version, nearer Ibrox Stadium. Another ultra group, The Blue Order, had once competed with the Union Bears in numbers and influence, and actually combined to challenge the club on matters such as security. But Ed told me they had taken a back seat in recent years after a power struggle within their Broomloan Stand section of Ibrox.

Regardless of which ultra group were present at Celtic Park, the reduced numbers meant I was unlikely to hear the sometimes controversial rendition of their 'Follow, Follow' anthem[31] given how outnumbered they would be. Yet I was pleased that I did not have to suffer hearing 'Simply the Best' by Tina Turner, which has been played before games at Ibrox since Rangers clinched their ninth consecutive title in 1997 against Celtic. With five games left to play that season, Hoops fans' nightmare scenario became a reality. A solitary goal from Brian Laudrup secured a 1-0 win at Celtic Park and effectively the trophy as Rangers went 11 points clear, although a brawl between Paolo Di Canio and Ian Ferguson stole plenty of the headlines.

Although it was the first encounter since Celtic clinched a second consecutive domestic treble, it was arguably the first time since Rangers' demotion in 2012 that they were going into the game from a relative position of strength. Had Motherwell's Peter Hartley not netted an equaliser against them in the fourth minute of injury time the previous week to secure a 3-3 draw, the visitors would have headed across town on top of the league. The lack of support had already reduced their chances of victory. Rangers were also going strong in the Europa League having just reached the group stages and were unbeaten in all competitions under new manager Gerrard.

The former Liverpool midfielder's arrival at Ibrox also added an additional narrative as Celtic manager Brendan Rodgers had overseen his somewhat premature departure from Anfield in 2015. The Northern Irishman's decision to rest Gerrard for a crucial European tie with Real Madrid contributed to his decision to depart. Rodgers was coming

---

31 Based upon the revivalist hymn 'Follow On', it became controversial when some Rangers supporters created alternative lyrics referencing the Pope and Vatican City that were considered sectarian, and vice-chairman Donald Findlay was even forced to resign in 1999 when he was caught singing that version on film

under criticism for the first time since arriving in Glasgow during the summer of 2016, after Celtic lost 3-2 on aggregate to AEK Athens of Greece in early August to miss out on Champions League football. Fans were also lamenting the bitter departure of star striker Moussa Dembélé to Olympique Lyonnais for £19.7m just 48 hours earlier.

After climbing the stairways with leaps and bounds, eager not to miss a minute of the action, there was no pause to savour the electric atmosphere that I often attempt when edging out towards my first view of a stadium steeped in as much tradition and history, but also hosting a fixture of such importance. The noise level had risen significantly in those last seconds before kick-off and we had reached our seats, luckily not disrupting too many people. Outed earlier as a Liverpool regular, Paddy's friends had joked that I would finally get to hear 'You'll Never Walk Alone' 'as it's supposed to be sung'. But they were wrong. The match was quickly under way, and I realised I had missed my chance, unable to recall whether I even heard it being sung while we were rushing through the turnstiles or being squeezed outside.

With both sides going through the motions during the opening exchanges, the home crowd seemed determined to increase the intensity with their reaction to every challenge or move towards the opposition goal, cheering each tackle made by Celtic or crying foul if a Rangers player even attempted to tackle their opponent and allowing me to locate the away support in a small section to my right, at the far end of our stand. That expected sense of disappointment arrived as I could barely hear them and, while hostile, the atmosphere was too one-sided. Not that I would admit it to those around me. I stood wondering if the brief silence an opposition goal could bring would also provide a sign of how fervent their support was. What was visually obvious among both sets of supporters, though, was the distinct lack of Scottish flags. There was a clear preference for the Union Jack among the travelling fans and the Irish tricolour adorning several of the banners displayed by the Celtic support.

Unlike Genoa, Rome or Lisbon before this, there was no elaborate choreography by the Celtic fans (although I could have missed it). Not that they had much room to do anything, crammed into a relatively small corner of the biggest of all football stadiums in Scotland. Alongside the Irish tricolour flew some green and white chequered or striped flags that were being energetically waved by fans. As was one Green Brigade banner I could see among those bouncing up and down and making themselves heard above the increasing rumble of applause filling 80 per cent of Celtic Park. A sea of enthusiastic bodies was dancing within the safe standing areas – sections 110 to 112 – that ultimately decided their placement, going wild through a mixture of delight and/or aggression towards their neighbours. This was no light-hearted attempt to better the opposition's tifos, but a collective effort to drown out the noise created from the visitors' section and generate one of the most intimidating atmospheres the Rangers players had ever walked out in front of.

* * *

The Green Brigade is also the only show in town when it comes to Celtic's supporters, formed as recently as 2006, describing themselves as anti-fascist, anti-racist and anti-sectarian, while credited with organising impressive pre-match shows such as an impressive full-stadium card display against Barcelona in 2012 to mark Celtic's 125th anniversary. The group had courted controversy, though. A protest against poppies appearing on the Celtic shirt in November

2010 brought widespread condemnation, and the club even moved to disband the Green Brigade towards the end of 2013. Ahead of that poppy protest against Motherwell, an increase in pro-IRA chants had also been reported and, given what I had heard earlier, those views are still clearly expressed without fear of punishment. Five years on from the attempt to reduce the influence of the Green Brigade, they are still very much front and centre of the support inside the stadium. A year before their creation, both Celtic and Rangers had agreed on a project aimed at eradicating sectarianism but little has changed, even if it is the actions of the few that dominate the headlines and ensure that an entire group of supporters is labelled as one.

A unit monitoring sectarian activity in Glasgow once reported that on Old Firm weekends violent incidents were almost ten times higher than normal. Meanwhile, in *How Soccer Explains the World*, Franklin Foer listed eight deaths and hundreds of assaults linked to the fixture between 1996 and 2003. In *Football Against the Enemy*, though, Simon Kuper raised an interesting question of whether the Old Firm rivalry might have overtaken the religious element of the hatred that exists given that fewer people class themselves as religious. The Celtic-Rangers rivalry and violent actions as a result have become as embedded in Scottish culture.

* * *

For those who have ever watched Celtic's combative captain Scott Brown play football, it will be no surprise reading that the midfielder was first to be booked on ten minutes for what was, if being polite, a robust challenge. The Scottish international seemed to thrive off controversy and his overly physical tackle sent Rangers manager Gerrard raging to the fourth official on the sidelines. The supporters around me congratulated their skipper and goaded the recently appointed Rangers boss in equal measure, while I reflected on the hypocrisy of the Englishman berating a challenge Gerrard made on countless occasions as a player himself, especially against Everton and Manchester United.

The relatively early booking for Brown continually had the home support incensed when any Rangers foul went unpunished, particularly in the case of striker Alfredo Morelos, who committed several needless offences and acted as the visitors' own public enemy number one with the noise within the stadium having settled to a more familiar level experienced at fixtures where sides are contesting a title decider, even in September.

Those were the only moments temperatures increased until Celtic finally looked set to make the breakthrough. On 25 minutes, a long-range free kick from Callum McGregor was more cross than shot, but Allan McGregor in the Rangers goal punched awkwardly away and single-handedly enthused the Celtic fans. Nine minutes later, Celtic attacker James Forrest controlled a headed clearance and sent a deflected volley from 25 yards crashing off the top of the crossbar. The crowd was now demanding a goal before half-time.

From the resulting corner, defender Mikael Lustig struck the same part of the goal frame with a header before an under-pressure Gers defence cleared the ball away and it sparked a chant of 'you're not Rangers anymore' on all four sides of Celtic Park. When McGregor pushed another chance away, this time a close-range effort from Odsonne Édouard just before the break, the home fans must have been wondering whether the discipline clearly instilled by Gerrard might deny them victory.

Listening to the expectant waves of supporters I followed towards the toilets at half-time, I failed to be convinced by their optimism and then had my mid-match reflections interrupted by a stadium announcement. 'It remains 0-0 in paradise.' How odd, I thought. The fans' optimism seemed to centre on the lack of touches Rangers had had in the Celtic box rather than a growing sense that the hosts looked to be struggling to finish their own chances.

Stood waiting my turn to approach the urinal, staring at the floor as you do, the determination to wear green and white was visible in the abnormal number of lime green Adidas Gazelle trainers being worn. I should have counted them for accuracy, but more announcements broke my train of thought. 'Take your place on the fields of paradise, and 'Tickets for paradise still remain for …' The widespread commercialisation of top-level football has many clubs cooking up a variety of marketing slogans, such as Liverpool's ridiculous 'This Means More' and Barcelona's narcissistic 'Mes Que Un Club' (More Than A Club). Referring to the stadium as 'Paradise' out loud sent a cringeworthy shiver down my spine as I stood there trying to focus on finishing the task at hand, aware of the backlog behind me such were the queues to relieve bladders.

The return to my seat coincided with a few Rangers players emerging and, as opposition goalkeeper McGregor jogged out almost alone, the level of vitriolic abuse aimed in his direction was unbelievable. I assumed it centred around a lifetime ban from international football imposed by the Scottish Football Association after a marathon drinking session with then-Rangers team-mate Barry Ferguson while on Scotland duty, followed by obscene hand gestures to television cameras while sat on the sidelines.

Therefore, their aggressive cries of 'rapist' in his direction came as a bit of a shock. It turned out that, in 2010, the courts had cleared McGregor of an alleged sexual assault of a young woman in Glasgow. But the home fans were not letting that stop their abusive guilty verdicts, with all sorts of unsavoury terms linked to the November 2009 incident.

This was in significant contrast to the respect shown by the Rangers supporters at Ibrox on 5 September 1931 when captain Davie Meiklejohn communicated news of a serious injury to Celtic goalkeeper John Thomson to fans, after a collision with Gers striker Sam English. Thomson's head had crashed into the attacker's knee and he later died of a depressed fracture of the skull. With the severity of the incident obvious as they stretchered Thomson from the pitch, the Rangers fans remained almost silent. What was also unique about the goalkeeper was that he was the only Protestant in a Celtic team full of Catholics.

The abuse had little effect on McGregor, though, who produced an excellent save from Olivier Ntcham shortly after the play resumed, somehow deflecting a powerful low drive heading towards the bottom corner on to the crossbar and reinforcing the sense that Rangers would leave with at least a point.

However, on 62 minutes, Celtic and Ntcham broke the deadlock. Gaining possession on the edge of their own box after two players had contested a high ball, which could easily have resulted in a Rangers free kick, Tomas Rogic drove forwards through the middle of the pitch with Forrest and Ntcham either side, as the noise inside the stadium increased in anticipation. Faced with two retreating Rangers players, the midfielder played the ball into the feet of striker Édouard, cutting across the 18-yard box, who passed to Forrest on the right flank. With the opposition drawn to the attacker, he slid the ball first time along the six-yard box to an unmarked Ntcham, who rolled it home amid a crowd already celebrating the goal and going wild.

I expected to get swept up in the feverish atmosphere in paradise, before the sound of Darude's dance anthem 'Sandstorm' drowned out the initial roar of celebration, being blasted out from every speaker possible, and the organic celebratory sounds generated from thousands doing their own thing turned into a two-minute rave inside the stadium, apart from the odd scream of ecstasy skywards by those around me.

One man in particular was wearing a classic green and black away shirt from the mid-1990s adorned with 'McAvennie' above a number nine. My mind was trying to remember whether the striker had even appeared for Celtic during that period. It turned out that Frank McAvennie had featured in the first 'Old Firm Shame Game' at Ibrox in October 1987.

McAvennie was sent off first, Rangers' Chris Woods soon followed the striker after the pair had a physical altercation. Defenders Terry Butcher and Graeme Roberts were also dismissed for their involvement. Despite the lack of players on the pitch, Rangers held on for a 2-2 draw, but all four found themselves in court for breaching the peace. Despite leaving Celtic in 1989, McAvennie had returned for a brief spell in 1992. The gentleman in front of me met my need for historical accuracy regarding shirt printing.

Whether it was the increase of social media or post-game government involvement, the third of the 'Shame Trilogy' – the second that infamous title-clinching fixture in 1997 already mentioned – appears to take prominence over its predecessors. In March 2011, managers Neil Lennon and Ally McCoist fought on the touchline and had to be separated. Lennon received a four-game ban and McCoist won an appeal against a two-match suspension. Rangers trio El Hadji Diouf, Steven Whittaker and Madjid Bougherra were all shown red during a fiery Scottish Cup replay played in front of a poisonous atmosphere, with 34 supporters inside the stadium arrested. Few will remember that Celtic triumphed 1-0 and, in 2019, McCoist would describe the incident as 'nothing, really' to BT Sport.

Celtic could have doubled their lead minutes later when another Lustig header flashed past the foot of the goalpost and, despite Morelos forcing a save from Craig Gordon, there had been something inevitable about the opening goal, which transferred any nervous energy around the stadium into celebration. Full of optimism for the final 20 minutes, they almost rewarded the fans when substitute Leigh Griffiths hit the post on 80 minutes.

There was still time for controversy when Ryan Christie threw himself to the ground after the slightest of touches from Connor Goldson on the edge of the box but, to the home supporters' disgust, the referee did not award a penalty, instead giving a free kick and booking Goldson. Brown's general behaviour in attempting to get the defender sent off was unsavoury but within character.

Then, on 89 minutes, the ball fell to Rangers full-back James Tavernier. His low shot from the right side of the box flew just past the left goalpost to a collective sigh of relief.

Before I knew it, the referee had blown for full time and relief had turned to ecstasy. The stadium erupted and the tannoy kicked in once more to the sound of Daniel Boone's 1970s one-hit-wonder 'Beautiful Sunday' with the Rangers players giving a quick salute to the pocket of travelling fans and heading straight for the tunnel. The backslapping and hugs from McAvennie shirt and co in front of me were short-lived, quickly turning their attention to the departing opposition players and aiming several V-signs in their direction while continuing to sing along to the music with smiles on faces. Despite this being just a few weeks into the season, they knew it was one of the few meaningful victories they would celebrate together and intended to make the most out of the experience.

With the post-match formalities completed and the Rangers players departed, the Celtic players made their way to our corner just as the in-house music jumped into the next decade with 'Just Can't Get Enough' by Depeche Mode, and they embarked on a lap of honour. People were tossing fragments of white paper in the air or standing on whatever they could find to rise above the rest of us and clapping along with the music. It felt like I was witnessing the end to a title-winning season, as they spent the entire three minutes and 38 seconds of the track drinking in the adulation. It wasn't their first Old Firm win by any stretch of the imagination. But there was something showmanlike as the players slowed their walk when approaching the visiting section, which was being held back and forced to sit through the festivities. As the players arrived, the home fans let out a collective roar, almost silencing the music playing. The visitors unleashed waves of inaudible verbal abuse and less-than-welcoming hand gestures to the Celtic team. Two sets of supporters more similar than either will ever be willing to recognise, I thought to myself. Two siblings provoking each other just for the sake of it and one biting back. The celebratory atmosphere continued when we rejoined Paddy and friends after the match, and we undertook a much quicker walk back towards the city along Gallowgate, which was useful as I was flying home just a few hours later.

When we reached Hoops Bar, we were told that it was already full with Celtic revellers and we could not enter. We sauntered instead a little further along to Bar 67 which I had passed earlier that morning. It was obvious, though, that it had similar issues given the queues outside and we then decided on The Phoenix, which we had just passed. Sinking a few beers, as the others concerned themselves with travel arrangements for the upcoming Europa League fixtures now that the title contest was over, I convinced them I could not stay one more night for some Irish hospitality with work awaiting in the morning.

5

The Budapest Derby –
Budapest, Hungary

BUDAPEST IS one of my favourite cities and one of the most beautiful in Europe, whether visiting during the inviting high 20°C heat during the summer months or insulated from the freezing temperatures and falling snow during winter.

Yet, until a few days before landing in the Hungarian capital, I had only momentarily considered the derby for the book. It was, however, at the top of the reserve list, should one trip not be possible. My intention was always to head to Tehran, Iran, in September 2018, to witness Esteghlal versus Persepolis, and not for the first time.

In January of that year I had booked four nights' accommodation in Tehran for early March but then asked for an authorisation number from the Ministry of Foreign Affairs of Iran relating to my visa. Unbeknown to me, UK passport holders were required to 'travel in the company of an "official guide" at all times on a tailor-made trip with the itinerary predetermined, pre-booked and prepaid', as one travel agent confirmed. My wife, Stacey, will tell you how much I love an itinerary (providing I've made it!), but this was rather extreme.

There was an alternative solution. If I could find an Iranian resident willing to act as my host, they could lodge an application directly with the Iranian Foreign Ministry, allowing me to travel freely without the need of an escort. As you have probably guessed, the latter wasn't an option. After being quoted £320 per day for a package, and with time running out, I abandoned my efforts.

Ahead of the next fixture in September 2018, James Montague – author of books such as *1312: Among the Ultras* and *The Billionaires Club* – had kindly introduced me to a local journalist, Behnam Jafarzadeh. Once again, after contacting him out of nowhere, Behnam was equally generous in providing advice and guidance, and willing to join me at the match as well as facilitate an interview with Persepolis coach Branko Ivanković.

As it was then July, I thought I had plenty of time to arrange a visa, with or without Behnam as host, but world politics had adjusted the rules. I was now forced to use a prearranged tour provider and thought I had tailored a four-night trip perfectly with Pariza Travel, albeit touching down in Imam Khomeini Airport at 1am and being transported straight to the Iran National Museum and at an eye-watering US$1,070 before flights, and with a guide having to join me and Behnam at the Blue-Red Derby.[32] I swiftly sent organiser Niloofar Rajaeeyan various documents, such as a professional CV, passport photos and a list of every country and city I had ever visited so that they could submit my visa application. Eventually I was asked to confirm my marital status and if I had any children (none, for those wondering), which yielded a strange response of, 'That is

---

32 Perspolis's primary colours are red shirts, shorts and socks whereas Esteghlal perform in an equally one block-colour-strip of blue

excellent. Both your CV and lifestyle.' Complete with a smiley face emoji.

A month later, though, Niloofar confirmed they had rejected the application without reason, but I could reapply in a couple of months. Whether it was the journalistic nature of the trip, I will never know, but Behnam thought it might have contributed.

I tried again in December 2019, and all was looking positive with the application until a US drone strike the following month saw my plans thwarted once again.[33] Niloofar then confirmed, 'American, British and Canadian passport holders can no longer enter sports complexes.' The Covid-19 pandemic would probably have put an end to my visit regardless of my visa application, though, in hindsight.

Although the visa rejection was a blow, I had kept in touch with fixture dates of the same-city derbies on my long list and, within 11 days, I had return flights to Budapest and accommodation booked. Tickets for the Budapest derby had not yet gone on sale but within days I had secured a ticket within the Ferencváros ultras section, as I had become a club member when visiting the capital in 2016.

Budapest was once three separate entities, until Buda, Óbuda, and Pest came together and assumed the current name in 1873, becoming the co-capital of the Austro-Hungarian Empire until its termination after the First World War. Around 80 geothermal springs and a huge thermal water cave system are a significant selling point for tourists who flock there, with the Gellért and Széchenyi baths among some of the most renowned in the world. The

---

33 On 3 January 2020, Qasem Soleimani, an Iranian major general, was killed by a targeted US drone strike at Baghdad International Airport while on his way to meet the Iraqi prime minister. Soleimani was considered the second-most powerful person of Iran at the time

former is ideally situated at the bottom of the hilly Buda and connected to Pest by the 19th-century Liberty Bridge, which stretches across the River Danube. Széchenyi's heated outside pool is particularly picturesque as the sun sets in winter months.

A walk along the famous waterway is another captivating attraction, with it hard not to stumble across the subtle Shoes on the Danube Bank memorial that was constructed in 2005 to honour the Jews persecuted during the Nazi occupation of the city. Budapest and the rest of Hungary remained under significant Soviet influence until full liberation in 1991, but the country appears to have grown stronger and stronger since. With a fondness for unpretentious eastern European cuisine and craft ales, though, it is at night when the city's appeal increases tenfold, regularly lurching between the skeletons of previously neglected buildings transformed into trending ruin bars and scattered conveniently across Budapest.

* * *

Like many Hungarian teams, Újpest were originally formed as a sports club in 1885, when not yet resting within the Budapest city boundaries (becoming the fourth district in the 1950s) and named Újpesti Torna Egylet (Gymnastics Club of Újpest). In 1901, though, they united with the football club Újpesti FC, who had begun playing the sport two years earlier. Therefore, some consider the 14-years-younger Ferencváros as the *Liláks'* (Purples) junior. After several residents from the city district of the same name and first president, Ferenc Springer, founded Ferencvárosi Torna Club in 1899.

Ferencváros are another of those on my list to play in green and white. Some believe that they took inspiration from the country's first sports club, Budapesti Torna Club, who played in red and white stripes, Ferencváros exchanging red for the third colour on the national flag. Another adaptation was that fellow-founder Kornél Gabrovitz, through a passing fondness, asked the daughter of a coffee-shop owner to select the colours. Green and lilac were chosen but the latter faded to white after washing, luckily for fans of replica shirts considering the thought of that brash combination of colours.

Traditionally, Ferencváros's local rivalry was with MTK Budapest – Magyar Testgyakorlók Köre Budapest Futball Club (Hungarian Practitioners Circle Budapest Football Club). The *Fradi*[34] had won eight of the 12 championships since formation, and five consecutive titles between 1908/09 and 1912/13. However, immediately afterwards, MTK secured a historic ten in a row. As the 1920s ended, though, with Hungarian players and coaches being exported across the world, Újpest established themselves as the third of a trinity of Budapest giants and soon become Ferencváros's major rivals, although that would not have been immediately apparent after losing their first encounter at the Sorkosári úti Stadion 2-0 on 19 February 1905, and the return fixture 3-1, as the *Fradi* finished eight points ahead of them as league champions.

With Ferencváros embarking on a promotional tour of South America in 1929, where opposing fans would applaud the team from pitches across the continent, Újpest turned professional and would win their first Nemzeti Bajnokság I (National Championship) and dominate the next decade, winning the Mitropa Cup at both the beginning and end of

---

34 The nickname *Fradi* is shortened from the German Franzstadt, Ferencváros being the ninth district of Budapest. The team is also frequently called the Green Eagles as their colours are green and white

that period. The second Mitropa Cup, under the tutelage of historic Budapest-born coach Béla Guttmann, had arguably sparked the rivalry between the clubs, after defeating Ferencváros 6-3 on aggregate, including a memorable 4-1 win at the *Fradi*'s Üllői úti Stadion (now the Groupama Arena). The same year, they also pipped them to the league title by a single point. Clinching the Coupe des Nations in 1930[35] might have already intensified the competition between the pair as well, though.

MTK had won the 1935/36 and 1936/37 championships, but the Second World War would soon have a significant impact on them as a leading club. In 1941, with Hungary under German influence, MTK refused to comply with a ruling that sports associations could not have members or their spouses identifying as Jewish, and the following year the club disbanded and several members were killed. When deportations of Jews began in May 1944, president Alfréd Brüll got transferred to the Auschwitz death camp and was never seen again, having believed his safety assured, when returning to Hungary a year earlier. Újpest counterpart Lipót Aschner was much more fortunate when an electronics company bought his freedom while at Mauthausen camp and he quickly fled to Geneva, Switzerland.

The *Lilák* remained competitive, with Hungary selecting nine of their players for a fixture with Italy in May 1947, but Soviet occupation severally impacted both clubs. With MTK trying to re-establish themselves, Ferencváros were renamed in 1950 as ÉDOSZ and lost their club colours, after being consumed by the state food workers union, and later became

---

35 The Coupe des Nations was an early form of the European Cup/ Champions League and was last won by Újpest against Slavia Prague in 1930, triumphing 3-0 in the final in Geneva, after all four rounds were played across eight days

Kinizsi. Their right-leaning tendencies saw them depicted as the opposition of the government.

That fitted the narrative between them and Újpest, who were renamed as Budapesti Dózsa Sport Egyesület (Budapest Dózsa Sports Association) by the Soviet Ministry of Interior and then Újpesti Dózsa Sport Club in the late 1950s. The *Lilák*, in particular, struggled for success in the years that followed, winning just two titles during the 1950s and 1960s, but they came roaring back in the next decade and dominated once more with nine championships between 1969 and 1979 and extended their supporter reach throughout Hungary.

Success would not last, Újpest having won two league championships since that heyday and the *Fradi* just seven in three and a half decades. However, remaining on somewhat of an equal footing has allowed the rivalry to evolve and intensify in the preceding years, becoming the fixture attracting the most spectators domestically each season.

* * *

My bus journey from the airport was unspectacular, particularly in the dead of night, with little in the way of sights to see until crossing the bridge over Könyves Kálmán körút Üllői út. Out of the darkness I could glimpse the green hue of the tastefully lit Ferencváros Stadion, known as the Groupama Arena, growing ever bigger as I moved closer. As the bus descended, a sudden loss of bearings struck me. Ferencváros's world-famous statue, an eight-metre-high stainless-steel eagle sculpture by local artist Gábor Miklós Szőke – the biggest bird monument in Europe on creation in 2014 – was missing.

Within seconds, though, the 16m wingspan of the huge 15-tonne figure quickly came into view further down the road. I later found out that, to accommodate a new business development on the south-west side of the stadium, the monument had to be moved. Now positioned on the adjacent corner, nearer the club offices and entrance to the traditional home end for supporters, it certainly felt a more prominent position than randomly slapped on the wide open stadium plaza.

On the morning of the game I decided to make an early start and visit some previously unseen sights. Pulling open the heavy wooden door of my accommodation building, leading out on to Király utca, the flashing blue lights of a police van greeted me. Surveying the street, there was a huge police presence despite being only just past 9am. I knew it was a fixture often marred by violent clashes between the two sets of fans, but starting this early was a little extreme, I thought to myself.

Rather than indicating that I would spend my day steering clear of warring supporters, the local authorities were simply policing (somewhat overzealously) an event at the nearby Zeneakadémia concert hall. The match would be requiring sizeable resources as the day progressed, though, with local newspaper headlines focused on an expected capacity crowd of 22,000 and how hooligan elements of the fanbases would be out to cause havoc before the game. *Ripost* kept things simple, with the headline 'Important? It is more than important'.

It was immediately hard not to associate any potential crowd disturbances with Ferencváros and, in particular, their ultras, the Green Monsters. While the team had struggled to make an impact on the pitch outside of Hungary in recent years – qualifying for the UEFA Europa League group stages in the seasons after this visit – the ultras had ensured that they remained infamous across the continent, engaging in bloody battles with foreign opponents, such as Dynamo Kyiv, Hajduk Split and Millwall, and appearing unsympathetic to innocent bystanders caught in the crossfire. They justified their violent and intimidating actions as extensions of the battle the team would have on the pitch and rarely apologised for them. However, they saved their best efforts for encounters with Újpest, normalising the use of chains, belts, baseball bats and even tasers.

Without a league title since 2016, Ferencváros were sitting on top of the Nemzeti Bajnokság, unbeaten and ten points ahead of their city rivals in eighth place. The belief that this fixture would impact the final standings was questionable considering that it was just eight games into the current campaign. Even with Újpest finishing third behind their hosts the previous season, an accurate reflection of the gap in quality was, once again, the points difference between the pair. Újpest were nearly 20 points behind their rivals in 2017/18, although ultimately finishing with the same prize of Europa League qualification. Ferencváros were certainly no stronger on the continent that year, exiting the competition to Maccabi Tel Aviv at the first qualifying stage. Újpest remained in the contest one round further, before losing 7-1 on aggregate to Sevilla.

Once the sightseeing was over I found myself back on the bus, after maintenance work foiled my attempts to reach the Groupama Arena by metro. Although it would have been nice if there had been some warning the line was not running before purchasing a ticket, rather than a burly security guard abruptly gesturing for me to head back towards ground level. Fortunately, public transport in Budapest was cheap enough not to worry about the lost forints. Travelling above ground also has its benefits, making it far easier to survey the crowds shuffling their way to a stadium or amassing outside bars and judging when best to disembark to join them on their journey or find refreshment.

I took my cue to leave from the sight of the Fradibox Fight-Club on the opposite side of Üllői út, which had four huge 6ft-plus men standing outside dressed head to toe in black. Even from some distance, their veins bursting from their supplement-induced muscles and minimal gap between any of their heads and shoulders convinced me that, should the widely reported pre-match violence come to pass, the quartet could hold their own in hand-to-hand combat and probably relish the battle.

Although it was late September and with the sun having nearly retired for the evening, as I stepped off the bus, there was no sign of winter fast approaching and chilling my bare arms. A woollen hat and scarf had remained firmly packed in my backpack since leaving England. After I continued on foot for a few minutes, Ferencváros's huge eagle sculpture came into view again, and it surprised me to see a queue forming for tickets nearby. Fortunately for me, as a Ferencváros member, I had purchased a ticket in advance online and, considering newspapers were announcing a sell-out, I assumed that supporters were simply collecting pre-purchased tickets at the office windows. An eventual attendance of 20,675, though, suggested room for a few extra bums on seats ahead of kick-off at the 23,698-capacity stadium.

As I passed the ticket office I became conscious of the suspecting glances I was receiving from the locals. I wondered if I looked so obviously not Hungarian, despite my eastern European heritage, or maybe they were just surprised that anyone from outside Budapest would risk attending. They may have viewed me as a lost tourist, straying from the well-trodden sightseeing paths.

A general lack of supporters outside the stadium made me stand out more prominently while also suggesting that I may have made an error going directly to the ground and not researching parts of the city in advance where the fans may have congregated. I pressed on towards my intended target, the Szöglet Presszó bar, a well-known haunt of Ferencváros fans, via the Népliget metro station underpass. Soon I realised where everyone had been hiding.

The station was a huge rotunda full of bars at its core and several others scattered around its perimeter, and filling at pace with *Fradi* supporters. For a second I hesitated at the bottom of the stairs leading back outside, before turning back around into the poorly lit subway. Instinctively I headed through a tiny door, next to a public toilet which looked as though it would lead to little more than a utility storage room.

What I found upon entering was a windowless room barely 50ft x 20ft that looked similar to a poorly maintained chip-shop kitchen I worked briefly at as a youngster. The back wall behind a canteen-style counter was filled with previously bright-white tiles that now bore the buttery stains of nicotine smoke which filled many of the drinking establishments around Budapest. Adorning the remaining three walls was the garish bright-green paint that forms one half of the *Zöld Sasok*'s (Green Eagles) famous colours. The overwhelming stench was not smoke, though, but the mix of various heavy spirits on offer. On the benches lining the wall opposite the bar sat two misty-eyed elderly gentlemen, either contemplating where life went wrong or intoxicated by the near-empty vodka bottle on their table. Some significantly more youthful fans stood full of life at the far end of the homemade tavern, enjoying a mix of beers and spirit chasers, which seemed to accompany every meal in Hungary. Even breakfast! A vodka shot was served up with the delicious traditional Hungarian feast provided at Szamos Gourmet House in the city centre.

Behind the bar was a middle-aged woman with an expression on her face suggesting that outsiders were not always welcome. Yet somehow she was also threatening me, with a steely glare, to order something, before she ran out of patience. In my best, and repeatedly practised, Hungarian, I asked (while also pointing embarrassingly) for a draft beer. She maintained her tough-looking appearance and demanded 500 HUF (about £1.40). Then, after quickly responding, I advanced towards an empty table in the room's corner, pleased to have stumbled across the cheapest pint in Budapest.

A TV screen by the entrance at the end of the room was showing a Premier League encounter between Arsenal and Watford, which appeared to catch the interest of passersby, several of whom were arching their necks around the doorframe to keep check of the score despite no obvious allegiance to either club. I paid little attention initially as I had become conscious of the eyes around me pointing in my direction, probably questioning why I had ignored the more welcoming establishments available.

Thirty minutes into the action on screen, the noise from those gathering outside had reached a level impossible to overlook. Firecrackers were exploding within the confines of the metro concourse, augmenting the blasts. As the walls alongside me rumbled, it made me think of the ferocious conflicts that have left a lasting impact on the capital. Would they have used the metro as a bomb shelter, I thought to myself.

To escape the mayhem, more filtered in. A man in his late 40s instantly caught my eye, striding boldly through the doors wearing a bright-red t-shirt emblazoned with POLSKA (Poland) in thick white letters, although partially hidden by a long overcoat. Expecting orders to fly in from newcomers, I purchased two more pints (given the price) and found someone had placed themselves between my table and the vodka-drinking duo.

Their new companion could have been around 50 years old, but looked at least 20 years older through an over-indulgence of life's excesses. He had himself a single bottle of red wine, but was pouring each serving into a thin, tall, 300ml tumbler rather than a traditional wine glass. Or opposed to directly from the bottle that I assumed he once had done. With my two drinks, I somehow felt accepted by the hard-drinking trio. After a few moments surveying the other new arrivals I concluded that 'Mr Red Wine' was possibly on his second or third bottle as he struggled to keep his balance despite being seated, but kept his eyes firmly fixed in my direction. Sheepishly lifting my gaze from the table, I realised that rather than looking at me, he appeared to be staring through me. I'm unsure he even knew I was there, to be honest. His eyes were a cloudy shade of red that almost made it impossible to separate the iris from sclera.

This uncomfortable episode was suddenly, and gratefully, broken by a silver-haired man entering the bar and downing a shot of vodka, screaming something incoherent loudly before quickly disappearing, that sparked a short-lived spell of singing from those now lining the bar.

Whether the burst into song was a call to arms or not, there appeared a sudden surge of supporters entering. In particular were several bulky shaven-headed men and another resembling the character Gumbo, wonderfully portrayed by Lee Ross in cult classic film *I.D.*, all wearing Ferencváros 1928 t-shirts. The tops varied in design but, as I discovered later, they referenced the year in which the club won the Mitropa Cup against SK Rapid Wien[36] to collect their first non-domestic trophy.

Although I initially assumed they might be one of the many ultra groups associated with the *Fradi*, they soon looked far less imposing when several of them began coughing and spluttering because of the increasing amount of smoke filling the room. The revelry beyond our bunker continued to rise in volume and creeping inside.

While that was going on, a man in his 70s had shuffled in with the help of a walking stick before asking for one of the unused chairs at my table, placing it just a few yards away and taking his seat. Moments later, though, his face was turning red and he was shuffling uncomfortably as he attempted to remove the first of many layers of clothing he was wearing. From my position, I could see that the zip on his coat had separated from the clasp at the bottom and opened up to his chest despite the zipper grip still safely fastened beneath his chin. Without a shared language to rely upon, we embarked on a sequence of comical facial expressions and gestures as I attempted to communicate my willingness to assist. Eventually, I just grabbed the bottom of his coat and pulled down the zipper with brute force and ignorance. When the zipper returned to its intended position, smiles broke across both our faces, sharing a nod of the head in each other's direction. He then squeezed my forearm affectionately and we went back to sitting in silence.

Witnessing the struggle, some young men to our left lent over and enquired where I was from, noting the zipper

---

36 The Mitropa Cup was one of the first major trophies that pitted European sides against each other and began in 1927, but was officially the La Coupe de l'Europe Centrale or Central European Cup. In 1951, after the Second World War and continent on the mend, the tournament was revived, but it was eventually discontinued in 1992

interaction, during which I must have muttered something in English. They had assumed I was Hungarian, or at least living and working locally. Clearly my eastern European heritage was allowing me to blend in, or I was right to assume that few tourists frequented this bar.

Discussion quickly moved on to my allegiance to Liverpool and I was surprised to hear that they 'supported' West Ham United – for no other reason than believing the London club is renowned for football-related violence; I feared they had just watched *The Football Factory* and *Green Street* one too many times. Even pointing out that current Ferencváros goalkeeper Péter Kurucz – who started his career with Újpest – once made a solitary substitute appearance for the Hammers back in 2009 made little difference. All they wanted to talk about was their exaggerated, I sense, hooligan activity. What would have happened had I told them I supported Chelsea, I wondered. They told me how little they feared English fans now in what appeared an attempt to highlight how dangerous they were, but that just appeared youthful embellishment. During our interaction, one of the more drunken members of the group insisted on showing me where a recent scuffle had left him with a broken nose.

Although not directly associated with Ferencváros's Green Monsters, they told me they were off to fight with their Újpest counterparts, which was some relief given that the language barrier had become something of a problem, particularly as they slurred their words. As was establishing how much they were exaggerating the details of their battle stories. As they exited the bar they gave a few fist pumps, cheers of 'Liverpool, Liverpool', and much laughter, which suggested there was an element of boyish mockery during the tipsy exchanges. With two-thirds of the customers' gazes firmly fixed upon me now, especially from a middle-aged man missing all of his teeth directly opposite, I decided it was time to find out what the commotion was outside.

* * *

Coming from Hungary's most well-supported club, it is easy to see why the Green Monsters have become infamous throughout Europe. Yet, with supporter groups outlawed until 1989, while still under Soviet occupation, they were only formed as recently as 1995. Not that this prevented vicious clashes or violence before that historic juncture with rival factions that had evolved organically, battling for supremacy away from the pitch.

These seem to have remained as hooligan groups such as Sector 2, Új Generáció or EEE,[37] that will occasionally clash on club matters, but rarely seem to have fought for terrace superiority. This is not dissimilar to Újpest. Hooligan groups like Angol Brigád and Korps had influenced the Ultra Viola Bulldogs '92, formed three years before the Green Monsters. Post-Soviet developments, when the availability of footage or publications from European championships increased, have, however, resulted in a heavy English and Italian influence. Although, political ideologies have less influence, with most ultras or hooligan groups in Hungary of a right or far-right leaning.

In fact, the Ferencváros and Újpest groups came together in April 2015 to boycott fixtures at the Groupama Arena, when opening the new stadium coincided with the Hungarian Football Federation supporting Ferencváros's decision to enforce a card-based entry system that required biometric scanning of fans. Both clubs had the support of

---

37 The E.E.E group take their name from the Ferencváros club motto 'Erkölcs, Erő, Egyetértés' (Moral, Power, Accordance)

Újpest mayor Zsolt Wintermantel, who insisted that their 'basic rights had been violated', and 'without fans, there is no good atmosphere and no good match'.[38]

It was a surprising show of solidarity considering the widespread violence a year earlier, when rival groups clashed at the Újpest-Városkapu metro station during the 2013/14 campaign, leaving two supporters in hospital with serious injuries. When the match at the *Liláks'* Szusza Ferenc Stadium ended in a 2-1 defeat for the home side, Újpest ultras began throwing projectiles and breaking into the Ferencváros enclosure, which resulted in tear gas being fired at the warring factions and escalated the rioting that continued long after the final whistle.

* * *

Squeezing through the crowd that had formed around the tiny doorway, I could barely see more than ten paces in front of me through the dense smoke. Had it not been for the lack of panic from those quietly sipping their beers, you could have been walking into a burning building. When striding further into the fog, the strong green hue to the clouds made it clear it was, once again, the work of pyrotechnics. This adds to the choreography in and outside of stadiums across Europe but has been lacking in English football.

As I crossed the hallway I had to sidestep others emerging suddenly from the bright-green clouds, before leaning against a cold, tiled wall and absorbing the lively crowd. Few were hanging around and were instead marching past, looking to escape the smoke-filled enclosure as quickly as possible, protectively clutching scarves or small flags over

---

38 'FTC-Újpest: "There is no rally without fans!" – Signed by Wintermantel' (Nemzeti Sport, 2015)

their airways and shielding the occasional youngster in tow. A few recurring uncovered faces of two or three young men would pass, clearly circling the metro station with billowing thick green fog from smoke canisters held aloft, often just as visibility improved.

Head bowed, I checked my phone to see how far away the kick-off was when a sudden flash of light close to my right startled me. Just two yards away a portly man in cargo trousers and black hoodie had ignited another flare while taking great pleasure in those stopping to take photographs (myself included), as he held the bright-red light above his head, bellowing out what I assumed were pro-Ferencváros chants. With the sparks raining down beside my face, it might have triggered an alarm of some sort. Considering the constant flow of pyrotechnic smoke and flares for well over an hour, though, it was unlikely that it was a fire alarm now bursting into a high-pitched song. Yet it became my cue to locate food to supplement a stomach full of ale.

With my mind switched to finding sustenance, it did not take long for the smell of hotdogs being served nearby to break through the burning stench. The bar was as packed, if not more so, than the last, so I joined a long queue with time to further practise my ordering skills. This time I was greeted by a much friendlier face before sputtering my way through, 'Két sör és egy hot-dog kérem?' At least, I thought I had ordered two beers and a hotdog.

When the second pint of lager was placed in front of me, so was another. And another. And another. I turned to the person next to me and asked if the beers were his, and if he wanted them, such was my embarrassment at my attempt to speak Hungarian, but also that they had cost so little. He responded in near-perfect English to decline my offer, but also inquired what I thought I had requested, then he translated this to the bartender. Apparently, as well as believing that I had ordered eight beers, I had handed over significantly more cash than needed. It was returned, thankfully, while the additional beers went to the next willing customer. I finally had some food in my hand and struck up meaningful conversation with a Ferencváros supporter.

After quick introductions and discovering that I had a Ferencváros membership, it turned out that Dániel Karafiát was a member of one of the *Fradi* ultra groups and he asked whether I would like to join them for the match. The approachable Dániel was far removed from the stereotypical impression of a Ferencváros ultra or hooligan splashed across newspapers or dominating many ultra-indulging websites.

Barely 5ft 9in, Dániel was slim and slightly built, and a project manager for a creative solutions company. The only characteristic in keeping with any thug-like appearance was a closely shaved head, definitely more out of necessity than choice with little hair left on a polished balding scalp. In contrast, his companion Róbert was far more physically imposing, if not threatening, standing at least 6ft 3in, weighing 18st or more, and with large, menacing eyes which almost looked through you. When accompanied by a well-meaning smile this could appear sinister, but more frequently it put me at ease.

Dániel and Róbert were grabbing a few drinks on their way to meet the rest of the ultras and invited me to follow them into the ground and meet them, promising a much more accurate reflection of the Green Monsters. As we headed through the biometric turnstiles, I noticed that neither had been required to scan their wrists for entry. Dániel explained that the ultras had negotiated that, while a few would pass legitimately through the gates, the majority were not required to undertake such security measures. This allowed the Green

Monsters to return to the stadium on 4 November 2017 for the visit of Debreceni VSC.

This was no big secret, with one leader of the Green Monsters, an individual known as a *Capo*[39] detailing conditions of the return agreement which allowed the ultras' terraces to be accessed by just 500 people and undertaken through alternative types of membership cards. A 'normal' card, which I owned, required biometric scanning, whereas it was optional for holders of B category cards. The latter would display their photo and date of birth. Interestingly, it also specifically forbade violent acts against standard card holders. Violence inside the stadium was also banned. They did not advertise that when joining back in 2016 and I was unaware of this before attending!

However, while the Green Monsters' reappearance at the stadium ensured a return to the passionate support that had been absent for the previous two and a half years, it also resulted in tragedy. The first capacity crowd at the Groupama Arena was forever marked by the first stabbing at a Hungarian ground, during a brawl of over 50 people which also saw another spectator suffer serious head injuries. For their part in the disturbances, Ferencváros received a 3m HUF fine and were made to close any areas that housed ultras for three fixtures. This was where I got a little confused trying to piece together the mocking youngsters' stories of stabbing Millwall fans and running Chelsea supporters out of Budapest.

The Millwall incident happened in October 2004, when their fighting was almost certainly limited to the school playground, infamous for two supporters being stabbed before a UEFA Cup tie. In attempting to unpick their more

---

39 *Capo* is the Italian word for boss which was often used with organised crime groups and the Italian mafia, and popularised through movies such as *The Godfather*, *Goodfellas* or television series *The Sopranos*

realistic claims regarding the Chelsea fixture, Dániel was a great help, clarifying that it was more likely, with the Groupama Arena chosen to host a UEFA Europa League match between the Premier League side and MOL Fehérvár FC a few weeks later. Certain groups would take advantage of being able to welcome the English side's famed hooligan element to their city.

With the anticipation building, Dániel punctuated my nervous excitement, telling me he would first be required to ask permission for me to join the ultras. Therefore, I stood for what seemed like an eternity in the middle of the concourse for the pair to return. When they did, Dániel revealed that a 'head' (which might have got lost in translation) wanted to meet me first.

We walked past a few huge concrete pillars until we moved right towards a group of tall and imposing middle-aged men, not dissimilar to those seen outside Fradibox earlier, dressed almost identically in dark jeans or combat trousers and a black coat or hoodie. Dániel informed me that Ferencváros ultras tend to wear black and Újpest white and, I thought to myself, that their opponents drew the short straw given the difficulty getting many stains out. Particularly blood, for example! As we approached, the group parted, leaving a solitary individual standing front and centre, although the colossal kinsmen remained close enough that they looked like his personal security guards. Despite the intimidating welcome, they greeted me with a warm handshake, but a face refusing to issue anything close to a smile. Then it was straight into the questioning which, I imagine, was only marginally less thorough than had I got to pass through Iranian immigration.

The primary focus centred on whether something connected me to the police, regardless of whether that was the Hungarian, UK or maybe even extra-terrestrial law authorities. Given my inability to address them directly, I decided not to joke that my brother had been working for Hampshire Constabulary for the previous 18 years. Once satisfied that I was not some undercover police officer, their focus switched to my attempts to write this book. Their concern was not with how many copies they could distribute around the Green Monsters, but if I might look to implicate or possibly publicise any illegal activity. There was little unease about any violence I might witness. It was seen more of a badge of honour to cherish.

Minds at ease, they treated me to a friendly embrace complete with backslapping and cheek-kissing which, through an eagerness to welcome me, included each of the dozen or so people standing around us. We then enjoyed a few more pre-match beers and eventually moved as one up the steps leading on to the terrace.

I could see all four sides of the arena preparing their choreography. Along the pitch-length stand to our left, opposite the substitutes' benches, supporters were holding aloft what I thought were green and white pieces of card. After a closer inspection of those being held in our section, though, they looked like pieces of black bin liner, and I assumed the rest were similar bits of plastic. There was also a small spot of yellow in the centre of the stand, but my position and angle made it difficult to make out the mosaic design. Those directly across from us were also creating another green and white plastic display and, while easier to see, it was difficult to work out exactly what it was they had attempted to create. Next to them, in the far right-hand corner, were the Újpest supporters, themselves unfurling a huge purple-and-white-striped shirt that almost covered their entire section.

Before I could gain any insight on the visitors, though, Dániel leant in to point out that the ultra 'old boys', of which I now felt an honorary member, predominantly stood in Sector 16. After 'allowing' the younger, and certainly more energetic, ultras to graduate to a position directly behind the goal, these elder statesmen were now tasked with watching over the upcoming generation and ensuring they stuck by the principles and unwritten rules of the ultras. He also enlightened me on the B-Közép, who had preceded the Green Monsters, something I was previously unaware of. In a similar changing of the guard, the B-Közép had been the original ultra group but split ahead of the move to the Groupama Arena. The majority seemed to have transferred with the Green Monsters to the new stadium, keeping a nice consistency, still standing in the B sections from which the original group gained their name.

As we stood observing the final pre-match rituals, they released an eagle from high within the roof of the stadium, just like Lazio and Sporting CP, and it circled down towards the falconer, who almost always seem to be approaching their late 50s and sporting ridiculously long hair not befitting their age. The fans joined a rendition of the club anthem 'Fradi Induló' as they paraded the bird of prey around the perimeter of the playing surface, stopping just before the last few verses to allow the entire stadium to perform a wonderful *a cappella* rendition.

With the game about to get under way, our numbers almost doubled after another large, male-dominated group arrived, looking as though they had just left a Mixed Martial Arts (MMA) contest or, at the very least, an extremely punishing weight session in the gym. Gripping embraces started being delivered all around me, with a brief hesitation at which I noticed a curious look from one newcomer while hugging Róbert. The steely gaze was made as the new arrival's chin briefly rested on the top of his shoulder.

Again Dániel, who was relishing his role as tour guide, disclosed that they were supporters, more specifically 'hooligans' from the Polish side Śląsk Wrocław. They have a friendship, almost brotherhood, with Ferencváros ultras and regularly travel to fixtures. This made me aware of a handful of Polish flags on display within our section of support. It is some dedication, considering there are some 500 miles between the two cities. Újpest appeared to have a similar close relationship with those across the border, proudly hanging a large flag of the republic above the entrance to their section.

The two sets of supporters left notable pauses between chants, to allow for the volleys of abuse to be traded across the stadium, and then there was a sudden break in the festivities. I had missed the players gathering around the centre circle ready to observe a minute's silence. To my left, Dániel was standing with his head slightly bowed in preparation and drew a crucifix across his chest with a finger as the quiet began. That those around me were mourning the death of the legendry Hungarian international István Géczi[40] two weeks earlier, and not just a former Ferenváros goalkeeper, was no doubt crucial to fans of both sides showing their respect impeccably, and it had brought the stadium to a standstill.

It was a moment of calm before that beautiful eruption of vitriol, spilling out from the terrace a split second after referee Viktor Kassai put his lips on his whistle. The volume inside the arena instantly returned to its ear-splitting level and was

---

40 Géczi had a 16-year career with Ferencváros but also won a silver medal at the 1972 Summer Olympics and played in the 1966 FIFA World Cup finals and UEFA European Championship in 1972 for Hungary

the sign for home supporters to unveil a huge banner in front of us, unflatteringly suggesting that Újpest were the team of the police, or at least willing to hide behind the authorities in an act of cowardice when the two sets of supporters come to blows before or after fixtures.

There was one such incident during the 2010/11 campaign. When Újpest recorded a 6-0 victory at the Szusza Ferenc Stadium, Ferencváros collapsed midway through the second period. Their supporters decided they would retain some honour by launching a full-scale attack on their neighbours. The *Fradi*, though, became embattled in fights all around the stadium and across Budapest, largely with police who, at that point, increased their reputation for protecting the *Lilák* fans.

Buoyed by the feverish home support, Ferencváros immediately charged down the right wing and sent a low cross towards the six-yard box and goalkeeper Filip Pajović pushed Davide Lanzafame's delicate flick around the post. As a lone striker, it was soon clear that the hosts would channel most of their attacks through the journeyman Italian and he was equally happy accepting the responsibility, forcing Pajović into another save midway through the first period and then sending the home supporters into hysterics as they appealed for a penalty after a clumsy tackle on Lanzafame on the edge of the area.

The rest of the half followed a similar pattern. Wave after wave of Ferencváros attacks was repelled by the Újpest defence which, if penetrated, was saved at the last moment by their able custodian. Just towards the end of the first half, midfielder Vincent Onovo gave the Újpest fans faint hope of an expected lead, but Ferencváros goalkeeper Dénes Dibusz saved comfortably. That prompted a small pocket of supporters in front of us to direct monkey chants towards the

Nigerian. With UEFA sanctioning Hungarian national team followers and those of Ferencváros multiple times in recent years, there was little surprise at their actions.

However, what did shock me on my visit back in 2016 was the careless abandon shown by Ferencváros supporters of all ages who would suspend a purple monkey soft toy from around their necks at most home fixtures. Despite *Capo* Kubatov Gábor promising 'ultras are not making monkey sounds because they are racist, but because they want to make the coloured footballers angry,'[41]the act clearly has some racial motivation.

Dániel ushered us off the terrace for a 'quick pint' but, despite leaving minutes before the half-time whistle, we joined a swell of supporters trying to squeeze towards the refreshment kiosk. That allowed more of the ultras Dániel knew to recount stories of fighting with Millwall fans and share their fondness for West Ham, if only because of the east London club's rivalry with the Lions.

When we returned pitchside, the match had already restarted and sectors B2 and B3 were being illuminated through a wall of flares at the front of the terrace. Some supporters deviated from synchronised circular swinging motions into figures of eight as additional green smoke canisters merged with the flares' off-white smoke. With the initial sparks of red from the flares, it fittingly presented the colours of the Hungarian flag. The pitch, submerged in fog, was out of sight. All that was visible was the fuzzy glow of flares still being waved frantically.

Although the smoke eventually cleared from the playing surface, it remained little more than a blur for me as Dániel

---

41 'Ferencvaros capo: Don't mix racism with fanaticism! We aren't racists, we are fanatics!!' (Hungarian Ultras, 2018)

and Róbert had wedged me between them and our whole terrace was bouncing up and down in unison. Some, like us, linking arms across our shoulders and shuffling side to side.

Soon afterwards, Ferencváros took the lead. Lanzafame instantly controlled a low cross drilled along the edge of the box and nudged the ball a yard away from his body, allowing the ex-Juventus youth to spin 180 degrees and fire a shot into the top corner of the net.

The stadium exploded in celebration, as did what remaining pyrotechnics the Green Monsters had available, and I overlooked the awful European techno track that began playing from the loudspeakers. A few minutes later, while we awaited a corner, there was a pocket of activity within the crowd just behind the goal nearest to us that was attracting a noticeable amount of attention from our group.

I could see some younger members of the Green Monsters waving and pointing at their counterparts as more flares burned in front of them. However, it was not flares providing the flickers of light, but the flames from a material they were holding.

It turned out that Újpest had won the 2018 Magyar Kupa Final at the Groupama the previous May and, in that moment of ecstasy, they had left behind a couple of banners. Róbert mentioned that the Újpest fans were not willing to meet 'in the woods' to reclaim their possessions, originally agreeing on some hand-to-hand combat but not showing up, and Ferencváros supporters were now burning those banners as punishment, with little concern for the obvious safety issues this was presenting and a request to stop repeated over the stadium tannoy.

Once the banners were all but incinerated, the ultras started their own version of the thunder clap made popular by Icelandic fans at Euro 2016, calling out 'Fradi' as their palms slammed together. Given that several supporter groups seemed to adopt the motion after that tournament, I suspect it was a newfound phenomenon in the Groupama Arena. Although it was far more wholesome than the fascist salutes that followed during the arrival of the crowd favourite, Dániel Böde.

The 32-year-old striker was coming to the end of his time at Ferencváros after falling out of favour with coach Serhiy Rebrov, and was desperate to score. In a ten-minute cameo, Böde saw a shot clawed away by Pajović, thrashed a volley well over the crossbar, and, in the final minute, was foiled at the last moment when trying to take the ball around the Újpest stopper.

There would be no last-gasp recovery from the visitors, though, and plenty of the home fans had long departed, such was the confidence that Ferencváros would continue to victory. I waited with Róbert and Dániel to join in the post-match festivities, but it wasn't long before we were walking out of the stadium with supporters singing at the top of their voices as they headed to their respective forms of transportation home.

Living outside the city centre, they said their goodbyes and pointed me in the tram's direction, with the metro out of action, and I jammed myself in, unsure of when the next one might depart. The journey was less than 15 minutes but felt much longer. The jubilant crowd bouncing up and down in song meant that the tram would sometimes come to an abrupt halt, either through the sheer weight in numbers or the driver worrying that the carriage might topple over. It slowly regained stability as travellers departed, and when we arrived at our final destination, the singing had stopped and frolicking was reduced to a few friends jostling each other playfully.

When I reached my accommodation, I stepped into the communal area to find a dozen guests playing music and drinking beers at the start of a night of revelry, and retired to my room, wondering if they even knew of the passion, excitement and action that had been taking place less than three miles away. Or ever would.

6

Clássico das Multidões –
Rio de Janeiro, Brazil

IN 1981 – the year I was born – Liverpool first attempted to gain official recognition as the best team in the world when facing Brazilian giants Flamengo in the Intercontinental Cup Final having declined to contest the 1977 and 1978 editions after winning the European Cup. Knowing that had always drawn me to the famous red and black hoops of the Rio de Janeiro side, who also had the legendary Zico receiving global plaudits. Despite the attacker's finest displays being confined to footage from the 1982 World Cup, images are imprinted on my memory via VHS as much as the Diego Maradona-inspired 1986 edition or the drama of Italia '90.

That glorious failure of Spain '82 was the catalyst for my 30-year Brazilian infatuation, and South American football, with its beauty and glamour extending beyond stadiums to the beaches of Rio and the world-famous carnival which seems to encapsulate the warmth, sensuality and extrovert nature of the local *Cariocas*.[42] The rivalries I had experienced

---

42 Rio locals are often referred to as *Cariocas*, meaning warm, fun and friendly people

so far on my journeys were full of atmosphere and intensity built on long-standing and deeply ingrained hatred across both fanbases. One of the interesting aspects of this trip was whether that friendly and happy-go-lucky attitude portraying the Rio natives would soften the animosity between Clube de Regatas do Flamengo and Fluminense Football Club, which was built, like many other rivalries, on a social divide.

As Rob Smyth highlighted in *Kaiser: The Greatest Footballer Never to Play Football*, the vibrant, vivid images we lust after when watching a mid-morning travel show or, as older readers might recall, flicking through a travel agent brochure are only one side of a city. Rio also has high crime and violent incidents, and challenges with corruption that contribute to high levels of poverty. That many issues reside within the favelas, however, allows the social elite or the many tourists to ignore them until confronted with them.

With almost seven million inhabitants, Rio is the second-largest city in Brazil and sixth in the Americas. It is one of the most famous places in South America and certainly the country's primary traveller attraction, welcoming millions of visitors each year to its stunning beaches, World Heritage sites and party atmosphere.

The open approach to tourism made travel and entry as easy as most European cities but, even ahead of the summer peak, the distance made the trip more expensive. I also knew that, in a city with high crime rates, it was best to pick suitable accommodation. In the end, given the cost, it became a ten-day trip with Stacey. Even if she knew the primary reason for travel, the outlay could be justified. Although famed as a holiday destination, the port of this seaside city remains one of the busiest in Brazil and, considering I had enjoyed Sporting CP v Benfica in Lisbon just five months earlier, I found it interesting that Rio had been an essential source of revenue for the Portuguese royal family. There were shared similarities with how this rivalry had come about.

* * *

Known as the 'Sons of Rio's Elite'[43], the wealthy Oscar Cox founded Fluminense in 1902. He was also credited, along with 19 friends, with organising the first football match in the state of Rio de Janeiro. Born in the city to English parents, Cox was sent away to study in Lausanne, Switzerland where he developed a love for football that he felt compelled to share with the Brazilian public. The matches were intended to be glamorous cosmopolitan social events for the higher echelons of society. Fluminense are still regarded as the club of the upper classes, even if the social divide between the two supporter groups no longer exists in such simple terms.

Despite becoming the first established club in Rio, that historical link to the elite has arguably contributed to Flamengo dwarfing Fluminense in terms of support across the country. It is estimated that the *Rubro-Negros* (Scarlet-Blacks) draw support from 25 per cent of Brazil's population of 210 million population, referred to as the *Nacao Ruben-Negra* (Ruby and Black Nation). In comparison the *Fluzão* (Big Flu) has just 34,000 members. In fact, it is thought that the Flamengo fanbase within the city is double that of all the other eight Rio clubs combined. You get the distinct sense walking the streets that the shirt is more authentic than the Brazilian national side, while their appeal to the socially deprived was increased early on by training on public land. With minimal resources during their formative years and some of the most famous black stars like Domingos Antônio

---

43 Bellos, A., *Futebol: The Brazilian Way of Life* (Bloomsbury Publishing, 2014)

da Guia, Leônidas da Silva and Zizinho starred for the side as they collected several titles during the 1930s and 1940s.

The club's continued success has attracted many middle-class fans, and a few within higher society, but more within the lower classes, so much so that the term *Flamenguista* is slang for a slum-dweller and opposition fans will chant 'ela, ela, ela, silencio na favela' (she, she, she, silence in the favela). It's hard not to relate that to the 'sign on, sign on' calls still aimed at Liverpool and Everton supporters in 2022. Links with the underprivileged did not disadvantage the *Rubro-Negros* or lessen their appeal, with clubs in six different Brazilian states naming themselves Flamengo in honour of the Rio original.

A neighbourhood in the city's south, their foundation in 1911, like Benfica, resulted from disgruntled Fluminense players seeking football elsewhere. However, unlike in the Portuguese capital, they were joining an established rowing and sports club (established in 1895) who were adding football to an expanding offering of sporting activities to members. Fluminense might not have lamented losing virtually the entirety of their side over 100 years ago, as they prevailed 3-2 in the first encounter between the two sides at the Estádio das Laranjeiras.[44]

Trying to establish the success of the two sides over the next few decades, until the professional era began in 1934, is quite difficult without a degree in Brazilian sporting administration, especially once professionalism was introduced. At one stage, four groups contested mini-leagues to progress to the next stage, and teams with the best overall record would join the winners of those leagues. Confused?

---

44 The Brazil national football team played its first match in 1914, at the Estádio das Laranjeiras, beating Exeter City of England 2-0

You should be! Unlike in Europe, the state championship in Rio de Janeiro held more weight with clubs and supporters, and could take nine months to complete. The national Campeonato Brasileiro, which began in 1971 through expanding the Rio and Sao Paulo state championships, would last for a little over four months. To complicate matters, the order of competition would be reversed for no apparent reason and, almost every year, the format and dates appeared to change. That still continues today as they wrestle aligning with a European calendar.

A national championship, however, could not replace the long-standing and deep-rooted state rivalries. At the start of the 1980s, when records became easier to interpret, the pair were almost neck and neck in national titles with Fluminense leading Flamengo by 23 to 20, but the *Rubro-Negro* success on the world stage appeared to see their popularity soar. As interest grew in the Brazilian national team, boosted by the star-studded teams that appeared between World Cup successes in 1994 and 2002, relatively barren spells came for the two giants. Flamengo won just one national title but maintained state dominance. However, it was Fluminense who had the most remarkable of decades, with near-relegation punctuated with a famous triumph over their most hated rivals.

In June 1995, Flamengo had fought back from a two-goal deficit to get level and stay on course to lift another Rio state championship only for Renato Gaucho to score an astonishing late winner with his stomach to give Fluminense the title. Within 12 months, Flu were ending the national campaign second from bottom and were about to be relegated from the top flight until several questionable deals within the corridors of power resulted in a sudden expansion of the league to 26 clubs and brought redemption. It was a sign that, despite the popularity of Flamengo, the original aristocrats of Brazilian football still held significant influence. Failing to learn from their flirtation with the second tier, they then finished second from bottom again, despite an enlarged competition, and were relegated. The club began to freefall and were staring demotion to the third tier in 1999. A complex series of administrative and legal wrangling, though, saw them somehow reinstated to the top flight once more.

* * *

After we touched down in the city famed for its carnival at around 8pm, Galeão International Airport was subdued as we sauntered through the well-lit yet empty white corridors towards immigration. We removed the additional layers of clothing that were now unnecessary with the Rio summer approaching. Pre-booking a taxi to our Copacabana accommodation was a straightforward decision to make, given our late-night arrival and the city's much-publicised issues with crime rates. And it wasn't long before our choice appeared justified. Cruising along a stretch of motorway and scanning the horizon for famous landmarks, and football stadia, a vehicle travelling alongside caught my attention. Protruding from the partly opened windows of an unremarkable-looking car were high-powered rifles, which, on closer inspection, appeared firmly grasped by multiple armed police. Looking ahead stony-faced, as reluctant as I was for our eyes to meet, eventually our cars parted and we continued our journey south to catch up on some much-needed sleep.

With a few days until the action would get under way at the Maracanã Stadium, we set off early the following morning for the Estádio da Gávea by Lagoa Rodrigo de Freitas. It continues to act as the training facilities and administrative offices for Flamengo, despite only hosting youth fixtures since the 1990s. Lagoa Rodrigo de Freitas had a starring role in 1941 for a match known as the *Lagoon Fla-Flu*. With Flamengo needing a win to take the championship, league leaders Fluminense could settle for a draw. Flu were winning 2-1 with six minutes remaining but Flamengo levelled the scores. Rather than run the ball into the corners, as has become commonplace in the modern game, the Fluminense players began launching it into the lagoon as they sought to run down time. However, Flamengo had seen this tactic coming and placed several rowing crews in the lake to fetch the ball as quickly as possible. Beginning life as a rowing club came in handy. This did not deter Fluminense, though, with the process repeating itself until the match was being played in darkness and Flu hanging on to secure the title. Flamengo would take solace in winning the next three championships between 1942 and 1944.

As the country's most well-supported club, small groups were having photographs alongside the statues and club crests that adorned the walls. One fetching version covered the black parts with feathers, acknowledging another nickname, the *Urubu* (Vulture). The club shop bustled with customers filling their baskets with merchandise. Stopping to admire the stylish shirts Flamengo had for the current campaign, I debated how much use a man my age would get out of a football shirt, but my focus remained on the ticket desk at the back of the store and I walked purposefully towards the counter. I requested a match ticket in the 'noisy section', as the cashier described it, and for the biggest game in Brazilian football, at a cost of less than £5. I could see Stacey looking at me, unsure whether the visible delight on my face was because of the price or that, after travelling 6,000 miles, my attendance was now confirmed.

With the ticket tucked away in my wallet, we crossed the hallway to the club museum and got transported back to 1981, and that Intercontinental Cup Final. They had dedicated an entire room to the triumph and shirts were hanging for each one of that successful team, with Zico's standing out above all others. The Rio native's emergence in the early 1970s coincided with two decades of constant success for Flamengo and he amassed 378 goals from attacking midfield in 506 games from 1971 to 1983, after joining their ranks as a youngster of prodigious talent. With Zico dictating play, Flamengo won six state championships, three national titles and, more importantly, a first continental triumph in the 1981 Copa Libertadores, which would bring worldwide recognition. It would take 37 years before they would hold that trophy aloft again.

After two seasons in Italy with Udinese, Zico returned to find more success – in the most stunning fashion, writing himself into the history books of the rivalry and becoming a permanent hate figure for the Fluminense supporters. With the Brazilian international overseas, Fluminense had won three consecutive Rio state championships and were optimistic of reaching a historic fourth straight title as they began the 1986 edition at the Maracanã against their bitter rivals. While it is unclear whether the Flamengo players knew of the banners in the Fluminense dressing room proclaiming that they had already won the championship, the homophobic chants directed at Zico spurred him on and he hit a hat-trick.

Later that season, the attacker hit all four goals against Fluminense during a 4-1 win. It was the only time he played with 1982 World Cup team-mate Sócrates, and Flamengo not only ended *Fluzão* hopes of a fourth title but lifted the crown themselves.

Convincing Stacey that the Maracanã tour was one of the must-see trips while in Rio (thank you, TripAdvisor!), we filled the next 48 hours with a walk along Copacabana Beach to its fort, a visit to Sugarloaf Mountain and various other famous monuments. Yet I never envisaged matchday starting at the bottom of the Corcovado mountain, attempting for the second time to see Christ the Redeemer. Dense fog 24 hours earlier required us to use much of our imagination, squinting at a blurry silhouette of Mr Cristo through the cloud, shuffling around the viewing platform and unable to see our sightseeing companions.

When the Brazilian sunshine came bursting through a gap in the bedroom curtains at 6am, we set off after breakfast to complete the task. Getting there was the straightforward part. A 30-minute Uber ride cost just £2.73, despite the Rio traffic. On arrival, though, we found that the next available trip up by train was not until 3pm; somewhat problematic with Flamengo-Fluminense starting at 5pm local time. Then we were told that minibuses leaving immediately were available and we began the long, hot, arduous pilgrimage. In search of views so picturesque, most visitors still spend more time taking selfies squeezed among the crowd than of the panorama.

With Cristo Redentor ticked off the itinerary, it was 12.30pm, but, as I had set my heart on attending Vasco da Gama against Cruzeiro the following day, I had one more errand to run before focus could switch to the Maracanã. With a metered taxi pulling up I thought it couldn't cost that much, given the earlier Uber bill, and we climbed in. Almost as soon as we joined the slow-moving traffic down the mountain, though, the meter had already surpassed our morning fare and, unable to communicate with the driver, it was obviously not going to be cheap. We weren't helped by him revving the engine so hard that the meter would tick over at an even faster rate, somehow believing that we wouldn't notice.

Eventually Google Translate came to our aid and, according to our dishonest chauffeur, it turned out that the Vasco club offices at Marina da Gloria did not sell tickets. We instead needed to head directly to the Estádio São Januário. The driver also became the latest in a growing number of people warning that the surrounding area was one of the most violent neighbourhoods in Rio. I'm not sure what he uttered into his smartphone, but 'are you sure you want to go to the dungeon' is what was robotically fired back out at me. Never one to miss an opportunity to visit a new stadium and atmosphere, the journey had cost too much to turn back.

When we finally arrived, I tried to join a short queue outside four triangular, face-sized holes in the stadium wall without being noticed, but soon had plenty of company. My height alone singled me out among the band of diminutive locals surrounding me, and I congratulated myself at the decision to leave my mobile and wallet in the taxi with Stacey. With obvious concern for my safety, our driver exited the car and came to act as a sort of interpreter, but by this point I had already handed over the small amount requested and made our way back – not because of any impending danger; rather, there were now just over three hours until the kick-off of the game I had gone to experience, and I had run up a taxi bill of R$200 (£25).

* * *

The actual match, a few days after the *Clássico das Multidões*, was just as eventful as getting tickets. Concerned with the safety of the walk between metro and the Estádio São Januário and unable to use my mobile internet, such were the charges in South America, I took an Uber from the hotel and arranged that Stacey, when notified by text, would order the return trip. During the drive to the stadium, my driver ran another driver into a central reservation filled with water butts, casually switching on his wipers to clear the spray from his windows as we continued on our way. When we arrived, he dropped me about 50 yards from the ground, and I was approached by several shady-looking gentlemen. However, I had no intention of sticking around and was tackled by a female steward, looking out of place, and ushered towards my entrance.

Having chosen to stand with the most fervent supporters, before taking my place on the terrace I made a beeline for the toilets. I had been warned there was limited running water and electricity in the area, but finding two toilets filled, I assumed, by buckets with faeces was a shock. The smell alone was unbelievable, let alone the visual spectacle.

For different reasons the display on the terraces was just as amazing. Having stuffed my mobile into my underwear, I eventually dug it out to take some videos towards the end of the first half when things got even stranger. I only took around £30 in Brazilian real and left my watch at home, but grabbed some beers from a mobile kiosk.

Positioning myself a few rows up but along a wall of the terrace, I had noticed a man, somewhere around my age, enjoying the game, but also surrounded by a handful of women less interested, and around 30 minutes into the game an older man had approached. They had a quick discussion, he handed over some cash and departed with one girl. Being able to arch my head over the wall, I watched them enter the toilets together. As the women came back 10–15 minutes later and received an approving nod of the head, I can only assume she provided a specialist service of some kind. Maybe a massage, of sorts? It was such a bizarre interaction that I became transfixed on the group, until they spotted my inquisitive looks.

Soon it was time to text Stacey, and you can imagine my horror when the message would not send. BT later confirmed that my contract thought I had gone over a pre-set limit, despite having not touched any of my additional usage charges. I decided I would have to walk the 20 minutes to the nearest metro, having not wanted to, and started watching those departing around 85 minutes. I saw an older man, maybe 60, with two teenage children, so I followed close behind and uttered 'metro' to him. He gave an approving nod and I continued, confident I was heading in the right direction. Independent from the group in front, though, some locals set upon me, trying to engage me in conversation. I shrugged my shoulders a few times and, despite a few surrounding me, I kept pace with the others. A tour guide had warned me, first not to take too much money, and second, do not run. 'If you run, they'll shoot you in the back, and they have shot you for nothing.' We eventually walked so far from the stadium that they got bored and headed back. When we reached the metro, another man that had been following close by tapped his front pocket and rubbed his fingers together to suggest they were trying to relieve me of my valuables.

* * *

After dropping Stacey at the hotel in our expensive taxi ride, I grabbed my Flamengo-Fluminense ticket from the safe and headed straight to the nearest metro station. Over the last decade, both sides of the divide had struggled for national success, but they remained competitive at state level. Flamengo had not won the Campeonato Brasileiro Série A since 2009, and Fluminense's last two triumphs came in

2010 and 2012. In *World Soccer*, Tim Vickery wrote that the 'Brazilian game had been stripped of so much of its talent, which had had a clear effect in the quality',[45] resulting in unpredictable title races and reducing the chances of long periods of one-club domination.

Flamengo added continental success over their rivals to their list of achievements, though, as they met in the quarter-finals of the Sudamerica Cup in 2017. Trailing the second leg 3-1 at the Maracanã, Flamengo netted twice in the second half to advance to the semi-finals 4-3 on aggregate. But their inability to win the competition will have softened the Fluminense disappointment. That victory was a sign that Flamengo were going places and at the halfway stage of the campaign they were among the favourites for Série A having led the standings for the majority, although everything was still to play for, with just eight points separating first from sixth place. Fluminense were nowhere to be seen and I sensed from those I spoke to that the match would be one-sided.

Having toured the famous stadium earlier in the week, the journey would be a familiar one – but with added trepidation after witnessing a fellow tourist have their valuables stolen at gunpoint leaving the Maracanã. Had we not stopped to use the toilets, it could have been us. Heading back to the metro they had stopped to take a picture from the bridge leading to the station, only for a youngster to cycle up and point a handgun at their chest. As we watched in shock as they handed over what looked like a smartphone and wallet from just 50 metres away, I had been snapping away with a DSLR camera. A woman ambling down the slope with hands full of shopping bags gestured frantically to hide it so I stuffed

---

45 Vickery, T., 'Title race reaches midway: Six contenders but a poor title race' (*World Soccer*, 2018)

it in the rucksack on Stacey's back and we navigated our way on to the train without incident.

I took the advice of a writing acquaintance and one-time Rio resident, Suhayl Al-Sammari, and stopped in Botafogo to see if I could, as I often do, befriend Flamengo supporters on their way to the match. As I stood on the platform at Cardeal Arcoverde it was approaching 3.15pm and a fear of missing pre-match festivities outside the ground left me tailgating a group in red and black who had joined me at the station. With the vast number of Flamengo shirts sported by the Rio public, it could have been a regular day in the city but it was unlike anything I had ever experienced before. From small child to elderly grandmother, every couple of steps you would encounter another Flamengo crest on a member of the public. I also found it strange that I never saw European club shirts on display. Instead, it was the many colours of the teams in Série A, almost as if football outside Brazil did not exist.

Stepping on to the train, though, even more *Mengão* shirts confirmed that I was right to head straight to the Maracanã. The carriage steadily filled with more and more bodies, sucking any fresh air from our cocoon and, after the previous encounters and high crime rates, I noticed how much my smartphone and wallet bulged from my short pockets. I expected a change of train to deliver some respite from the claustrophobic heat, but the 35°C temperature above ground had already penetrated the subway network. So I did the best I could to mop the ever-increasing beads of sweat from my forehead. When the next train pulled in, those desperate for a seat had congregated on the opposite platform, squeezing past those exiting, as the rest of us watched on disapprovingly for the doors on our side to open. When they did slide apart, though, to my relief, a chilled, air-conditioned breeze caressed my face, making the last leg more comfortable than expected.

With the sun setting, the renovated Maracanã was a stunning sight as I left the metro into a warm, fresh South American evening, and considerably more welcoming as I followed hundreds of spectators shuffling towards the stadium. A bridge crossed a busy road and arced left before descending and the sizeable home support Flamengo would call upon when the match got under way was obvious. Four out of five people were wearing an official or unofficial piece of Flamengo merchandise. The decision to wear a salmon-coloured polo shirt, intended to highlight a lack of preference for either side, was unnecessary with the odd Fluminense replica shirt walking among the waves of red and black. Any clashes between supporters were possibly being played out well away from the stadium.

Being keen to make my way to my entrance gate and yet to get my bearings, I inadvertently walked three quarters of the perimeter of the stadium, being asked at regular intervals whether I needed a ticket and finding myself assessing the fashion sense of the women in attendance, much like the courage and self-confidence required to stroll Copacabana Beach in the smallest of G-strings, not satisfied with modelling an ill-fitting male replica shirt, as in the UK back in the 1990s when female-specific shirts were unheard of. Shorts just exposing the bottom half of the buttock, a staple of those I passed, were supplemented with a tight-fitting replica t-shirt manufactured with a plunging neckline to promote their ample cleavage and exposing the odd half nipple. The more daring, and I would say younger, attendees donned little more than a bikini top in team colours. Rio does fashion in a particularly powerful and sexual way.

As I approached the large bronze statue of Brazil's first World Cup-winning captain, Hilderaldo Bellini, outside the main entrance to the officially named Estádio Jornalista Mário Filho, the huge numbers congregating outside forced me to double-check my entry point and seek sustenance. My only meal of the day had been the hotel breakfast. I approached a generously proportioned middle-aged woman standing behind a tiny pop-up table and a cooler box, but dressed more for comfort than style. Deciding that the snacks on offer would not satisfy my growing appetite and the smell of barbecued meat filling the air, I requested a couple of bottles of beer and stepped aside from other customers only to realise that they still had their tops on. Walking confidently back to notify her of the error, I asked that she open them for me and a wide beaming smile spread across her face. Taking a bottle from my grasp, she twisted the cap off and I departed with an uncomfortable laugh.

Several pyrotechnic explosions close by lessened any anxiety growing over how stupid I had looked or who saw me. They also almost made me choke on my first mouthful. Proudly displayed on an entrance ahead of me, as I basked in the early evening sun, was the name of former editor of *Mundo Esportivo*, Filho, who encouraged supporters to bring fireworks, drums and more into stadiums in the 1930s. They credit the current carnivalesque atmosphere at Brazilian stadiums to his initiative. However, it wasn't the party animal in Filho that was the driving force behind his idea, but an attempt to sell more and more papers through increasing interest in football. His importance grew to such a level that, at just 26 years old, he was once one of the most influential sports journalists in the country. Eventually having the national stadium named in his honour showed that his approach worked. It was he who dubbed this biggest of fixtures as 'Fla-Flu', although also adopting the nickname of *Clássico das Multidões* (Derby of the Masses), given the size of the respective fanbases now.

The next stop was the barbecue stalls and, as always, I ordered too much, getting excited by the look, smell and price. What is it about random meat on sticks that is so tempting? I then tried to fade into the crowd, observe them, and bathe in the sunshine, only for some Flamengo supporters five or six paces away to notice me standing alone and a 40-something man ushered me over with a hand clasping a beer. It could have been a family, although they seemed too friendly with each other. They had come prepared. I noticed a cooler box filled with beer in the middle of the group when a young member reached down for a drink.

Although not quite yet hitting a carnival-like atmosphere, there was a positivity and easy-going attitude rarely experienced at such historic and intense rivalries as I stood mute among the Portuguese chattering, lamenting that I had not focused on learning languages earlier in my life. A scooter crawled past, ridden by a young man in a Flamengo shirt and a girl of similar age in a Fluminense shirt along for the ride, displaying the friendly mood outside the ground. The crowd, still increasing, had spilled out on to the main road. The sound of car horns attempting to clear a path became so consistent that they faded into the background.

What I noticed, though, was the filtration of poverty from the local neighbourhoods. Weaving their way through the crowds were pockets of small children, collecting empty cans or surrounding fans in bulk and pleading for any money they could spare. Hanging back from one particular group of five or six youngsters was a child, little older than three years old, and unwilling to approach the thousands of strangers towering above them. Then, from within another set of supporters, a teenage girl emerged and knelt down before the youngster and handed them some cash, either to ensure that they would not return home empty-handed or to make them more comfortable undertaking this unappealing, but vital, activity.

While their tender age adds an element of sadness to their actions, it was more heartbreaking seeing grown – yet weary-looking – adults also wading through, scooping cans into enormous plastic bags. When I finished another beer, and spotted an elderly gentleman approaching with a less impressive haul of aluminium in two standard carrier bags, I stepped out into his path to make my donation. The gratitude with which he welcomed my contribution was such that my heart sank and tears could have shed.

I took that as my cue to head inside. Making my way through the maze of steel railings into the sheltered concourse, I soon realised how soaked in sweat my polo shirt was and headed to the bathroom to wash my face and relieve myself of several street beers. Such was my discomfort, I had overlooked the party taking place around the hallways. A wide variety of music (some sort of samba/hip-hop mashup) was playing out through loudspeakers. Beers were flowing and fans were dancing around as if they had already won the game. Originally seen as a sign of Flamengo's historical superiority over Fluminense or the current condition of the two sides, it might just have shown how the colour and beauty of Brazilian music penetrates life throughout the country. Different regions have expressed themselves through their own individual musical styles that have migrated to the city over the years, such as the samba, Sertanejo and Bossa Nova. It may simply have been the *Charanga* (an out-of-tune band), that Alex Bellos in *Futebol* noted as becoming popular in 1942 through the efforts of state functionary, Jayme de

Carvalho. Seven decades later, Brazilian football seems unthinkable without music. There was certainly no time for quiet apprehension, and the thought that defeat could lurk behind their public show of positivity.

Much like Rio de Janeiro itself, the concourse was awash with red and black and I even spotted a 2014 German national team away shirt, designed in honour of Flamengo. Considering *Die Mannschaft* had worn it when they embarrassed the Brazilian national team 7-1 at the World Cup, that was an interesting choice and not something you would see in England.

I got more beer from a small stall operating, independently it seemed, despite the official kiosks and being ignored by those queuing in large numbers. I then climbed the dozen steps towards my section and took my first peek at a full Maracanã and its underwhelming playing surface while forced to shield the low afternoon sun from my eyes, now only two-thirds visible as it set behind the roof of the stadium but still cooking those unable to escape its glare. I showed my ticket to a steward to receive some direction, but he just shrugged his shoulders. It turned out the shrug was not to show that he had not understood my request, but that he did not care where I sat once in. My use of the stadium numbering system convinced me that I had at least placed myself somewhere in the vague vicinity of where I was supposed to be.

There were now just 15 minutes to kick-off so I scanned the stadium in search of the visiting fans, spotting a condensed pocket of Fluminense supporters in the opposite corner. There was a poor turnout considering that it seemed Flamengo had given them around a third of the capacity available. I wondered if the atmosphere would be even more spectacular if the 52,924 in attendance were not scattered across an 80,000 venue. With most supporters being packed into the cheap seats alongside me and continuing the party atmosphere, I could see the Fluminense fans jumping up and down in unison but I could hear nothing from across the vast bowl. With Brazil the last of the Americas to abolish slavery, in 1888, football remained elitist until black players competed at the top level domestically. Carlos Alberto was one of the first. The speedy Fluminense attacker used to whiten his face with rice powder, attempting to be accepted, and became so popular that the club nickname 'Rice Powder' stuck and fans continued to throw talcum powder in the air ahead of big games. Having seen this homemade spectacle on *Transworld Sport* during my childhood, I was eager to see it in person. Visibility did not allow me to see if they still undertook the act.

It was the hottest I have ever been at a football match, and I could have done with some personal hygiene products to make me more pleasant to stand next to. While the surrounding majority continued to dance to the *Charanga*, I felt the sweat dripping from my elbow. I didn't even know an elbow could sweat! Then, as I watch drop after drop fall towards the concrete floor, I realise that my grey tailored shorts were a shade darker because of the moisture they had absorbed. Even more sweat was running down my shins like some rather disturbing water feature.

When they announced the Flamengo team, 21-year-old midfielder Lucas Paquetá received the largest cheer from the home support despite the club agreeing on a sale to AC Milan before they had received the benefit of his undoubted potential.

I could not take my eyes off those around me also struggling with the temperature, though. Welcoming, if non-verbal, greetings were made with two young men on either side of me and the one to my right had come prepared, using a flannel to mop the sweat from his face and arms. I turned around to survey the rest of the fans and was greeted by the bare chests of a group of men behind me, each one soaked in sweat, and even more across the crowd. A handful of women had also stripped down to their bras to join those who arrived in bikini tops. Could I take off my shirt in such an unfamiliar setting, I thought. Would it be culturally inappropriate for a non-Brazilian to do so? However, spotting a woman in a Fluminense shirt three rows behind me broke my concentration, plus a lack of confidence that my physique would provide a respectability to the act having prepared my body for winter, not summer.

Turning towards the lad on my left, I saw in his eyes that he was considering the same thing. That was it. We were now locked in this uncomfortable, sweaty struggle together, as the referee blew for kick-off.

The samba-like atmosphere suddenly turned into a deafening eruption of noise in encouragement for the home side. At that moment, I struggled to recall such an energetic, exuberant crowd. Despite the fanatical home support, it was Fluminense who first broke with purpose, striker Luciano da Rocha Neves sending a powerful 25-yard drive straight at goalkeeper César Bernardo Dutra. The shot was fumbled into the path of an onrushing Fluminense player and an intake of breath from the home crowd allowed the excited cheers of the visiting support to be heard for the first time. With the game setting off at an amazing pace, Flamengo had two chances of their own through Paquetá's header, and a wayward strike from defensive midfielder Willian Arão sailing high over the crossbar.

I glanced down at my watch and just seven minutes had passed, but felt like 30. Exhausted just watching the game played at such speed and absorbing the intensity sweeping down from the stands, there was no time to draw breath as Victor Vinícius Coelho dos Santos – aka Vitinho – curled an inviting in-swinging cross into the box on 11 minutes and Fernando Uribe headed past a motionless Júlio César Jacobi. As the Colombian wheeled away in celebration, the stadium exploded and I found myself among a sea of arms and legs jumping up and down excitedly, strangers squeezing my shoulders from behind. I screamed into the distorted faces of those around me.

Then I realised that, during the celebrations, the shades that were hanging from the buttons of my polo shirt had snapped and a lens had disappeared. Great amusement for the boy on my right, who pointed this out to his girlfriend. Two huge pyrotechnic explosions from behind then vibrated through the concrete floor, frightening a girl in her 20s in front of me, still basking in the emotions of an opening goal. She had drawn my eye to her almost immediately after taking my place as she was wearing huge, almost novelty-sized, sunglasses and sporting a Carlos Valderrama-styled mop of thick curly blonde hair.

The goal relaxed the hosts as they dominated proceedings while the crowd settled into the more expected carnivalesque atmosphere, although the volume would rise every time another goal-scoring opportunity presented itself. I also realised how involved I was becoming in events, releasing a familiar scream out of 'eh! eh!' in disapproval of a tackle I felt outside the laws of the game. Whether it was a Brazilian thing, the referee seemed willing to let a lot of challenges go without penalising them. They would be fouls in England, and certainly in European competition.

On 30 minutes the players and fans got a well-deserved break. Play was stopped by the officials to take on some much-needed refreshments given the stifling conditions and I took my seat for the first time. My companion to my right took this moment to tell those around him about my broken sunglasses, which were now in several more pieces at my feet. His girlfriend was still disinterested and happy munching through a family bag of crisps.

With half-time approaching and two of an additional four minutes of injury time already played, Flamengo won a free kick for an overzealous Fluminense tackle just in front of us. Vitinho stepped up and sent over another wonderful cross from the set piece, and Léo Duarte sent another header into the Fluminense net. It was the perfect way to send the supporters skipping towards the concourse in search of relief or refreshment as others partied.

To say that the celebrations continued throughout the break would be an understatement. After a quick toilet stop and grabbing another couple of beers, I just stood in awe at the sights in front of me. The spacious hallways of the Maracanã were not only full of radiating smiles and congratulatory embraces, but hordes of fans dancing to the music booming out of speakers. The voice of an MC somewhere on a microphone was singing what I assumed was a classic Flamengo anthem. In front of one of the official Flamengo merchandise stalls were half a dozen shirtless young men and a couple of girls dancing to samba beats. You could have mistaken it for the dancefloor of a beachfront bar in the Balearic Islands, filled with Club 18–30 revellers.

As expected, the interval and a two-goal lead had calmed the crowd outside somewhat. I returned to my place in the stands with some new companions: a young family occupying the seats in front of me, and a man in his late-40s and boy around ten years old to my left. I was in the right seat, if you are wondering.

Flamengo made a quick start to the second period when a deflected Paquetá shot on 50 minutes bobbled into the path of Uribe, who scrambled the ball into the net in a very un-Brazilian way and sent the fans into raptures. The young boy beside me looked a little frightened by the aggression of some of those celebrating around us. I decided a physical gesture was better than any verbal attempt to make him feel more comfortable about the chaos, and I received a welcoming smile in exchange. I looked towards his father and received a friendly wink, thanking me for the effort. It filled the youngster with the confidence for another interaction. After using my frame as leverage to stand on a seat for a better view of the pitch and resting his hand on my shoulder for balance, he asked my name and where I was from, then wanted to know if I was a Flamengo supporter. Although I said 'yes', I think he realised that it was a recent development. After I discovered that his name was João, he insisted on a selfie with his dad's phone. I can only assume he wanted to tell friends he met some strange 37-year-old Englishman who travelled thousands of miles just for a football match. We then took another on my smartphone to show Stacey, who likes to know I've made friends when disappearing off on my own. Even if João is much younger than those I befriend in bars.

It was now 6.30pm, yet I was still sweating and paying more attention to my surroundings than the action in front of me. The arrival of Orlando Berrío from the bench seemed to lift the crowd. I was half expecting to witness some journeyman Brazilian footballer or a legend returning from a career in Europe, like ex-Porto, Werder Bremen and Juventus schemer Diego Ribas da Cunha, who made a cameo against Liverpool in the 2019 FIFA Club World Cup Final. Berrío, though, was an unspectacular attacker who had failed to shine in the famous red and black since arriving from Atlético Nacional 22 months earlier.

I scribbled this strange incident into a small notepad, which I used to keep track of incidents I wanted to remember, and this sparked João's father into life. Leaning over his son, he asked 'look at player, no?' and 'scout?'. I thought to myself that this was the talent factory of Brazilian football and they must have had countless scouts coming over and prising away their most promising footballers. There was no underlying aggression or concern to his questioning. Maybe they like to see players such as Paquetá leave to progress. I responded in broken Italian and hand gestures, 'no, io scrivo un libro' (no, I am writing a book). He seemed satisfied with my explanation, but realised that the language barrier between was too vast to warrant any attempt at more detailed discussion. We were both relieved that some form of scuffle broke out away to our left, which caused a couple of dozen police officers to appear, kitted out in riot gear and carrying, what I believe he explained to João, tear-gas launchers.

As they walked past like a horde of stormtroopers, I then became transfixed on the Flamengo ball boys. At the very least, on average 25 years old, they were probably the first ball 'men' I had ever seen at a professional match. How quickly they brushed aside the trouble was another sign of how the atmosphere in Brazilian football stadia had changed since the 1970s and 1980s. They had been described as 'crazy' and needing forced segregation of supporters, yet violent clashes still broke out and sometimes escalated to guns being pulled on one another.[46] With just five minutes and injury time remaining, the Fluminense fans had had enough. Few

---

46 Downie, A., *Doctor Sócrates: Footballer, Philosopher, Legend* (Simon & Schuster UK, 2018)

actually remained in the arena. They may have even missed a late header from Luciano which brought a flamboyant, if needless, flying save from Dutra. That gave the Flamengo fans one last piece of action to cheer, even though they were departing in their hundreds. Maybe a victory over your bitter rivals is not worth staying around to celebrate if facing them so often and in various competitions. I awaited the final whistle and then shuffled out with the rest of the crowd, chanting 'Zico, Zico, Zico'. Not, I assume, to remind me once again how the attacking legend helped crush Liverpool's hopes of world recognition.

Beyond the turnstiles, the Brazilian evening was much cooler and a breeze came rushing past my hot and sweaty legs, in a moment of much-needed refreshment. When I approached the end of the concrete ramp out of the stadium it amazed me how many street vendors were still operating post-game, but less so that many of the homeless were still sweeping up empty cans or asking for spare change from those leaving. It could have been pre-match, given the early start.

Then, as I paused, contemplating whether I should purchase one last beer or barbecued snack, a minor panic broke out. What I assumed, looking back, were gunshots caused several locals to hurry away from the entrances and spectators started running away from the venue. I followed the lead of a middle-aged man next to me who darted behind a large concrete and steel structure with a child and we knelt, staring at each other for what felt like an age but was probably just seconds. A police vehicle, I think, made its way through the fleeing crowd, firing shots into the air. Although it felt like you could hear them hitting the metal perimeter fencing, it was difficult to judge whether they were overhead or echoing from a distance. After they had passed, I joined the man and his son marching towards the metro at a pace that may well have won someone an Olympic medal in that stadium two years earlier.

Once we had reached the metro, few seemed worried about making the first train home. Happy to be there unscathed, I stood in silence and watched an older couple who had done well to keep pace with me as I scurried towards the station. Her head buried in his chest and visibly shaken, he caught my gaze and raised an eyebrow that made me think that this was not a unique experience. I looked down at my watch once more and, despite the excitement, realised it was only 7.30pm. It would be two hours before I would reach the hotel, such was the wait for an available train with spaces. One young mother started breastfeeding her child, standing on the platform. I wondered how infrastructure, built for a World Cup four years earlier, was so inept, or how they coped in December 1963 when a world-record crowd of 194,603 witnessed a goalless draw between these two sides at the Maracanã.

Eventually I boarded, yet there was still a nervous anxiety filling the carriage. Then, as we reached Estácio Station four stops along, there was a sudden outburst of mild celebration. Those in red and black were tapping out the beat of songs on the handrails and singing, bringing back a sense of post-game normality to the evening as we headed safely home to our loved ones, remembering the words of 1994 World Cup winner Bebeto who said, 'At its best the Brazilian game is a euphoric fusion of sport, dance, art and sex, and everyone is at it,'[47] and the *Clássico das Multidões* had them all.

---

47 Smyth, R., *Kaiser: The Greatest Footballer Never to Play Football* (Yellow Jersey, 2018)

7

Intercontinental Derby – Istanbul, Turkey

MY FIRST visit to Istanbul, to watch Liverpool lift the UEFA Champions League trophy, would be hard to surpass in terms of drama. Yet this football-crazy city, full of more than just two highly charged fanbases, was ripe to host one of the most passionate same-city encounters in world football I could attend.

Back in 2005, the locals we encountered, whether Beşiktaş, Fenerbahçe or Galatasaray fans, were always quick to remind us of the links between them and the Merseyside club, especially the latter of the famous Turkish trio. Several former Reds players had worn the famous *Sarı-Kırmızılılar* (Yellow-Red Ones) colours of Galatasaray back in the mid-1990s. More recently, though, Dirk Kuyt left Liverpool for Fenerbahçe and netted the winner for the *Sarı Kanaryalar* (Yellow Canaries) against their hated rivals, Galatasaray, in March 2013.

Also, 16 months after vacating the managerial hot seat at Anfield, Graeme Souness took the reins at Galatasaray and, despite overseeing a disastrous year in Turkey, became an icon for the *Aslanar* (Lions) supporters. Finishing the

1995/96 season 16 points behind bitter rivals Fenerbahçe, the Scot spent the campaign being derided for failed British signings – Barry Venison, Dean Saunders and Mike Marsh (who one particular fan kept referring to as 'Mark Marsh') – an error he would repeat later at Benfica.

Souness grabbed the opportunity to leave with a little pride intact, though, when Fenerbahçe and Galatasaray met in the Turkish Cup Final. Taking a 1-0 first-leg lead, secured with a Saunders goal, to the Ülker Stadium, it was the Welshman's injury time strike that secured a 2-1 aggregate victory and stopped the *Sarı-Lacivertliler* (Yellow-Navy Blues) dominating domestically. That alone was not what brought Souness his slice of infamy, though. As he and his players celebrated in front of the travelling supporters, a huge Galatasaray flag attached to an 8ft pole made its way down from the stands and, after waving it joyfully, the former Glasgow Rangers boss turned and ran to the centre circle, planting it in the turf after the third or fourth attempt at breaking ground. The still-running TV cameras caught the act live and sent the home fans in the stadium into widespread anger. News of his exploits made headlines across Europe, but I still expected Souness to remain something of a hate figure given that the season became a blot on the most successful period in Galatasaray's history, only to be proved wrong when visiting 23 years later.

Souness has cult-hero status with Galatasaray fans, who refer to him as 'Ulubatli Souness' after Ulubatli Hasan, a heroic martyr who in 1453 placed a flag during the siege of Constantinople while collapsing with 27 arrows adorning his person. The Aslan Ultras group even dedicated the pre-match choreography ahead of a derby on 18 November 2014 to the Souness incident. It wasn't just the fans who applauded his actions either. Souness expected the Galatasaray hierarchy to fire him post-game but instead they came running into the changing rooms with tears in their eyes, proclaiming it one of the greatest moments in the club's history. 'I've never kissed so many men in my life as I did after that game,' wrote Souness in his autobiography.

* * *

A legitimate legend of the club, though, is Ali Sami Yen (born Ali Sami Frashëri), who became synonymous during the early 1990s because of the ferocious welcome the home fans would give opposing sides when they visited the stadium named in his honour before opening in 1964.

While studying at Galatasaray High School in 1905, Ali Sami formed the Galatasaray football team with fellow students to take on sides, often comprising players from a single nation, like Greece or England. A founding principle was to have a side that played an English way, although it was likely that players were British rather than specifically English. Within four years they had clinched a first Istanbul league title and have remained a major force in Turkey ever since, helped somewhat through their association with the high school, with its own rich history since its foundation in 1481, and links to public administration, which has strengthened the opinion that they, at first, represented the city's higher classes.

Just as Galatasaray were taking their first tentative steps into the world of organised football, in 1907 a local group in the district of Kadıköy on the Asian side of Istanbul were forming Fenerbahçe, who soon became the second side to enter the Istanbul league. Their humbler beginnings allowed for the narrative that they became the club of the working classes, providing the familiar social element to this conflict and explaining why Fenerbahçe supporters outnumbered those of Galatasaray until their success in the late 1990s and their 2000 UEFA Cup Final triumph against Arsenal brought more admirers.

That Fenerbahçe rests on the Asian side of the city is likely to have influenced their fanbase. Over 90 per cent of Turkey's landmass is in Asia, which resulted in Fenerbahçe cultivation as the true Turkish club, playing on the regional and cultural differences between them and Galatasaray while any class divides between supporters are now a thing of the past. The history and prestige of both clubs entices fans from across the social classes.

One of the interesting things about this rivalry, and similar to Budapest, is Beşiktaş's presence as the third major force in Turkey. Founded in 1903, the *Kara Kartallar* (Black Eagles) have ensured that domestic competition has not become a two-horse race and they have a heated relationship with Fenerbahçe and Galatasaray. However, being the two most successful and widely supported sides in Turkish history, particularly after the league turned professional in 1959, had propelled Fenerbahçe-Galatasaray as a showpiece fixture.

I doubt the first contest between the pair on 17 January 1909, when Galatasaray triumphed 2-0, showed any sign of the animosity that would grow between the two clubs, at least until Fenerbahçe refused to part with the winners' shield to Galatasaray at the end of the 1914/15 season. Having won the previous two championships, Fenerbahçe were late to register and Galatasaray, among others, declined their appeals to be allowed to take part. Fenerbahçe were furious at the rejection. It then intensified the hostility when, on 23 February 1934, violence between the two teams on the pitch escalated into a full-scale fight that was mirrored on the terraces. Galatasaray coach Sydney Puddefoot was struck in the back of the head by Fenerbahçe goalkeeper Hüsametin, and the game eventually abandoned. They gave some players six-month bans.

* * *

My passion for travel and football has me regularly looking for new football and cultural experiences, especially ticking off several new stadiums in one visit. However, in the days before departing for Istanbul, my body and mind seemed consumed by an overwhelming desire not to travel. I had visited the city before, although briefly, among the chaos of a Champions League Final, and it was not a daunting destination for a solo traveller. In the previous five weeks, though, I had spent just nine days at home with the comforts that brings, like your own bed, after travelling between Rio de Janeiro, Turin, Liverpool and Milan.

Both physical and mental exhaustion had allowed an anxious feeling deep inside me to fester and grow to near-uncontrollable levels. Insomnia soon followed, and I spent the final few nights patrolling the house through the dead of night. A difficult few weeks at work, with little managerial support, increased the need to recalibrate mind and body. Yet I packed a bag, also covering the onward trip to Belgrade for Crvena Zvezda versus Liverpool in the Champions League. I considered taking a rare bath (rather than shower), but sat motionless in an empty house. Rather than relax, it felt like my mind was on standby, waiting to spring into action and, by the time Stacey arrived home, I was ready for another attempt at sleeping, telling myself there was no turning back.

Within seconds of my eyes drifting off into a natural state of slumber, though, it seemed like the alarm on my smartphone began ringing. The countdown had begun. The race was on. Despite believing that I had prepared everything well in advance, just before I was due to travel, the Turkish Football Federation had moved the fixture to Friday night. Sound familiar? I stared at the smartphone screen, well aware the match would kick off in just 12 hours' time, and I was still 1,600 miles away.

That Turkey had reversed a decision to return to Daylight Saving Time – remaining three hours ahead of the United Kingdom – softened my lingering anxiety. The reality, though, was that I would have just under four hours between the plane hitting the tarmac and referee Fırat Aydınus blowing his whistle. There was a short-lived moment of panic when I thought they had cancelled my train to London Gatwick Airport. However, it must have been an inaccuracy or technical glitch with Google and I was soon watching the British countryside speed past outside.

The journey through the terminal was unproblematic, easing my nerves further, and there was a welcome surprise when I realised that Turkish Airlines both fed and entertained you on board. I selected the first movie on the menu, *The Equalizer 2*, starring Denzel Washington. There was a certain symmetry in watching a film where the main character spent the duration timing each activity to perfection, just the type of meticulous planning the trip had already required and now needed to succeed, so the pilot announcing we would arrive early was very welcome.

The Ottoman conquest in 1453 resulted in Constantinople becoming the formal name of the city known around the world as Istanbul. Until the fall of the Ottoman Empire in 1923, and five years later, other countries agreed to use Turkish names for their cities rather than translations of Latin scripts, and Istanbul was born in 1930, although Ankara has been the country's capital since 1923. Like many major cities in the world, and some visited for this book,

Istanbul held a strategic position, between the Black Sea and the Mediterranean, and controlled the rail networks to the Middle East, helping ensure that it remains the cultural, economic and historical centre of Turkey, with a population of around 15 million people. Part of the city's allure, though, is that it plays host to both Europe and Asia. A third of its residents live on the latter of the two continents.

As the plane approached Istanbul, thoughts started turning to the task at hand. I figured that, if visiting the toilet just before our descent, there would be no need to go again until in the stadium or maybe half-time, such was my level of paranoia. I had also picked the closest seat possible to the front of the aircraft to make a speedy exit. We somehow lost 25 minutes between landing and doors opening. Three hours and 35 minutes to go, I thought to myself. Trying to remain calm as I marched toward passport control, I was relieved when I saw the long queue for those getting a visa on arrival having secured mine online a few weeks before. When I turned the corner, though, there were around 300 people shuffling their way through the metal barriers at a snail's pace. To make matters worse, as I edged along behind them I started sweating heavily, partly through nervousness but also because I had misjudged what an average temperature of 20°C would feel like still wearing a jumper and jeans.

Removing my coat, I attempted to ignore the beads of sweat trickling down the side of my face and focus on identifying the quickest route to the exit doors – an immediate left after the passport desks, for those of you finding yourselves in a similar situation in the future. I should have mentioned that, although the match was starting at 9pm local time, I had been told under no circumstances could I collect my ticket later than 7pm or access the stadium with anything more than a man bag.[48] I convinced myself that, in the two hours available, I could taxi 25 minutes from the airport to the hotel then travel another 25 minutes towards the Türk Telekom Arena. By the time I walked unchallenged through passport control, though, it was already 6.15pm.

This forced me to head straight to the stadium. Worrying about what to do with my rucksack, if or when I had my ticket in hand, I brushed aside the random individuals offering taxi services at arrivals and made a beeline straight for the private hire desks. Although I might have worn a look of desperation, I was determined not to get ripped off. I had already checked prior to leaving, and an Uber was around TL130 Turkish lira (about £7). As expected, a friendly-looking gentleman quoted TL450 and my expression turned from desperation to shock. Rather than dwell on the fact that they needed a calculator just to type in the numbers four, five, and zero, I recalled two things I had learned on previous trips: the Turkish people are some of the friendliest you can meet but they also love to haggle, almost taking enjoyment from it.

In April 2000 two English supporters tragically died when Leeds United travelled to Istanbul to face Galatasaray. They were stabbed the night before a UEFA Cup semi-final and defined the British image of Turkish supporters. The intense partisanship of fans in the country is the element that, for me, sets it out as one of the most desirable destinations to watch football. But it also allowed the British to portray an image of savage hooligans, especially with the violence-filled mid-1980s still fresh in the memory of the English public. As John McManus highlighted in *Welcome to Hell?*,

---

48 Much like the classic ladies' handbag, a man bag is an informal small bag, most commonly with a shoulder strap, carried by a man to hold small personal items. On European away trips you will see several male Liverpool followers using the man bag to store their matchday essentials

the incident created a frustrating preconception of supporters and a misguided belief that Turkey is a dangerous country to travel to for football. That is far from the truth if you choose to visit and open yourself up to the warmth and hospitality of the local people, and get a feel for the true Istanbul.

We both appeared satisfied when settling on TL200 for the taxi, and aiming to transmit my urgency, I tried to march him towards the exit before realising that I was being handed over to someone else. Outside, a man in his 50s greeted me with an earnest smile but a slight look of concern born from an inability to communicate in English, as I attempted to question whether he knew if Galatasaray would honour my tickets if I arrived after 7pm, which was now almost certain. His response was to smile some more and let out a loud laugh, giving off a bit of an evil villain vibe from a 1980s James Bond movie.

With light traffic, the journey between Istanbul Atatürk Airport and the Türk Telekom Arena should have taken around 30 minutes, meaning I would arrive just in time to collect my ticket. However, just as we started speeding along the motorway, we met with a collage of brake lights growing ever closer. My plans had not allowed for rush hour and over 50,000 people making their way to the stadium. My driver at least understood my growing concern about missing the game yet his constant screams as we sat stationary, of something which I assumed translated to 'go, go, go', did little to lighten the mood in the minivan I found myself trapped in. He then told me when he thought the traffic would clear, using fingers to underline the estimated minutes. Which it didn't. Next he switched to random guesses of when I could expect to reach my final destination.

After building 18 new stadiums between 2007 and 2015, Turkey has a phenomenal amount of grounds and could

easily host a major tournament. For all the investment in
the facilities inside the stadium, though, the transport routes
continue to be a nightmare for fans with horrendous queues
being experienced on a weekly basis. However, hearing that
the authorities denied Galatasaray's home a second access
road because of the conduct of their supporters sounded
ridiculous. It was difficult to find out if a particular incident
would have resulted in the rejection. But as the transport
issues became apparent after the arena opened in January
2011, trouble at the Şükrü Saracoğlu Stadium on 12 May
2013 might have been a contributing factor. During a
fixture beset with racist chanting by home Fenerbahçe fans,
which the hosts won 2-1, a Galatasaray hooligan stabbed
young Fener supporter Burak Yıldırım to death as they left
the ground.

In the wake of crowd disturbances across the country,
for some time spectators required a Passolig card to attend
fixtures. It would be no different for an overseas fan. The
process is quite simple. For around £5 you need to register
online and, if in Turkey, you can collect your card from
various locations. You then load the games you wish to attend
on to the card. I could have got a ticket from the club. All that
was available, though, was within the neutral sections, and
I wanted to experience the intensity of the Aslanlar Ultras
(*UltrAslan*). Therefore, I paid a little over face value online to
a supporter through an independent ticketing site, who then
transferred the ticket on to my Passolig card which, I hoped,
was still awaiting me at the Galatasaray ticket office. By then
I was preparing a speech if I had to plead for the release of
my card, while also resigning myself to the prospect of a tout
outside the stadium being my only way of gaining access.

My driver started pointing ahead of us with purpose,
towards an illuminated structure in the distance, just visible

between two high-rise buildings. The Türk Telekom Arena was finally in sight. Before I could say 'drop me here', though, we had passed by as he insisted he knew an alternative route to the motorway exit that was already bursting with cars queuing, and increased my angst tenfold. In hindsight, we were not moving at all fast and I would have been better off asking him to pull up on the hard shoulder, taking my chances crossing the slow-moving procession of vehicles on the motorway. All he achieved with his route was to join the traffic jam further away.

With the Türk Telekom again out of view, Google Maps was suggesting I had another 15 minutes to travel, and it was now 7.45pm. My patience snapped and I insisted he find somewhere to stop and allow me to walk the remaining distance. However, he was unwilling to let me leave without insisting upon another payment for his personal efforts, but considering that he had added to my journey time I refused, explaining as best I could that his associates had already taken an enhanced fee and he was delivering me some way from my intended destination. I think the Istanbul metro could have resulted in a similar arrival time and with much less agitation.

For the last few minutes of our journey together, an increasing number of Galatasaray shirts had been walking past the van. So I joined the steady flow of jerseys southbound, hastily consuming a sandwich purchased back at Gatwick, until the stadium was almost upon me. That was not obvious because of how the move to the Türk Telekom had displaced Galatasaray from their traditional neighbourhood and, from my experience, that often lessens the vibrant atmosphere around the surrounding area.

Galatasaray have inhabited an impressive seven stadiums during their history, but for most of the modern era they had occupied the Ali Sami Yen Stadium in the Mecidiyeköy district. Regardless of location, the *UltrAslan* has always created a terrifying and intimidating atmosphere for opposing players and fans, but the Sami Yen gained a certain notoriety in the 1990s. In November 1993, after an astonishing 3-3 draw with Manchester United at Old Trafford, the ferocity of the stadium was credited with helping Galatasaray secure a goalless draw in Istanbul. However, while it ensured progression to the next round of the Champions League, Onur Bilgiç, who I spoke to just before heading to Turkey, believed that it was just as important in raising awareness of the fans and club across Europe.

Infatuated with Galatasaray before even setting foot in the Sami Yen, Onur recalled a 4-1 away win over Fenerbahçe when he was just seven years old and watching on TV on 11 April 1993. Galatasaray overwhelmed their hosts with goals from Tugay Kerimoğlu, Hakan Şükür and Torsten Gütschow, despite playing half of the match with ten men after the sending off of Mert Korkmaz. Onur assured me, though, that while moving further away from central Istanbul had impacted on the aura around the ground, and limited bars to find ultras, it had not diluted the experience inside the arena.

The home fans who by then were filling the stadium could have confidence in victory over their bitter rivals. Fenerbahçe were in freefall after a terrible start to the 2018/19 campaign. At the start of the season they had appointed three-time Eredivisie winner Phillip Cocu as coach, but they had sacked him four days before my visit after a 3-1 defeat at home to Ankaragücü left them 15th, just one point and one position from the relegation zone. They had also failed to reach the Champions League group stages after losing 2-1 on aggregate to Benfica. The hierarchy blamed Cocu for failing to capitalise on a creditable 1-0 loss in Portugal. Fellow Dutchman Erwin Koeman would take charge of this fixture, but as he had assisted Cocu's few months at the helm, they expected little to change.

Galatasaray, in contrast, had begun the season steadily if not spectacularly, sitting in third place but within striking distance of the leaders. The *Aslanlar* were also happy to be back competing in continental competition after being banned by UEFA for two seasons as punishment for breaching financial fair play regulations.

Onur lamented the constant cycle of financial difficulties over the previous few years that had affected all three Istanbul giants, noting the inability to sign significant foreign talent, without the slightest suggestion that they may have contributed to their financial troubles. He sounded positive that the situation had forced Galatasaray to give chances to young talent, who may previously have had their career progression blocked trying to oust an ageing star. But then he expressed his displeasure at how quickly they departed to provide some much-needed income and told me to look out for Ozan Kabak.[49] Onur was right to suspect that the 18-year-old was next to move in order to raise much-needed funds, as he had joined VfB Stuttgart within three months.

Eventually reaching the ground and looking down from the motorway flyover, I could see a bright sign reading 'Ali Sami Yen Spor Kompleksi' (Ali Sami Yen Sports Complex), which appeared to hang above the main perimeter gate. At the bottom of a couple of flights of stairs ahead was an entrance to a metro station and several hundred people

---

49 Ozan Kabak would spend four months on loan at Liverpool at the start of 2021, but with the 2020/21 season played predominantly without fans in attendance due to the Covid-19 pandemic, I never saw him live in a Liverpool shirt

congregating in the space between the two. I had arrived at an entry point exactly where the ticket office was situated and it was still very much open. Around a dozen windows were operating but there were no organised queues, just a mass of bodies shuffling among themselves, and I was struggling to see anyone leaving with a ticket in their hand or a smile on their face.

Making my way down the stairs, I focused on one window that appeared to be handing something out and forced my way past anyone hesitating. It was difficult to understand whether they could not find my Passolig card, if it had ever been created, or if they even bothered looking. After handing over my passport they just supplied me with a temporary card made from paper-thin cardboard, but it provided none of the crucial information I would need, like gate, row or seat number. Maybe they assumed I could access an electronic invoice? It was lucky I had not given them the printed copy of the payment receipt. At this point I realised that, while the Passolig card should stop touting and banned fans entering the stadium, it does neither. At least a dozen individuals had offered me tickets while I queued.

That weekend in the city, Kasımpaşa and İstanbul Başakşehir were also playing. Getting tickets at face value for the former was easy, with another temporary card issued ahead of kick-off, whereas Başakşehir was a different matter altogether. The current Süper Lig leaders were facing Beşiktaş and, because of the recent transgressions of their supporters, there was a partial stadium closure as well as a ban on non-Başakşehir members purchasing tickets. Seeing them available from touts at Galatasaray, though, I took a chance, setting a limit of twice face value (about £30). A local was happy to slip the ticket office a financial incentive, to transfer a ticket to yet another flimsy Passolig card and it became clear that this was common practice. The stewards at the entrance gates gave nothing more than an additional glance when a black silhouette (not my picture as standard) flashed up on their scanner.

My next concern at the Türk Telekom was a backpack full to the brim with my belongings. With kick-off fast approaching, I saw an opportunity at the congested entrance gates that were swimming with bodies. Lowering my bag between my legs, I shuffled along with the rest of the crowd until I faced security. Scanning my Passolig card and checking my face against that which was showing on the device (submitted when purchasing my never-to-be-seen card), they chose not to request my passport and waved me through. Me and my bag were in, or so I thought. Within a hundred yards there was a second, less-congested checkpoint. This time I decided confidence would be my best ally and attempted to stroll through unnoticed when they questioned the bag. I told them they had checked it at the previous gate. Through again. It was only when I reached the entrance to my section that security attempted a thorough search. However, after the removal of the second or third piece of underwear and maybe realising it was ten minutes before kick-off, they decided I was of minor threat and waved me in.

With a near-capacity crowd of 49,929, not far short of the record of 52,044 set against Real Madrid on 9 April 2013, a wall of noise almost stopped me in my tracks as I raced up the concrete steps and looked out on to the vast arena, the steep daunting stands looming over me from all sides and brimmed with supporters awash with red and gold. When Galatasaray used the Atatürk Olympic Stadium while temporarily homeless, the fixture had attracted a record crowd of 71,334 on 21 September 2003. But that seems like it was stealing a record-breaking opportunity from their regular homes and I cannot imagine it generated anywhere near the same atmosphere.

With the supporters already going through their repertoire of songs, there was a noticeable wind swirling around the dome despite all four corners being closed to the elements and packed with fans. After soaking up the emotional scenes around me, I edged towards my position only to find three men blocking the seat. Wanting to at least wedge my bag underneath I pointed as best I could, with a backpack in one hand and the printed ticket receipt in the other, expecting a shrug of the shoulders or a reply in Turkish I could not understand. One of the trio responded in near-perfect English, though, and told me that in Turkey I could stand anywhere I liked. Turkish fans simply policed the system themselves, allowing friends and fan groups to congregate together. I'm not sure whether I had sat in any of the seats, or even rows, assigned so far in these games (maybe the second Rome visit?).

Watching as I placed my Passolig card into my wallet gave the young man to my right, a reason to introduce himself as 'Daan with two as', while explaining that I could have downloaded the app rather than gone to the ticket office. While that could have saved a few precious minutes and a lot of anxiety, the Passolig website was so basic that I am not convinced it would have worked anyway.

About 5ft 9in tall and of a slender build, Daan could have been 30 years old, but his sporting a baseball cap, tracksuit and expensive-looking trainers had me questioning whether he was younger. As did the dark, meticulously shaped and groomed beard. Another of the men could have been Daan's twin in both facial appearance and build, whereas the third, called Jeroen, despite sporting a thick, unruly beard and a portlier frame, had a much more youthful face. I apologised for my non-existent (not even a hello or thank you) Turkish and commented on their impressive grasp of English. Daan admitted this was because they were not Turkish residents.

Onur had mentioned that introducing the Passolig card in 2013 had increased the non-local attendees at Süper Lig fixtures and second- or third-generation Turks. Born in the Netherlands to Turkish immigrants, the trio were cousins and travelled regularly from Rotterdam where they also supported another side known for their fanatical support, Eredivisie club Feyenoord.

The ultras beginning their pre-match display cut our conversation short. Daan encouraged me to hold aloft an A2-sized piece of red card placed on each of the seats as we became part of an enormous display covering the Tribune Pegasus end of the stadium. Positioned around a dozen rows up from the corner flag allowed me to just about make out the display. The top tier was covered in red, apart from four stars and a number 21 (denoting the championships won by Galatasaray at the time) displayed with gold placards. From the upper terrace they rolled down a narrow banner, the width of the stand, just as the Champions League anthem began playing from the loudspeakers. The club was well aware of what the *UltrAslan* had planned. The banner read 'SIZIN HAYALLERINIZ BIZIM GERÇEKLERIMIZ' (your dreams are our realities) and just above our heads was the picture of a digital clock showing 20:45, the typical start time in Turkey of Champions League matches. Even I, after Daan's translation, knew that this was the Galatasaray supporters mocking Fenerbahçe's inability to reach the group stages of the competition a few months earlier, although I had not realised that it was also referencing them failing to achieve that aim for over a decade.

As the public address system fell silent, I noticed the booming sounds of drums beating and we joined in with the cries of 'Galatasaray, Galatasaray, Cim, Bom, Bom', as the fans' exhibition moved into phase two. Those initial chants were part of the Galatasaray anthem 'Nevizade Geceleri'. Therefore, when those around me started passionately belting out the lyrics in full, I retreated into a wide-eyed appreciation of the spectacle.

Fixing my gaze on the evolving display to my right, the stand was now half red and half gold, while the top tiers had rotated their pieces of card to create the Champions League logo and on our level was the year of Galatasaray's formation. Even the message draped from the stand above had changed, now proclaiming 'BİZİM HAYALLERİMİ DÜNYADAN DAHA BÜYÜK' (our dreams are bigger than the world). Then a huge material image of coach Fatih Terim rose from the middle of our level to top off an impressive piece of choreography. This was Terim's fourth stint in the Galatasaray hot seat and, considering what he had achieved with the club, the supporters will always revere him.

Galatasaray won three consecutive championships from 1970 to 1973 but Fenerbahçe were just as strong, collecting half of the league titles between 1964 and 1975. The *Imperatore*'s (Emperor) first spell at Galatasaray coincided with an unparalleled success both at home and abroad. In the 1999/2000 season, Terim won a record-breaking fourth title in a row – of seven they would win between 1993 and 2002 – along with the Turkish Cup and lifted the UEFA Cup after a penalty shoot-out victory over much-fancied Arsenal. The tactician had an unsuccessful two-season return in 2002. When the league started swinging back and forth between the two sides regularly, Terim recorded back-to-back triumphs when called upon once more a decade later.

With Terim having taken the reins again around 18 months before my visit, Galatasaray were reigning champions again under the 65-year-old. A true legend when you also consider that, as a player with the club, he became captain at just 23 and made 505 appearances over 11 years.

The *UltrAslan* displays have not always been so wholesome and light-hearted. In 2006 they displayed a racist banner aimed at Fenerbahçe's Brazilian-born Turkey international Mehmet Aurélio,[50] stating that 'insan Mehmet olamaz, ancak Mehmet olarak doğabilir' (one cannot become Mehmet, but only born as Mehmet). The Turkish national anthem gets played just before kick-off and, as the majority belted out the words with an obvious sense of pride when I was there, I stood in silent respect. Daan and his cousins singing along were born in the Netherlands, but it was clear they felt a close connection with their family heritage, or wanted to feel closer to their fellow Galatasaray supporters.

Just before the referee blew his whistle, the crowd broke out in excitement. Keen to get me involved in the festivities, they attached me to a chain of bodies bouncing up and down, and strongly encouraged me to copy the next chants and gestures. It was later explained that the words were something derogatory in relation to the Fenerbahçe fans' mothers' genitals. They placed the *Sarı Kanaryalar* supporters high to my left on the third tier of the stadium as they had not travelled in huge numbers. Daan suggested the team's current form embarrassed them and they were also protesting against new president Ali Koç for issues both on

---

50 Born Marco Aurélio Brito dos Prazeres in Rio de Janeiro, Mehmet Aurélio played as a midfielder for CR Flamengo and Olaria in his homeland until moving to Turkish side Trabzonspor in 2001. After joining Fenerbahçe, he made 176 league appearances for the club and was naturalised in 2006, winning 44 caps for Turkey

and off the pitch. Somewhat unfair, considering he would have inherited the unsustainable debts that besieged clubs across the country. However, even greater numbers would have struggled to be heard among such intense home support and from such a position.

Like Galatasaray, the Fenerbahçe Ultras group appears to incorporate the entire fanbase, although a breakaway group, Genç Fenerbahçeliler (Young Fenerbahçe Fans), did form in the late 1990s, intending to break from historic violent incidents that gave an unfair interpretation of ultra groups' evolution. However, the murder of one of their prominent leaders, Mehmet Altunkaynak or *'Dadaş Mehmet'* (Daddy Mehmet), while leaving a teahouse in 2017 suggested that breaking those ties and changing perceptions will be difficult.

The passion and intensity, and certainly hatred, between the two sets of fans makes the *Kıtalar Arası* (Intercontinental Derby) so fascinating to those on the outside, but allows it to creep towards incidents of violence with ease. In 1996, Fenerbahçe Ultra leader Sebahattin 'Sebo' Karabul stabbed to death a Galatasaray-supporting 'friend', Celal Kurtuluş, in a bar, when a post-derby debate progressed into a fight between the pair. Such incidents were common in the 1970s and 1980s when the rivalry was arguably at its most extreme, as were street battles and kidnappings that characterised the feud between the opposing groups, not just in Istanbul but across several areas of Turkey too. An adamant Onur, though, was quick to assure me that there had been no 'significant violence' between the fans for some time and he was unaware of recent deaths from clashes.

Since early 2001, the *UltrAslan* has been the major power for Galatasaray, from when multiple groups agreed that the team's dominance under Terim and growing European exposure and popularity required a more united support.

This allowed for the spectacular demonstration I had just witnessed, but I was a little disappointed that they did not follow it up with a flare display after reading about a fixture with Fenerbahçe being delayed because of Galatasaray fans setting off 3,000 ahead of kick-off and an opening training session being abandoned for a similar issue. Daan ended my childlike expectation that they were holding them back for later by revealing that huge fines issued had all but ended their use in stadiums.

I stood in amazement at the sound this cauldron was creating. The noise was rising from our position close to the pitch and was trapped beneath the roof surrounding the stadium. Remaining at such a high level for a ridiculously prolonged period, it appeared to have reached maximum potential and left me unprepared for what came next.

Attacking the end where we were situated, Fenerbahçe won a corner and the *UltrAslan* switched from chanting to sustained, high-pitched whistles. At the start of crucial European fixtures at Anfield, the stadium often does similar when the opposition gain possession, but this was like nothing I had ever experienced before. Expressing my admiration to Daan and the others was impossible, and trying to compose my own thoughts was just as challenging.

Soon afterwards, the opening goal of the match arrived. Galatasaray attacker Younès Belhanda swung over a corner kick which Serdar Aziz headed downwards and, as Fenerbahçe goalkeeper Harun Tekin looked set to save, a spinning Ryan Donk instinctively flicked the ball over him and into the net. The Türk Telekom exploded in celebration. Daan and his cousins grabbed me once more, this time for a group embrace, and then broke for independent jigs of delight. Galatasaray dominated the rest of the half, as expected given their league positions, but the limited goalmouth action was a reminder that such encounters are often a war of attrition. A small touchline spat just before half-time raised temperatures inside the stands, but nothing compared to what would come later.

At half-time there were few fans rushing for refreshments. The consumption of beer to top up alcohol levels witnessed in Budapest, Rio or Lisbon was almost non-existent. Onur mentioned that a drinking culture exists in Turkey, despite a large Muslim population, but it is limited to the city centre ahead of games. I wondered how an atmosphere could be that furious and intimidating, aggressive even, if not supplemented by alcohol. That, in my experience, is when the line between passionate support and violence can sometimes spill over.

The following day, at Kasımpaşa v Antalyaspor, I realised how little alcohol Turkish fans need to create a compelling atmosphere when spending pre-game in a cafe sipping 20 pence cups of black tea (much cheaper than pints of lager) with Kasımpaşa supporters. Yet, when we moved inside the barely full 14,234-capacity Recep Tayyip Erdoğan Stadium, I watched them perform with just as much passion.

During the break, Daan gave Fenerbahçe little chance of recovering and started speculating that Galatasaray could avenge a 6-0 defeat to their bitter rivals on 6 November 2002. Fenerbahçe hosted the reigning champions, who also included several members of the Turkey squad that came third at the 2002 World Cup finals, and completely outplayed them. Considering that Galatasaray were ahead by a solitary goal, his comment showed how dominant they had been and how deep that loss had affected supporters. Galatasaray still held the record for the fixture's biggest win, though, 7-0 during the 1910/11 Istanbul league campaign, but that was before professionalism. It was Fenerbahçe who took that initial professional title in 1959 after winning a two-legged championship final 4-1 on aggregate. Back then, the competition was split into two regional group stages. Fenerbahçe topped the Beyaz Grup and Galatasaray the Kırmızı Grup.

Amid the tranquillity of half-time, multiple firecrackers detonated among the Fenerbahçe fans, who were leaving in large numbers. Before we could start speculating why, Jeroen leaned over and reported news filtering through via social media that a Fenerbahçe supporter had died in the away end. In the days after the game it was confirmed that 22-year-old student Koray Şener, who had travelled from outside Istanbul to attend, had suffered a heart attack before the match. When news reached the stadium confirming he had died at a local hospital, the Fenerbahçe Ultras exited in solidarity, although some suggested that it was a manoeuvre intended to have the match abandoned and save further humiliation, which seemed possible four minutes into the second period.

Fenerbahçe partly cleared another corner from Belhanda to the edge of the 18-yard box and the onrushing full-back Martin Linnes drove a powerful low shot arrowing into the corner of the net, sending the home supporters into raptures and us bouncing up and down once more.

Rather than demand that the players sought more goals, though, the crowd began cheering 'ole' with each Galatasaray touch of the ball. The players started passing the ball among themselves and were so passive that they allowed the visitors to get back into the game. With just under 30 minutes remaining, Fenerbahçe took their opportunity to punish them.

Awarded a penalty courtesy of a VAR consultation, Mathieu Valbuena was standing in the distance in front of

Galatasaray goalkeeper and captain Fernando Muslera. A barrage of abuse rolled down from the four terraces around the diminutive playmaker, before deafening whistling just as the referee signalled he could take the kick. It did not faze the former French international, and Valbuena stroked the ball past the Uruguayan shot-stopper. With a few Fenerbahçe fans still in attendance, albeit celebrating, the few seconds of silence throughout the stadium was chilling until the home fans sparked into life with both teams fighting over a loose ball in the Galatasaray penalty area.

You could feel the concern around the arena. Fenerbahçe without doubt attempted to capitalise on a shell-shocked home side and were level within four minutes. With Galatasaray retreating to a deep defensive block on the edge of their box, Valbuena cut inside from the left and laid the ball off to Jailson, and the Brazilian curled a wonderful effort into the far top corner. This time you could hear the few away fans celebrating, banging on the Perspex screens up in the heavens.

What had been a party atmosphere 20 minutes earlier took a huge swing in the other direction. The Galatasaray fans became aggressive, not towards the visitors initially, but their own players for allowing the match to slip from their grasp. Goalscorer Donk had an altercation with a handful of fans beside the touchline as he went to take a throw-in. Whether it was racially motivated is open to question, but it was as angry as I have seen a player get with their own supporters in 35 years of attending fixtures. The match was halted as the Dutchman left the pitch to confront the offenders. But there was a line of riot police surrounding the perimeter, blocking his path.

In hindsight it was probably a good thing that Fenerbahçe missed a late chance on 85 minutes, because the end of the match descended into chaos without a late winner. Arriving from the bench on 78 minutes, striker Roberto Soldado did little in the game other than raise his own blood pressure during a series of arguments with the Galatasaray defence.

When the teams came together at full time, a full-scale brawl broke out with several Galatasaray players and staff chasing Jailson around the pitch in classic playground style. This incited those inside the stadium, and one fan broke through the police barrier to join the fighting. Soldado appeared to have said something out of turn to Belhanda, but Jailson then hit out at the Moroccan international, who had Galatasaray team-mate Badou Ndiaye in support. The episode resulted in six- and five-game bans for Soldado and Ndiaye, respectively, while an eight-match suspension for Jailson suggested that he was the antagonist of the skirmish. Coach Terim was even issued with a touchline ban of seven games for insulting the referee.

Now unable to exit their compound, the away supporters continued to celebrate a valuable point as a growing number of Galatasaray fans attempted to break through the Perspex to get to them, fuelled by the shame of squandering a two-goal advantage to a Fenerbahçe team thought to be in disarray. Daan believed these to be older members of the *UltrAslan* who had migrated to the upper tier of the Tribune Sud, describing it as a natural evolution that allowed for younger, more energetic fans to continue what the others started, but placed them much closer to the Fenerbahçe support.

A lot of Galatasaray fans had headed home from the other end of the stadium, but, as they were unable to reach their adversaries, the home supporters left were fighting among themselves, or the police and stewards. You could feel the angst of the *UltrAslan* at our end, who were shouting aggressively at their own security, and had flooded into our section where a partition separated us from the Tribune Est running along the length of the pitch.

Without warning, Daan's more athletic cousin scaled the Perspex wall and we watched him scampering along a row of vacated seats. With a little help from fellow supporters, Jeroen was soon over as well. I turned to my right and Daan had a raised eyebrow and suggested he should follow to ensure the pair stayed out of trouble, and we said a quick goodbye.

It was an unsavoury and unnecessary end to what had been an eventful and entertaining fixture, played alongside one of the most ferocious atmospheres I had experienced. I stuck around for another five minutes. But any longer and I would have only witnessed more *UltrAslan* growing angry at the infighting. I had not developed such an immediate bond with Galatasaray that I wanted to join them. Filtering out of the arena and across the forecourt towards the metro, the atmosphere was subdued, with most of the aggression left inside the stadium and faces on the carriage to the city centre sullen.

Before I knew it, I was exiting the underground into the dark Istanbul night and heading south to my accommodation until I spotted a small kebab shop with a handful of customers and highlights of the match playing on a small television. I was about to turn around given the limited capacity but the owner ushered me in and pulled up a chair alongside some locals in deep discussion, then took my order. The language barrier was too great to ask or understand their feelings on the game, but it was the perfect discreet and relaxing end to a frantic 24 hours.

8

Superclásico – Buenos Aires, Argentina

A MUCH-NEEDED break between Istanbul (apart from the journeys on the way to the 2019 UEFA Champions League Final) and the next derby voyage was the perfect preparation for perhaps the biggest of all those I would attend.

Twelve months earlier, Argentinean giants Club Atlético Boca Juniors and Club Atlético River Plate had met in the CONMEBOL Copa Libertadores Final for the first time. Crowd violence that characterises fixtures across the country, though, tarnished South America's showpiece club event, which resulted in the second leg being switched to the Estadio Santiago Bernabéu in Madrid on 9 December 2018. Tickets for their encounter in Spain were much easier to access, but there is only one way to experience the *Superclásico*: on the streets of Buenos Aires. I shared the view of legendary Boca playmaker Juan Román Riquelme, who said, 'Playing the final at the Bernabéu won't be the same, it's sad. It will be the most expensive friendly in history.'[51] Stacey and I were

---

51 AS, *Riquelme:* 'Playing the final at the Bernabéu won't be the same, it's sad' (AS, 2018)

also leaving for Bali from London Gatwick the day after the match, which would have required a lot of rearranging. The interruption between the end of the 2018/19 European season and this trip also provided the opportunity to undergo some minor surgery.

I had spent the month before travelling to Argentina recuperating in the back garden, soaking up the sunshine, and unable to move very far from the sofa or sun lounger. That left me an impressive, if I say so myself, bronze glow, and with greater confidence that I could blend in, unlike on my October 2018 visit to Brazil, when my colourless face, arms and legs made it difficult to convince anyone that I had not stepped right off the plane and on to Copacabana Beach. The decision not to use the Madrid clash as a warm-up to the main event, though, soon felt a little foolish once I went in search of tickets.

The editor of *Outside Write*, Chris Lee, was quick to respond, introducing me to an English writer living in Buenos Aires, Sam Kelly, whom he thought could help with obtaining a ticket for the *Superclásico* even if one of Sam's first responses quoted prices of 'hundreds of dollars' above face value. His friend operated a tour company in Argentina, meaning tickets would be legitimate.

Several issues contribute to such high prices, such as the scarcity of tickets versus high demand and a surcharge added by those supplying the tour operators. Sam was also the first to suggest that I could try getting press accreditation as I would 'make them feel special' travelling all that way and improve my chances. The fixture taking place at the Estadio Monumental Antonio Vespucio Liberti (more commonly known as El Monumental) meant more tickets than Boca Juniors' Alberto José Armando Stadium, otherwise known as La Bombonera, even if demand still outstripped availability.

The Barra Brava[52] (fierce gang) also have a stranglehold on ticket resale to tour groups, which makes purchasing riskier and even more expensive. Sam was unsure of the appetite for the fixture since the moved Copa Libertadores Final, and said, 'It might make things even spicier, but on the other hand, might not.' The contest was unable to become any bigger or more important. His contact from the LandingPadBA showed more concern for my chances of getting in.

The crowd trouble that saw the final moved to Madrid made it almost impossible to have confidence in the clubs' own ticket allocations, with random, if thorough, inspections, heightened security and fewer reliable alternative ticket providers as they were being arrested or shunned by club administrators and River Plate were under investigation. Therefore, things were becoming complicated for non-members seeking legitimate tickets and guaranteed entry.

The contact's statement that 'this will be a tough one, more so than any *Superclásico* we have ever attended in my ten years of operating' did not fill me with confidence. Sam had at least noted that several fixtures – Racing Club de Avellaneda v Godoy Cruz, Argentinos Juniors v Gimnasia, and San Lorenzo v Unión de Santa Fe – were all taking place in the city that weekend, making some Primera División football possible. He also advised that, positioned within a considerable slum area, San Lorenzo was better visited in the company of a guide.

---

52 The Barra Brava are organised supporter groups common throughout Latin America. However, the fanatical nature of their support has often spilled over into violent incidents with rival fans and the police, while they have also been known to have links to, or been involved in, organised crime

Ultra groups controlling the resale of tickets have long been an issue in Buenos Aires, if not Argentina overall, with ticket touting an enormous industry that has resulted in internal clashes between Barra Brava groups. However, the 2018 Copa Libertadores Final had appeared to instigate an attempted clean-up, with tickets reaching $2,000 or more, prompting prosecutors in the city to open an investigation on their illegal resale. As well as the Barra Brava's historic management of the resale market, since the late 1970s they had also possessed immense influence at the clubs they followed with the members earning money undertaking minor repairs on stadiums, and clubs recognising their wider application.

Within grounds they would often play a central role in the gun and knife violence on the terraces, while away from fixtures they would help blackmail players, often at the request of directors, to serve their agenda, threatening to disclose illegal recreational drug use, adultery, and anything that could give a club leverage in contract negotiations or convince a player to seek employment elsewhere. European clubs might have ultra groups intimidating players from the terraces or at the training ground, but in South America it went much further. They could control a player's life. They even suspected the great Diego Maradona of paying his 'tax' to the Barra Bravas. The majority, and most regular source, of their income, though, was through free tickets handed over by directors which they would then sell on at ridiculous profits.

With the personal lives of players in the modern era more wholesome, or at least more scrutinised and visible, than their 1970s and 1980s counterparts, the Barra Bravas have less influence over the 21st-century player and seem to be clinging on to their match ticket empires. With stadiums also modernising and embracing new ticketing and turnstile technology, there is an opportunity for clubs to, should they want to, sever historic connections to the illegal redistribution. That River were under investigation would suggest that they were not quite ready for a messy divorce between the club and the Barra Brava.

Around three weeks went by until an email from LandingPadBA announced that 'especially limited' *Superclásico* packages may be available, costing between US$350 and $650, but only to be announced just before the game after the completion of negotiations with their ticket brokers. There was no sign whether that might be a week or a month.

Through a fear of missing out or handing over around £500 for a single game of football, I reached out once more to Sam, who explained my plight to some more contacts in the capital: River member Remi Lehmann, and Tom Nash, who he thought could also be able to put me in touch with someone. Throughout my travels, the helpfulness from individuals whom I had never met before has always surprised and overwhelmed me, especially considering how persistent I can be.

I contacted my accommodation in the middle-class neighbourhood of Palermo, an area of the city advised by both Sam and LandingPadBA, who told me not to worry. They would have prices for tickets 'one week ahead of the game'. A misplaced confidence on their part as the front desk had no knowledge of ever supplying guests' tickets when I arrived.

Tom had already returned with the email address for the head of press at River Plate and, when my initial approach yielded no response, another for someone in charge of international relations, and then confirmed himself that

River had received my request, but were dealing with a long list of enquiries which required 'rigorous checks, as there are a lot of people in South America who try all sorts of tricks to get a ticket'.

Things took a positive turn 12 days before the match. As long as I could provide a request from a recognised publisher, River Plate seemed to confirm my ticket. Forza Italian Football editor David 'Dov' Schiavone leapt into action, emphasising the website's additional interest with ex-Roma midfielder Daniele De Rossi having just signed for Boca Juniors.

When the former Italian international confirmed he was heading to Buenos Aires, he announced on Twitter that he had 'lived for 20 years in a country [Italy] where football is lived 24 hours a day' and rather than take a quieter route to retirement he 'chose to come to a place with the craziest fans in football'.[53] That was what I was hoping to experience in Argentina myself. Before Dov had time to press send on his email, I had booked a return flight to Buenos Aires for the costly sum, because of my deliberating, of £960. I would be spending just over 72 hours in the country.

Whatever the year and whatever league structure dreamt up by the Argentine Football Association (AFA), Buenos Aires has remained a dominant part of the domestic top flight with 12 of the 24 teams competing in the 2019/20 Superliga Argentina de Fútbol based within the Greater Buenos Aires area, allowing me to attend three matches inside 24 hours as suggested by Sam. If I could have navigated the local buses better, it may have been more.

* * *

53 'De Rossi makes surprise switch to Boca Juniors', *World Soccer*,(2019)

Genoese immigrants founded both Buenos Aires giants in the early 20th century, within the confines of La Boca dockland area. River Plate came first, in 1901, when clubs Santa Rosa and La Rosales became one under the English name given to the Río de la Plata estuary that those who established many of the first football teams in the city had seen splashed across shipping containers, while helping build the port. Four years later another group of Italians, alongside some Greek settlers, decided there was room for another team in the area, and assembled to create Boca Juniors.

On 2 August 1908 the two teams met for the first time, with Boca recording a 3-1 friendly victory over their neighbours. By the time they had also registered what remains the biggest win in the fixture's history, 6-0 on 23 December 1928, the rivalry between the pair had already intensified. River were now situated in the more affluent suburb of Belgrano with many linking their *Los Millonarios* (The Millionaires) nickname to the apparent socio-economic advantage they held over their rivals. It's just a part of the narrative, though.

River had been looking to vacate the La Boca area since their foundation, also holding fixtures in Sarandi and Recoleta. The move to El Monumental, though, did not arrive until 1938. During those early years, River Plate had spent vast sums of money on star names like Carlos Desiderio Peucelle and Bernabé Ferreyra, their informal moniker stemming from rivals believing that the millionaires' club were looking to buy success and secure their place within the upper echelons of Argentinian football.

That contributed to the opening-day postponement of every fixture in 1931, when all 12 teams, including Boca, disassociated themselves from the AFA. The clubs insisting that the association must allow teams to move from amateur status to professional, considering the increased investment. *Los Millonarios'* determination to leave their immigrant roots behind, though, angered Boca Juniors supporters and the subsequent rich/poor storyline has dominated and intensified the encounter over the last century.

With River Plate continuing to outspend the rest of the competition, they secured the 1936 title against Boca with two fixtures remaining. An ill-tempered 3-2 triumph saw one of the first demonstrations of violence breaking out between the supporters while also signalling a power shift and growing financial divide between the pair. Until that point, River had secured just two championships compared to Boca's nine.

* * *

Considering I had no assurances that a ticket for the match would await me in Argentina, I approached the check-in at London Gatwick with an unusual sense of contentment, especially as the cost of the trip alone would mean that, once I arrived, I would do my utmost to make the most of my limited time in the country with or without seeing the *Superclásico* from inside El Monumental. With a wedge of US dollars stuffed in my wallet, I was determined that I would find some way into the famous arena. Although the person on the airline desk, questioning whether I knew it was winter in Argentina, had me wondering whether I would soon spend some upgrading the light jacket I was wearing.

I ensured I made the most of the sleeping time an overnight flight provided, to reduce any tiredness later the following day. It was a welcome surprise landing at 8am to mild (by British standards) weather even if the grey cloud consuming the sky above Ezeiza Airport reminded me more of the climate in Belgrade, where I was heading just after

South America. As did the scenery outside when the bus headed down the motorway towards the capital, passing the somewhat underwhelming AFA headquarters just after exiting the airport. That must make it difficult for national players to slip past unnoticed looking to enjoy the Buenos Aires nightlife when reporting for international duty.

After already having taken in Genoa and Lisbon, Buenos Aires was another example of the transformation these cities, and sometimes countries, experienced through their international seaports, and the impact that remains. The capital still has an enormous influence on the Argentinean economy, accounting for almost a quarter of gross domestic product (GDP). It is the commercial and industrial hub of the country, with just under two million inhabitants.

Even with gloomy skies overhead and soaring concrete buildings, I fell in love pacing the streets, through the Italian-style palaces and interesting architecture of less physically imposing buildings within the traditional *barrios* (neighbourhoods), often stumbling across colourful murals that artists have provided to add a touch of beauty and promote a vibrant street art scene.

With so few football stadiums close to the metro network it forces you to navigate the bus system or commuter rail networks and I often set off on foot, if time, distance and weather allowed. It is the best way to discover the beauty of Buenos Aires. Unlike its South American cousin Rio de Janeiro, it felt more European, influenced by the huge worldwide influx of immigrants and a wide-ranging mix of ethnic groups and cultures including a significant number of Italian immigrants, such as those arriving from Genoa who played a major role in creating both Boca and River, and resulted in the former sometimes being referred to as the *Xeneizes* (Genoese). It is believed that at least 60 per cent of the population now has at least one Italian descendant. I would liken the city itself to Madrid, maybe because of the considerable Spanish migration to Argentina between 1857 and 1940.

When the 1940s got under way, *Los Millonarios* further increased their credentials as the main Buenos Aires rivals to Boca with the River side that became revered throughout the country, if not the continent, thrashing Boca 5-1 at El Monumental to claim the 1941 title. Expanding the Alberto José Armando Stadium, by securing a loan to add a third tier, was higher on Boca priorities. That development finished in 1953 and resulted in the 'Bombonera' (Chocolate Box) nickname, but Boca remained competitive enough to claim both 1943 and 1944 titles.

As with the rich and poor tags that the two clubs hold, that entertaining *La Maquina* (The Machine) team is one reason that elegant play, rather than determination, is associated with River, another motivation for both Remi and Sam choosing River as 'their club' when moving a decade ago. They also expressed their antipathy for how Boca often took a win-at-all-costs mentality into fixtures, focusing on grit and resolve, rather than entertainment and technical ability.

After obtaining tickets for the Racing Club match the following night with relative ease and settling in to the Malevo Muraña Hostel, it was soon time to head to The Gibraltar, a pub just north of the La Boca *barrio*, where I had arranged to meet Sam to discuss life in Argentina and the *Superclásico*. Before that, I allowed myself a few minutes to observe several pieces of Maradona memorabilia scattered around my accommodation, almost exclusively depicting one of my childhood heroes in the Argentina kit rather than giving any indication of the owner's club allegiance.

* * *

The diminutive genius would end his career in the *Superclásico*, Riquelme replacing him after 45 minutes on 25 November 1997 at El Monumental as Boca triumphed 2-1 against *Los Millonarios*.

Boca were on the rise at the time after electing president Mauricio Macri, winning four Copa Libertadores during his stewardship. The first success, in 2000, came after a memorable quarter-final win over River. Trailing 2-1 from the first leg, despite a stunning Riquelme free kick, legendary striker Martín Palermo returned from a six-month absence with a knee injury to score the winning goal from the substitutes' bench – now known as the golden goal on crutches. Ironically, 11 years later he would break a leg celebrating a goal for Boca.

Maradona's heyday in Boca colours came almost two decades earlier in a short-lived spell at La Bombonera. The attacker's 28 goals in 40 league appearances were almost solely responsible for winning the 1981 Primera División, but also helped hide a perilous financial situation away from the pitch. Although his world-record sale to Barcelona for £5m after the 1982 FIFA World Cup eased Boca's money troubles, the players still threatened strike action over unpaid wages in 1984 and, with the club in serious threat of bankruptcy, they sold future World Cup-winner Oscar Ruggeri to their bitter rivals.

* * *

Wedged between two thin multi-storey apartment blocks, the well-maintained, painted red-brick fascia made it difficult to miss The Gibraltar and, despite arriving early, it already had several customers outside smoking. Inside resembled a traditional British pub, with light reflecting off the shiny dark walnut furniture and wall panelling, and covered with nautical-themed imagery and decorations. Whether due to the wide selection of reasonably priced craft ales, excellent food or remaining open until the sun comes up, it became packed with local *porteños* (people of the port).

I was told that Sam would wear an orange polo shirt, to help him stand out from the crowd. However, he need not have worried. With a significant mop of untidy strawberry blond hair and pale complexion, plus a strong resemblance to American actor Jesse Eisenberg. With a similarly slight physical build accentuated by a pair of thin narrow jeans that just overlapped some red Adidas Gazelle trainers, he was different in appearance to those I had assessed each time the doors swung open.

As courteous in person as he had been in his emails, with a distinctive well-articulated English accent, Sam was clear in his determination to head straight for the pool tables. With several friends greeting him, this appeared something of a Friday-night ritual. I took a seat on a bench overlooking the tables. Sam then placed down a fire extinguisher-style water bottle, which proclaimed itself a 'thirst extinguisher', giving some insight into his sense of humour and willingness to acknowledge a geeky appearance.

What I found fascinating, given his unthreatening physical presence, was an alpha-male swagger around the pool table. The longer I watched Sam swat away opponent after opponent, with his meticulous studying of geometric angles, the clearer it became that he had earned this respect through his sporting prowess. If pool counts? But over simplifies the admiration others had for him, and that Sam was just an engaging person to be around.

Sam continued to write extensively on Argentine football, but admitted he had fallen out of love with the

Genoa supporters in high spirits ahead of the Derby della Lanterna in May 2022, despite the threat of relegation.

Sampdoria fans on the Gradinata Sud in full voice before kick-off at the Stadio Luigi Ferraris in February 2014.

In January 2020, a message in lights from Lazio fans to bitter rivals Roma is poorly delivered.

Sporting CP fans Jérémy, Guilherme, Mariana and Manuel enjoy a sun-drenched stroll towards the Estádio José Alvalade.

Goalkeeper Rui Patricio is nowhere to be seen behind the smoke flares hurled at the pitch in May 2018.

In September 2018, Celtic supporters look on in frustration as a clogged underpass at the stadium has them stranded outside shortly before kick-off.

Paradise being heavily marketed at Celtic Park ahead of the Old Firm clash with Glasgow neighbours Rangers.

Ferencváros supporters burn Újpest flags, that had been left at the Groupama Arena during a recent domestic cup final.

A solitary Fluminense shirt can be seen amongst the sweltering Flamengo support at the Maracana in October 2018.

The Galatasaray supporters display a special message for Fenerbahçe, after their Istanbul rivals failed to reach the Champions League.

Balloons rain down from the tiers above as the River Plate fans celebrate during the first Superclásico since defeating Boca Juniors in the Copa Libertadores Final.

The River Plate supporters savour the last few minutes of sunshine covering El Monumental during the Superclásico of September 2019.

Partizan Belgrade fans are engulfed by their own pyrotechnics moments before kick-off in the Eternal Derby with Red Star.

Crvena Zvezda choose the perfect moment to unleash a sea of flares at the Partizan Stadion in September 2019.

The Real Betis party reaching its peak on the side streets just a few yards from the Estadio Benito Villamarín.

The Seville Derby delivered World Cup 1978 vibes, with a ticker tape display before kick-off between Real Betis and Sevilla.

sport a little. Maybe just River? A feeling I could appreciate. It had contributed to me seeking more and more footballing experiences away from Liverpool and also sparked the decision to embark upon this book. As life progresses, you encounter deaths, tragedies, love, and more, and get a greater perspective of victories or defeats. For a little while at least I was becoming a little cold to the yearly grind of following my team, and started focusing on discovering different football experiences. That, and Jürgen Klopp arriving in 2016 to revitalise Liverpool, reignited my passion for the sport.

With interest from outside South America in Argentine football at an all-time low, most of Sam's income was coming from proofreading, highlighted by the next day's fixture between reigning champions Racing Club and up-and-coming Godoy Cruz, which would demand a significant television audience, if Premier League clubs. Manchester City (champions) v Leicester City (challenging for UEFA Champions League qualification) was the comparative fixture of the time. Yet there was little appetite to broadcast beyond the continent, maybe even the country. Therefore, it was nice to hear the distinctive sound of Sam's voice commentating for the BBC on 2021 Copa America games late at night when back in England given how knowledgeable he is about football across the continent.

Whether Sam has gone back to attending matches regularly, though, is another matter as he described being mugged during one of his last visits to an Argentine stadium. Then he dented my confidence in getting a ticket by announcing it had been nine years since he last heard of someone buying a ticket from a tout and it being legitimate. Although that was for a fixture at La Bombonera, it gave us the ideal moment to discuss the dangers of attending fixtures in Argentina.

In his 1994 book *Football Against the Enemy*, Simon Kuper suggested that violence within Argentinean stadiums had softened, yet this contrasted with the AFA feeling compelled to act more recently. Violent incidents had risen to over 250 per season – resulting in an astonishing 2,255 arrests – as deep-seated tribalistic behaviours of neighbourhoods associated to clubs intensified among growing social unrest across the country. That same year, after the *Superclásico*, Boca *el Abuelo* (the grandfather) José Barritta shot and killed two River supporters while passing in a truck, and in 1998 it had got so bad that a judge ordered the suspension of all football and widespread CCTV installed at stadia. The latter never happened and bloodshed continued to rise.

When new regulations stipulated that visiting supporters had to leave first, they forced River fans to remain at El Monumental after a 2-1 defeat to Boca in 2002. The Boca faithful insisted on remaining to celebrate in the pouring rain. Riots quickly broke out between frustrated River followers and the police, resulting in multiple injuries, including some to innocent fans caught up in the chaos, unable to leave the stadium. Since the ban on away supporters in 2013, after a rubber bullet fired by police killed a Lanus fan during clashes after an encounter with Buenos Aires side Estudiantes, the Boca and River Plate followers congregate at their own stadiums to send the coaches on their way to a *Superclásico*. The images of full stadiums at open training sessions ahead of the 2018 Copa Libertadores Final were both astonishing and inspiring, but saddening if this is the only way to reduce violent incidents within the proximity of stadiums.

Unable to attend a match at La Bombonera, I squeezed in a tour of the famous stadium early the following day before making the Maradona pilgrimage to watch Argentinos Juniors in the day's first Primera División fixture. After sitting in the midday sun watching a 1-0 win for the hosts, the fact that I could navigate the bus system back to The Gibraltar helped lessen the anxiety about the lack of communication from River.

With Wi-Fi access established, I enquired with Dov whether he had heard anything, before sending a hopeful email asking about the progress of the accreditation request. To my surprise, the response from Lucila was prompt, if short. 'You can pick up the ticket from the Marketing Office in my name. I am here until 8pm.'

With it fast approaching 5pm and Racing Club to attend that evening, there was no time to even consider public transport, so an Uber was the only option. Traffic added 15 minutes to the half-an-hour journey, but I was one step closer to the *Superclásico*. After the security gate had waved me through and pointed me in the vague direction of an entrance, local journalist Martín Pérez Alonso came to my rescue.

He realised I did not know where I was going and explained he was also collecting some press tickets for colleagues at Marketing Registrado and accompanied me to the relevant office. It was lucky that Martin was there to act as my unofficial interpreter, the River staff insisting I produce an unknown piece of documentation. After a few moments, the vice-president of public relations, Marcelo Gastón Schottenfeld, joined us. He wanted some information on the book and also asked whether I would like to speak to the ultras pre-game. He took my mobile number to pass on.

However, as we left, Martin expressed his view that their desire to keep a low media profile meant it was unlikely anyone would make contact, and that was indeed the case. He then asked if I would be around long enough for him to take me to see the club he supported, second division

Ferro Carril Oeste (also in Buenos Aires), but, despite being unable to, we exchanged contact details anyway and went our separate ways hopeful that a future trip would allow a visit.

Boca Juniors were sitting on top of the table but the match wasn't likely to decide the title because the Primera División was just four games old. Therefore, everything in the build-up to this fixture revolved around the fallout from the Copa Libertadores Final, *La Final de Todos los Tiempos* (The Final for All Time). Described as the most unwelcome *Superclásico* ever, it matched the hyperbole off the pitch but for the worst possible reasons. Had the fixture taken place 12 months later it would have been a one-off contest, like other continental finals. Instead, it became the last Copa Libertadores Final to be staged over two legs and created the perfect conditions for it to be marred with violence and controversy with the domestic ban on away supporters not enforced by continental governing body CONMEBOL.

After a 2-2 first-leg draw at La Bombonera, the chance for River to win the trophy against their fiercest rivals, at home, had amplified the fixture's importance for *Los Millonarios* fans. We could say the same for Boca, who had the chance to inflict the ultimate humiliation upon the home supporters should they triumph. The powder-keg scenario many were predicting exploded, but before the teams had even entered El Monumental. With projectiles from all angles striking the Boca bus on its approach to the ground, a tear-gas canister made its way inside. The driver fainted, and vice-president Horacio Paolini only diverted a serious crash by grabbing the steering wheel.

Midfielder Gonzalo Agustín Lamardo required hospital treatment, as did captain Pablo Javier Pérez, with shards of glass removed from an eye. Police and stadium security failed to take control. There was no way of knowing how far past the 70,000 capacity the stadium had swelled to, with home fans gaining access without tickets. The world watched on as the incompetent authorities announced delay after delay and attempted to convince the Boca players to take to the field, then abandoned the match almost four hours after its intended start. 'We have been shown up as a society'[54] announced River coach Marcello Gallardo. He was not wrong and, after the visitors rejected attempts to play the match the following day, CONMEBOL announced two days later that the second leg would take place on neutral territory.

After late-night drinks celebrating in The Gibraltar after Racing Club v Godoy Cruz, where I got to taste a famous *Choripán*[55] sandwich outside the Estadio Presidente Perón, I was glad that kick-off in the *Superclásico* wasn't until 5pm. Having explored the fashionable, some might say hipster, neighbourhood of Palermo and getting some much-needed fresh air, breakfast and a mid-morning craft beer, I was soon salivating at the prospect of the next few hours in the heat of this Buenos Aires battle. LandingPadBA had insisted that the Belgrano-Nunez area, where El Monumental sat, was one of the safest in the city, even on non-matchdays, although I needed to be mindful of stumbling into places where the Barra Brava had gathered. However, post-Libertadores troubles, increased police restrictions creating a larger security perimeter around the stadium reduced the chances of that happening. Therefore, Tom had asked that I meet him at the Tienda de Cafè on Calle Mendoza, some two kilometres from the stadium.

54 Smith, R., 'In Buenos Aires, a Rivalry Stretches Passions to the Limit' (*New York Times*, 2018)

55 *Choripán* is a traditional Argentinean appetiser or snack consisting of grilled chorizo on bread topped with chimichurri sauce

Since arriving in Buenos Aires, it was hard not to be alerted to the upcoming clash between the two rivals. A Fox Sports marketing poster was present all over the city proclaiming 'QUE NO TE LO CUENTEN' (do not let them tell you), with a bucket hat-wearing cartoon head between club crests emblazoned with #ARRIBATODA (above all else). It was, according to the broadcasters, a match that had to be experienced live, sort of. As soon as I exited Carranza metro and headed north along Avenida Cabildo, I encountered this advertisement every 50 metres, just in case I'd missed the last one, usually still in view behind me.

I arrived around 1.30pm and the cafe was quiet enough to have the pick of most of the tables. I spotted Arsenal v Tottenham Hotspur on a small TV hanging from the furthest wall, though, and positioned myself in front, but I could not see those arriving. That mattered little, however, as I soon felt the imposing presence of someone standing behind me.

Despite my late-summer suntan, I still stuck out from the growing number of local customers enjoying some tasty-looking pastries. Tom explained that my red and blue checked shirt singled me out, with the average Argentine often forced to accept low-quality offerings from providers. Even after rising and extending my hand, Tom had a commanding physical presence, with broad shoulders and a good few inches above my six feet, but he joined the welcoming and warm faces I encounter on my travels, agreeing to meet without securing a ticket himself. Tom teaches English in Buenos Aires, but also runs a River Plate fan Twitter account, @CARP_English, and was the Argentinean football correspondent for World Football Index.

In contrast, alongside him was Remi, who would be in attendance, holding a *Los Millonarios* season ticket. Slightly unshaven and with a slimmer, more athletic build, Remi was sporting a well-fitting River Plate Adidas tracksuit top, and has been an independent journalist covering South America for various Dutch and Belgian media outlets from Argentina since 2013. Discussion expectedly started with my long, drawn-out mission to secure a ticket for the fixture and, despite being unable to get one himself unless paying hundreds of dollars, Tom showed genuine happiness that I had got sorted. With the country experiencing a financial crisis – inflation rising to 49.7 per cent during my visit – it was easy to understand why he was watching the match on television rather than parting with a small fortune.

A depreciating of the peso was hitting hard across society, with Remi highlighting that his wife's monthly salary had fallen by more than half, while he was benefiting from still being paid in euros. This was like both sets of players, who often negotiated to have their salaries paid in US dollars, but that didn't help the impact on the club's domestic income streams. This took us effortlessly towards the rich/poor narrative of the rivalry, diluted as both sides have gained supporters from across the social spectrum. It is far more difficult to identify the financial divide between the fans now. The pair likened it to Manchester City and Manchester United, with the balance of power and money switching sides, but the subplot suits both clubs with River comfortable acting like the wealthy team of the elite and Boca, the club of the lower classes, fighting against adversity.

It was River who were most recently demoted from the top flight, in 2011, and that dominates much of the mockery by the Boca followers, although the duo seemed to view a Boca fan dressing as a ghost with a huge B stitched to the front, calling River *El Fantasma de la B* (the ghost from B Division) with good humour. Maybe that was because, of the Copa Libertadores Round of 16 fixture on 14 May 2015 when Boca fan Adrian *'El Panadero'* Napolitano squirted River players in the face with pepper spray, resulting in Boca Juniors' expulsion, with *Los Millonarios* ultimately winning the competition. The first time they had done so since 1996, with the aid of a Hernán Crespo double.

The Los Borrachos del Tablon (Drunks of the Leaderboard) ultras did not take River's first relegation for 110 years so well though, setting the stadium on fire and leaving 65 police officers injured during multiple post-match altercations. With the groups having got involved with various criminal activity, including murders, it was unsurprising that I was told of an ambush of Newell's Old Boys supporters that left two of the visiting fans dead, or the mafia-style internal fights over the leadership of the group of the past decades.

Opening in 1938, El Monumental is a glorious historic stadium and I could not wait to be watching on from the terraces in a snowstorm of ticker tape and dodging toilet rolls, recalling the gritty VHS footage of the 1978 World Cup Final opening scenes. However, after visiting the compact La Bombonera, I got the distinct sense it would not create the same intense atmosphere given that the bowl-like design and running track kept the fans so far from the playing surface. Tom and Remi were once again in agreement and surprisingly unbiased, suggesting that, had they scheduled the second leg of 2018 Copa Libertadores Final at Boca's home, they would have been far less confident in their team's chances. Before we could lose ourselves in another discussion encompassing famous Boca victories at La Bombonera, though, Remi reminded Tom that we should have already started our journey to El Monumental, and left us to head towards his entrance on another side of the stadium.

We walked for around ten minutes along Blanco Encalada, until we noticed a large collection of River supporters congregating at the intersection with Montañeses. A huge white flag with a red stripe running through it was hanging from the roof of a pizzeria and surrounded by several rugged-looking men. Empty beer cans lay on the tables outside, but very few people were swigging from the aluminium containers or glasses. Surprised at a ticket checkpoint so far away from El Monumental, Tom soon realised that the wall of armed police in front of us was just a temporary measure to reduce bottlenecks at a later juncture, before pointing out that Avenida del Libertador, where the Boca bus came under attack ahead of their last meeting, was just within view ahead of us. Multiple police cars cruising past our eyeline signalled the impending passing of the away team convoy.

This prompted the start of vociferous chanting from those around me. Tom lost himself in the need to hurl abuse at the top of his lungs and displayed how long he had been in South America, rhythmically flicking a loose wrist held skywards in time with the singing in a gesture regularly used by supporters across the country while chanting. He tried to summarise what the song was about, but all I took from our conversation were the words, 'Everything in Argentina is either singing "fuck you" or about death.' Despite those around me looking distinctly middle-class, I was getting my first taste of the River fans' passion. The propellers from the police helicopter passing overhead increased the sense of anticipation building inside me as we could finally continue on our travels.

We converged upon Plaza El Salvador with those in *Los Millonarios* colours or official merchandise emerging from every connecting street. Several hundred had gathered in the park and settled temporarily, chatting and drinking with fellow supporters. As we continued walking towards the ground, a handful were waiting patiently to have their photo taken with a cardboard coffin in Boca colours placed high in a tree. Across the front was '9/12/18', the date of River's Libertadores triumph. When we reached the end of the green, El Monumental came into full view to our left as did hundreds of ticket inspectors in fluorescent aquamarine vests, signalling the end of Tom's journey on that occasion, and we said our goodbyes. We arranged to meet after the game, if our schedules allowed.

When I handed my passport over at the first checkpoint, the steward gave an intriguing look, although it was unclear whether it surprised them to see an Englishman in attendance or because of the type of ticket I had presented. Maybe he had been going through the motions with familiar documents until I appeared. It was a little unnerving, but I was soon through a fourth spot check and at the Museo River entrance where I had arrived 48 hours earlier, after frantically racing across the capital. Given the size of the security perimeter around El Monumental, there were minimal food and drink kiosks outside the stadium and Sam was right to believe that 'they would jack the police presence up' for this post-Libertadores clash, unlike the vibrancy around Racing Club. So I sauntered towards the turnstiles with more than an hour until kick-off.

As I walked through the gates, there was a money-making modern fan zone in operation with two 20-something girls dancing below a clown on stilts in the heart of an increasing crowd. A sense of disappointment came over me that the supposed biggest game in world football was not out of reach of those attempting to sanitise every facet of elite-level football and cash in. I could have been awaiting your average

Premier League fixture. A booming *reggaetón* tune was drowning out any natural atmosphere and another speaker was spitting out old crowd noise accompanying footage of historical games. I wondered if I should have remained there for longer, but I was encouraged to leave by several people looking just as discouraged by the corporate spectacle. Most were just breezing past the entertainment and heading towards the terraces.

With the evening sunshine disappearing behind the imposing stadium, I followed their lead. It first appeared that I was entering through a VIP gate as several of those walking in with me looked a little more affluent than your average fan. There was a touch of class about the marble floor and Roman-style pillars that lined the walkway, and well-dressed welcome staff greeting hospitality customers. I continued up a small set of stairs that eventually led around a corner and out to the already half-full arena being bathed in sun. However, wanting to get a sight of the pitch before finding my place, I looked out in horror at River and Boca players in full kit, flying into full-blooded challenges, before realising that the clubs' youth sides were completing the final stages of a mini *Superclásico*.

Despite the rickety wooden benches, El Monumental still looked magnificent. They had not renewed the ageing seating for some time, but it had seen regular refreshes. The previous layer of red paint was still visible in places where the most recent white coat had been applied so badly. I tried to picture Mario Kempes scoring in 1978, but the memory did not lend itself to a sunny afternoon. When the two youth teams walked off the pitch about an hour before the main event was due to start, the stadium was almost at full capacity with the focus on the senior players arriving from the dressing rooms.

I had taken my position some time earlier, but I soon became squeezed between a group of men in their late 20s who were keen to join the person who had been standing alongside me since I arrived. Three stood in the row in front of me, my original companion to my left, two others on my right, and another pair a couple of rows behind, who had stationed themselves in a space behind us to remain part of the group. They soon talked, at volume, across me, to make a point. Unaware of local seat allocation customs and with no need to move elsewhere, also being quite stubborn, I continued to observe the swelling stadium and ignored their awkward glances.

At that point I noticed the uniqueness, especially in a venue that size, of an atmosphere created without away supporters. There was an obvious missing ingredient, but the supporters sounded happy enough singing along to 'Thunderstruck' by AC/DC rather than hurling insults at their bitter rivals or baiting them with their Copa Libertadores victory. Before the stadium DJ heard the reaction to their next song choice, thunderous cheers raining down from all sides disrupted the party atmosphere. A quick glance at pitch level explained the change in tone. Franco Armani and the River goalkeeping team had emerged from the tunnel and provided an organic conclusion to the DJ set as the crowd en masse began their repertoire of pro-River chants. Two-thirds of the stadium within view was bouncing up and down in unison. When the rest of the home players appeared, to undertake their pre-match routines, the crowd were so worked up that there was little increase in volume marking their arrival.

Clear that I was unaware of what the surrounding fans were chanting, those in front asked where I had travelled from. Unlike the previous day, when admitting to being

English prompted the mimicking of spitting on the floor from my taxi driver, they appeared inquisitive rather than insulted. Those closest seemed obliged to introduce them with anglicised names – Paul (Paolo), Michael (Michele) and Matthew (Matías). Paolo's most notable feature was a nose as wide as it was long, but he had a traditional Mediterranean-looking face with a moderate olive complexion topped with thick, if short, black hair and full eyebrows. Paolo had been distributing sweets from a huge brown paper bag and offered me something, explaining that he was the only one of the group who spoke English with any confidence. Not at all surprising after struggling to communicate, even in broken Italian, since I arrived.

Even with the language barrier, though, Matías attempted to put me at ease with a joke I failed to understand. The comedian within the group, it was as if he attempted to reiterate this by dressing less conventionally than his peers, wearing an extravagant top-knot that was being tested to the limit by a hairline almost in line with his ears. Michele was far more intense, barely speaking, even to his friends, and yet to acknowledge my existence despite Paolo's introduction. With the number of regulars who had arrived and greeted those around me, I wondered whether his ambivalence to my existence was the annoyance that a much sought-after ticket had found its way into the hands of a tourist.

As is the custom, the stadium announcer started revealing the starting line-ups beginning with the opposition. Names also adorned the huge scoreboard by the Popular terrace. The supporters greeted this with the usual chorus of boos and whistles until it displayed the name of new signing De Rossi, which resulted in even louder jeers. I turn to Matías and uttered, to myself given the language barrier, 'Wow, he hasn't even played a game yet and they hate him,' only to realise I had forgotten about another of their veteran stars.

Boca Juniors legend Carlos Tevez had returned to South America in 2015, and when they listed *El Apache*[56] among the substitutes, the vitriol being aimed towards the opposition increased tenfold.

A child prodigy and 16-year-old debutant, Tevez had limited domestic success during his first spell – only winning the 2003 Apertura title – but excelled on the continent, capturing a Copa Libertadores, Copa Sudamericana and Intercontinental Cup. His most memorable moment against *Los Millonarios* came in the 2004 Copa Libertadores semi-final, scoring at La Bombonera to level the tie 2-2 on aggregate and winning 5-4 on penalties, but being sent off for imitating a chicken[57] during his celebrations. Violence soon broke out on the pitch and several players from both teams were also dismissed.

While the players were preparing for the upcoming 90 minutes, some River supporters became focused on their pre-game choreography while the rest continued their enthusiastic singing, passing huge strips of red and white material, about one metre wide, between us. They had unfurled the strips from the front row of the top tier, and now they were making their way to the bottom of our pitch-level terrace. The sense of occasion was intensifying and those in our section were jumping up and down in excitement. I stopped to admire the spectacle that it had created through the gaps in material flying overhead, to see it had been replicated all around the arena.

---

56 Tevez was born in the Buenos Aires area of Ciudadela in the neighbourhood of Ejército de Los Andes, which was also known as Fuerte Apache and led to his nickname of '*El Apache*' after breaking into the Boca first team

57 Rival supporters have often referred to River Plate as Gallinas (chickens) due to their ability to choke late in games

The detonation of several firecrackers seemed to signal an increase in tempo as collections of balloons rained down from the stands above us. Paolo looked back at me and grinned before turning to join everyone else making an aggressive chopping gesture towards the pitch as they chanted, while red flare smoke fell from the upper terraces. Although I could see a few small plumes from the lower level escaping from the mass of bodies nearby, with my heart pumping faster and the ferocious chanting vibrating through me, I did not even flinch during the endless firecrackers exploding around us. Amid the thunderous noise, the entire ground broke out into frenzied applause as the two sides emerged. One of the thick plastic ribbons hit me in the face as they were being detached from further down the terrace.

With the Boca players having not warmed up ahead of kick-off, this was the first sighting of their hated rivals and prompted an expected reaction. So I joined Paolo and friends in a hostile few rounds of 'Campione! Campione!' and unknown Spanish expletives before scanning the stadium for the last of the surviving pre-match decorations and the masses of homemade flags and banners. I looked up to see hundreds of balloons drifting across the perfect clear blue sky, wondering, as I composed myself, whether this was the wildest atmosphere I had encountered. Yet I might have been giving it greater weighting because it felt impressive without visiting supporters.

In contrast to that chaos, the first 15 minutes of the contest were quite subdued. Neither side wanted to cede possession or give the slightest advantage, no doubt fearing that they might never recover. While I recalled, Américo Gallego, River Plate's captain when they won the Intercontinental Cup in 1984, had noted, 'Finals are *Superclásicos*. You play not to lose, to keep nil in your goal, because if you can score, you know that 1-0 will be enough to make you a champion.'[58]

The two teams had again been paired in the Copa Libertadores, this time at the semi-final stage, just before I flew out. The first of two legs was to be played a month later at El Monumental. With plenty of the Primera División still to play, the Copa Libertadores was already taking on greater significance. Sam had warned me the game was unlikely to match the previous fixture, with 'the country still paralysed from the final' and unsure how they could build these games up any more after 'the "biggest" *Superclásico* ever'.

The experienced De Rossi almost let the occasion get the better of him, appearing to make a rash challenge inside the Boca box. The crowd erupted, hoping more than anything that the officials would award a penalty, only for the protestations to turn to jeers as they waved away the players' appeals. It became clear the visitors were using the fixture as a rehearsal for four weeks' time, continuing to invite pressure, but bringing a mistake and foul from defender Lisandro Ezequiel López. Whether it resulted from the 30-year-old's yellow card or was a prearranged moment, on 25 minutes the hardcore fans in the Popular Local section high to my right burst into life without warning. A cacophony of firecrackers began reverberating around El Monumental as more balloons drifted towards the pitch alongside increasing flare smoke, wonderfully backlit by the setting sun in front of me. The game was paused moments later to allow the removal of the inflatables and for Boca goalkeeper Esteban Maximiliano Andrada to clear the smoke from his eyes.

---

58 Wilson, J., *Angels With Dirty Faces: The Footballing History of Argentina* (Orion Publishing, 2017)

The continual aimless crosses into the arms of Andrada and the wayward shooting of *Los Millonarios* players allowed me to focus on a minor disturbance in the crowd. A handful of security guards forcibly removed a flag that had just been unveiled, taking it away before I could try to read the intended message.

Just before half-time, though, the crowd redirected their frustration at Boca striker Jan Carlos Hurtado, cautioned for raking his studs down the thigh of Paulo César Díaz Huincales as the River defender cleared a corner kick. At the break, it was difficult to avoid the falling temperatures with our terrace now in the shade. A small portion of the upper tier behind me remained sun-drenched, with some respite from the Argentinean winter. It was, no doubt, why so few spectators headed for the food stalls or toilets, and the second half was soon under way.

River were quick to dominate possession and five minutes in they gave the fans cause for optimism, but they probably wanted someone other than Lucas Martínez Quarta in front of goal as the central defender sent a panicked shot over the crossbar. Boca continued soaking up the pressure. De Rossi played a major role in defensive midfield, but was substituted on 65 minutes with his exertions catching up with his ageing legs. The whistles that accompanied him sauntering off the pitch made it impossible to hear who was arriving from the bench.

Rafael Santos Borré Maury fired a powerful shot straight at Andrada, bringing an audible collective gasp from the home supporters, and with just 20 minutes of normal time remaining it felt like the game was building to a memorable ending. Shocked by the volume of fury aimed at De Rossi, I never imagined that they could surpass it. Once again, though, up stepped Tevez to prove me wrong. The venom being spat in the former Juventus attacker's direction was difficult to watch, especially as I was unable to understand most of the words being used.

On 84 minutes, Boca broke down the wing through Sebastián Villa and Milton Casco dragged him to the floor moments before stepping into the penalty box. Tevez displayed his undoubted quality, curling a vicious free kick towards the back post that Armani just tipped over the crossbar.

A nervousness then came over the home crowd, now considering the possibility that they could still lose a match they had controlled.

That fear seemed to transmit itself to the players and, on 87 minutes, it forced Ignacio Fernández to hack down a Boca Juniors player about to break through on goal, just as counterpart Frank Fabra did in added time, during the last notable act of the match. After looking forward to celebrating their Libertadores victory and reinforce that they were the dominant force of Buenos Aires, many of the fans vented their frustration at full time. One supporter turned away from the pitch and smacked the seating with his palm three or four times in anger.

Rather than berate their wasteful players, though, the crowd began abusing the referee as he exited the pitch, with a small gathering of individuals moving down the terrace, despite the sizeable running track between them and the turf, to get as close as possible to the officials.

I retraced my steps back to where we had met, intending to greet Tom. The moonlight now provided a little visibility walking back across Plaza El Salvador, while I allowed myself a little chuckle, comparing the dispersing fans to zombies from the hit TV show *The Walking Dead*. As they shuffled along the grass with shoulders slumped, I could hear the audible groans while I advanced alongside them. I could not share that disappointment, though.

Action and goals may have been in short supply (again), but the atmosphere lived up to expectation and a trip that started with such uncertainty had delivered so much. I agreed with Sam's assessment that 'not a lot really happened' when speaking to the *Totally Football Show* ahead of the Copa Libertadores clash, but not entirely that 'no one really cared', as that was not what I witnessed on the faces of supporters.

I will be back to Buenos Aires as soon as I am able to.

9

The Eternal Derby – Belgrade, Serbia

A YEAR after watching Chris Waddle send a penalty soaring towards a jet-black Turin night sky – as England exited the 1990 FIFA World Cup against West Germany – I sat in front of the television again, watching the English attacker suffer another traumatic penalty defeat, with the scars of the previous year yet to heal. The Olympique de Marseille star was back in Italy and could not even bring himself to watch the drama unfold, sitting with his back to the pitch as his team-mates succumbed to a 5-3 shoot-out loss to Red Star Belgrade (as known then[59]), failing to lift a first European Cup at the Stadio San Nicola in Bari.

After a sensational run to the final, displaying technique far greater than their French opponents, few could begrudge Crvena Zvezda a rather mechanical and disciplined triumph. Darko Pančev sent the winning spot kick soaring into the top corner and I became fascinated by that team, full of names as unusual as my own eastern European surname.

---

59 In 2007 Red Star Belgrade became officially listed in their own language as Crvena Zvezda for UEFA competitions

During that 1990/91 campaign, then-Glasgow Rangers manager Graeme Souness sent coach Walter Smith on a scouting mission to Belgrade. Smith gave a two-word report of 'we're fucked'.[60] The man who followed Souness into the Rangers hot seat was accurate with his assessment when the then-Yugoslav club[61] inflicted a 4-1 aggregate defeat on the Scottish champions. The damage had been done during a 3-0 win in Belgrade.

Over the course of the next 12 months, I followed with interest as the Yugoslavia national team qualified for the 1992 UEFA European Championships in stunning fashion with a +20 goal difference from just eight matches, before war broke out across the country and the continental governing body excluded them from the competition. The nations formed by the conflict continued to shine and entertain spectators on the international stage. Most notable in the immediate aftermath were Croatia, who exited Euro '96 at the quarter-final stage and then finished third at the 1998 FIFA World Cup.

After also winning the 1991 Intercontinental Cup against Chilean side Colo-Colo, though, Red Star have since failed to reproduce those continental and world successes. What endured throughout the Yugoslav First League, First League of Serbia and Montenegro and the still-running Serbian SuperLiga was the fierce rivalry between Fudbalski Klub Crvena Zvezda (Red Star Football Club) and city rivals Fudbalski Klub Partizan, the latter more commonly known as Partizan Belgrade.

---

60 Souness, G., *Football: My Life, My Passion* (Headline Book Publishing, 2017)

61 Belgrade was the capital of Yugoslavia from the country's creation in 1918 to its dissolution in 2006

Formed within five months of each other, there has been a misconception that both were pro-Russian clubs or that the hostility between them stemmed from one of the pair having leanings towards their bordering neighbours. However, both are socialist, after establishing themselves in post-Second World War communist Yugoslavia.

Founded on 4 March 1945 at Belgrade University by the United Anti-Fascist Youth League, Red Star had links to central government and a long association as the team of the country's lower social classes, after defeating an army side and embarking on a long unbeaten run soon after their formation. This might have sparked Partizan's creation, as the football division for the Yugoslav People's Army, in October of the same year, considering how sport unites the masses. Partizan took their name from the paramilitaries that fought Nazi occupation.

It was over a year before the two sides did battle on the pitch, on 5 January 1947. While Red Star would win that initial encounter 4-3, helping spark the rivalry that exists to this day, Partizan won the reverse fixture by a single goal and lifted the championship at the end of the 1946/47 season. Red Star remained trophyless until winning the 1949 Yugoslav Cup against league champions Partizan, dominating during a surprising 3-0 victory. Captain Rajko Mitić would raise the Yugoslav League trophy aloft two years later, beating Partizan on the last day of the campaign. As their leader and prolific striker, Mitić would have an enormous impact on Red Star over the next decade. The club rewarded him in 2014 when they renamed their stadium in his honour. It had been known since 1963 as the Marakana, given that over 100,000 spectators would pack into the arena. It was given the nickname in honour of its Brazilian counterpart in Rio de Janeiro, which I had visited a year earlier.

Unlike South America, and my *Superclásico* experience in particular less than a month before, getting tickets for this fixture would be nowhere near as difficult. Unusual Efforts editor Kirsten Schlewitz lived in Belgrade, as did partner Uroš Popović, who was a Crvena Zvezda supporter and confirmed ahead of travelling that 'getting tickets is usually not that hard', as well as much less expensive than in Buenos Aires (had I needed to pay!). Tickets among either set of ultras would be around 500 dinars (about £3.50). Uroš suggested that they were likely to be available on the day of the match as well, although he advised me to purchase in advance. He noted that it had been some time since they had ventured into the ultra stands at the Marakana.

As a Crvena Zvezda fan, Uroš was unsure where the Partizan ultras gathered before games, but knew their three separate groups had been at war with each other. He urged caution if wanting tickets in those sections, as it 'might be a bit more dangerous than usual', but a huge police presence would likely prevent violent clashes around the two stadiums, which are only separated by a 900m stretch of road. What I found surprising was that Uroš and Kirsten were still undecided whether they would attend. This was a fixture known across Europe for its ferociousness and one of the few 'competitive' games of the domestic calendar.

Neither side has finished lower than third since 1990, when the competition was still the Yugoslav League. However, Uroš and Kirsten would meet me in one of the many (I would discover) craft ale bars that have popped up across the city and even purchase my ticket if needed.

With Uroš able to get a ticket with the Zvezda supporters next to the ultras, who were not fighting among themselves, I accepted the offer, but when prices were confirmed they were higher than Uroš expected. At 700 dinars they were still a fraction of Premier League prices, however. Yet, as I boarded my Air Serbia flight less than 48 hours before kick-off, I was still unaware of whether Uroš or Kirsten would join me. I had arranged to meet them at Samo Pivo on Balkanska Street first, though, some two miles from the Partizan Stadium.

The understandable presence of riot police began almost as soon as you exit the city centre area. Kirsten had mentioned that bars around the stadiums would stop serving alcohol three to four hours before the game began. Therefore, supporters, like us, would drink in the city centre ahead of the match, just as in Glasgow. I am yet to witness a significant reduction in the amount of alcohol consumed at fixtures like this one as a result of that approach. At least an early evening start time was nowhere near as restrictive as that imposed by the Scottish Football Association.

I decided I would use the same accommodation, having visited Belgrade a year earlier for a UEFA Champions League tie between Crvena Zvezda and Liverpool. The Pop Art Hostel had been very hospitable during that stay and the owner, Alex, was a superb host. As I would land just after midnight on Saturday morning as well, I knew Alex would make allowances for my late arrival. At least, that was the plan.

After squeezing into a rickety old minibus for the 30-minute journey from Nikola Tesla Airport, I was soon standing in front of the weathered six-storey building, looking much better in the dead of night. After climbing the gloomy concrete stairs, I found that the door had been left unlocked. Did they ever lock it? When I entered I was greeted by the familiar affections of Rocko, a placid and well-mannered Staffordshire bull terrier who only acts as a criminal deterrent to intruders until they meet them. As that was the only greeting I received, I took a seat on a long sofa under a huge pop art painting of Jimi Hendrix and checked to see if Alex had left any further information about which room I needed to locate, but there was nothing.

As I sat in silence, not to wake other guests, I sent Alex a message, checked emails, and scrolled through social media to pass the time. With my eyelids struggling to remain open, though, I soon made myself comfortable alongside Rocko on the sofa and fell asleep. Around 6am, Alex woke me in panic and apologised for too many drinks the evening before, which resulted in him retiring to his own bed. Alex is such a lovable and honest individual so I ignored the aching neck the sofa had inflicted upon me. I was just pleased to be stumbling, half asleep, towards my dormitory room.

I spent most of the next afternoon exploring the many craft bars around Belgrade before, the night ahead of the match, propping up the bar at the Three Carrots pub and watching another famous same-city derby, one just as attractive for its fan choreography as Istanbul – the *Derby della Madonnina* between AC Milan and Inter.

I was sat chatting with barman Gajan – so confident he resembled *Peaky Blinders* character Arthur Shelby that he changed his name on the cash register – with pub regular Radoslav beside me. It surprised me that both had little interest in the game the following day. Despite the 1900s English gangster persona, Gajan was honest enough to admit that, although a Partizan fan with easy access to tickets and the fixture being held on home territory, he was too frightened to attend. The last time Gajan had been present was on 27 May 2017 when the teams contested the Serbian Cup Final at the Partizan Stadium. A solitary Nikola Milenković goal secured a league and cup double for Partizan, *Parni valjak* (The Steamroller). Considering the duo's dominance of the league championship, it was surprising to hear that it was the first cup final between them since 2001. On that occasion they had met at the Rajko Mitić Stadium (as Red Star's home had been renamed), but Partizan had again triumphed 1-0 through a Saša Ilić strike.

Clean-shaven and with lights from around the bar reflecting off a well-polished bald head, and dressed in formal dark shirt and suit trousers, Radoslav's reason not to attend was far more personal and, to a certain extent, humbling given that I somewhat disregarded the ability to fly thousands of miles just for a football match. Myself and Radoslav had spent the last 30 minutes exchanging numerous hand gestures, broken English, and lots of blank facial expressions until Sofia, an International Relations student at the University of Belgrade, spotted our discomfort and joined the conversation. She helped with translating our exchanges, a task proving even more difficult given the live music filling the bar and streets outside.

Approaching his 60th birthday, Radoslav was too young to remember Partizan's golden era, when they became the first club to win three consecutive league titles and just missed out on their own European Cup triumph after losing the 1966 final 2-1 to Real Madrid in Brussels. Yet he took great pleasure in highlighting that Partizan had won more league titles than Red Star since the Yugoslav League ended. A run of six consecutive championships from 2008 to 2013 contributed to the current gap in league titles between the pair. Radoslav would not be in attendance because of the current economic situation, it having taken away most of what he called his 'social activities'. Even enjoying a beer, some live music and a football match on television was now undertaken in moderation.

There was also a raised eyebrow when Gajan expressed his fear of attending the fixture. Radoslav noted that in the early 1990s the violence was much worse and at its peak, escalated by the period of transition in Serbia. The decade culminated in a teenage Red Star supporter dying after being hit by a lit flare in 1999, launched from within the Partizan section. Crvena Zvezda still leave an empty seat in tribute to the youngster.

With the sun shining as I woke early the following morning, I decided on an extra-long walk across the city to Jedno Mesto, for their wonderful traditional Serbian breakfast and honey coffee, although passing a Burekdžinica and grabbing a meat-filled *burek*[62] can be almost as satisfying. The cross-city expedition was to succeed in a plan to stay clear of alcohol until meeting up with Kirsten and Uroš.

Despite a population of around 1.7 million people, Belgrade is quite accessible on foot and I have walked to some of the furthest points on the outskirts of the city when time had allowed on previous visits, falling in love with a grittiness displayed in the scattering of socialist blocks among the post-war refurbishments. It is between Republic Square and its fortress overlooking both the Danube and Sava rivers that most tourists gather. Knez Mihailova, a vibrant pedestrian walkway filled with coffee shops and smoke-filled bars, demonstrates the city's journey from chaotic communist era past to embracing the modern world, which was noticeable as I strolled from the centre along the greatly rebuilt Kralja Milana later that day.

I arrived at Samo Pivo almost two hours before our intended meeting time, which was unusual even for someone like myself, who sets their watch a few minutes fast to ensure they are never late. However, despite a variety of people

---

62 This freshly baked pastry dish is sometimes controversial with the locals who will argue long into the night over whether it should traditionally be filled with meat or cheese

coming and going over the course of those hours I sat bathing in the sunshine, there was never any concern that I would overlook Kirsten and Uroš's arrival and the distinct facial expression of those walking into a room, looking for someone they are yet to meet in person.

Although I had seen a few tiny avatars of Kirsten on social media, I had a vague idea who to look out for. Shoulder-length hair and a large pair of aviator sunglasses added an element of mystique before reaching my table. Kirsten appeared quite reserved, despite a warm, tight-lipped smile to put me at ease. A hipster-punk look might go too far in describing them, but their fashion sense extended exuberant and welcoming personalities. Yet I got the feeling Kirsten would not back down from a battle and will challenge stereotypes based, like I may have done in that instance, on attire.

Uroš, though, was displaying a laid-back, cool and geek-like vibe. Tall and slim, sporting a well-worn hoodie and a rucksack across both shoulders, Uroš wore a pair of thick, black-rimmed glasses across an ample nose and had a full head of floppy black hair, occasionally swept to one side with a hand. Born in Montenegro, 45 minutes from Dubrovnik in 1983, Uroš was more a local than any of us sitting around the table – Kirsten hailing from the United States – and grew up amid the Yugoslav conflict.

Despite being born 300 miles from the then-Yugoslavian capital, his love for Red Star began on 9 November 1988, watching on television as they held Milan to a second consecutive 1-1 draw in the second leg of a European Cup last-16 tie, before succumbing 5-3 on penalties. The atmosphere at the Rajko Mitić Stadium, and many of the stars who would later lift the trophy themselves, had left an everlasting memory. Maybe Uroš's formative years coincided with a significant period of success domestically and abroad. When

Red Star provided a small, but much-needed, distraction from the turmoil tearing Yugoslavia apart. Partizan remained competitive despite their rivals' increased exposure and won the last ever Yugoslav Cup Final in 1992, defeating Red Star 1-0 at the Marakana and eventually securing a 3-2 aggregate victory. That their neighbours lifted the last league title under a united Yugoslavian umbrella felt somewhat fitting given the closeness of the rivalry.

With the drinks and conversation flowing, time had passed us all by. Uroš abruptly announced that there was less than an hour until kick-off and was summoning a 'fake Uber' on his smartphone. Given my difficulties finding the bar, though, I was unsurprised that there was some confusion over our collection point. However, it gave Kirsten the perfect opportunity to hide two small bottles of Rakija[63] and also demand that I down one of the 75ml servings before boarding our transport. Despite becoming quite familiar with the Balkan favourite, the sharpness of the alcohol still generated a fleeting urge to vomit, and reminded me that spirits should follow at least ten pints of ale.

Because of the collapse of former Yugoslavia, domestic competition has very much become a two-horse race between the Belgrade giants and the rivalry had intensified. Ahead of this fixture, Partizan had won 16 titles and Red Star, to my surprise, just eight, while a solitary championship for FK Obilić in 1997/98 was a distant memory. Therefore, the fixture would have a significant impact on the title come the end of the season.

---

63 Produced from plums in the Balkans, Serbia's national drink is a 40 per cent ABV spirit. With around 2,000 official and several thousand unofficial producers across the country, it is offered with or after almost every meal in Belgrade

Crvena Zvezda had so far been flawless, winning six consecutive league games, but they sat third in the table. Qualification for the UEFA Champions League group stages had taken priority and resulted in domestic fixture postponements. Partizan had stuttered during the opening weeks of the season, although in reality a 'blip' in Serbian football was taking 20 points from a possible 24, and remaining unbeaten. Considering the impact the result could have, even at this early stage, Uroš and Kirsten did not appear the slightest bit fearful or concerned about a Crvena Zvezda defeat, buoyed by the fact they had triumphed over the previous two campaigns.

The journey was brief and we could have walked, despite the impending kick-off. It was interesting to be dropped within 150 yards of the stadium. No wonder Kirsten was hiding the Rakija before leaving, as they almost dumped us at the security checkpoint. For a moment I wondered whether the taxi we had ordered was an armoured vehicle, getting that close. We were hit by a cacophony of chanting rising from the arena when I swung open the car door. How had we not been able to hear this on our approach?

With few supporters ambling around the stadium we had arrived later than most, and the majority had already made their way inside. This made our entry quite smooth, although I had forgotten Liverpool's trip to Belgrade ten months earlier and was once again forced to deposit all loose coins into a random bucket, with no idea where this money would end up.

What I had remembered, though, was the intimidating atmosphere at the Marakana back in November 2018. With just a wire fence separating Liverpool fans from the Crvena Zvezda supporters, they showered us in spit throughout the fixture. So I could understand why anything that could get used as a projectile was being confiscated upon entry. During a historic 2-0 win for the home side that night, the whole stadium created one of the most intimidating atmospheres I have ever experienced and contributed to their team's victory. The choreography matched anything I had witnessed across Europe and the ultras remained for more than half an hour in taunting celebration post-game, in a way making staying behind more bearable.

After emerging from the dark concourse out into the Partizan Stadium, it looked like they had split the visitor section in two. What were most definitely the Zvezda ultras were positioned right behind the goal. Kirsten had described the atmosphere as 'pulsing with a fantastic energy' and the away supporters were doing all they could to fulfil that description, whereas the section in which we were situated, while also squeezed for space, was more subdued in its vocal appreciation of its team. With little room to manoeuvre ourselves, we were forced to remain standing just outside our entry gate but within a metre or so of a thin wire fence separating us from the Red Star ultras.

I then refocused my eyes on the playing surface as a hush of near-silence consumed most of the stadium. The players from both sides had gathered in the centre circle, with the Football Association of Serbia (FSS) ordering a minute's silence to mark the US bombing of the city two decades earlier. Kirsten quietly mentioned switching between identifying as an American and Canadian whenever talk of the atrocities entered discussion among locals. What was interesting was that, when attending fellow Belgrade side FK Rad v Radnik Surdulica, 24 hours earlier, there had been no such commemoration. Although, apart from a small hardcore following loudly chanting and making fascist salutes during pockets of play, you could have mistaken the atmosphere for an elongated minute's silence.

The momentary pause added an element of spectacle with the referee's whistle reigniting the supporters, as you almost felt the vibrations from the terraces rise through your body. Even our previously passive companions began bouncing up and down in unison, with the ultras close by. At the far end of the ground the home supporters had passed an enormous flag over their heads, depicting an army tank with a Crvena Zvezda shirt-wearing soldier standing in the roof hatch, and a club crest on the bonnet. Then they unfurled another banner along a row of fans just underneath with 'THE WHOLE COUNTRY KNOWS', but written in Cyrillic characters, which Uroš believed was a suggestion that Crvena Zvezda have connections to and have been assisted by the state or ruling party throughout the years.

The Crvena Zvezda ultras, known as the Delije (Brave), viewed the break-up of Yugoslavia as a triumph and this, alongside other issues, amplified the hatred between the two sets of fans. It was thought that Partizan's ultra group, the Grobari (Gravediggers), preferred Serbia's previous role as part of a unified Yugoslavia. Thus, the tensions between the two sets of fans have been as much political as relating to locality or sporting success.

Since the Delije came together in 1989 through various smaller fan groups combining, they have become as synonymous with Zvezda as any of the star names who have appeared for the club, not only for their vociferous support for their team but for the notorious reputation that they have formed during battles with opposition groups. After their formation, on 13 May 1990, as the conflict in the Balkans intensified, Red Star travelled to Zagreb to face Dinamo Zagreb for a game that saw one of the worst riots in the history of European football. Clashes between fans ahead of the fixture resumed inside the stadium and made their way on to the pitch, forcing the match to be abandoned, and fighting continued on the streets outside with each other and the Croatian armed forces. With Serbian mobster and paramilitary Željko Ražnatović, better known as *Arkan*, leading the Delije and enlisting many supporters in the Serbian Volunteer Guard during the Yugoslav wars, you could understand how their notoriety grew. However, like many ultra groups, the Delije were a tight-knit community that also supported the most vulnerable during a period of immense struggle with food, clothing and accommodation.

On the far side of the pitch, a small section of Partizan supporters had joined the ultras and ignited several black and white flares, and became completely engulfed in a thick plume of grey smoke. Although a gentle breeze was carrying the cloud away to our left, they witnessed little of the action on the pitch for several minutes. We began inhaling a smoky scent of pyrotechnics mixed with the sweet aroma of freshly cooked popcorn being sold around the stadium.

The Delije reacted as expected to the attempted performance of the home supporters, and started an energetic rendition, if unoriginal, of 'daj gol, daj gol, daj goal, hajde Zvezda daj gol' (score a goal … come on Zvezda, score a goal) in rhythm with a constant drumbeat pounding from within the mass of bodies filling the terrace. That was until an exploding firecracker thrown towards our area provided a huge echoing bang that startled the majority in the visiting section and produced an abrupt cry of 'fucking hell' from Kirsten. Moments later, Zvezda's captain, Marko Marin, prepared to take a corner at our end of the stadium and was caught by surprise when another hurled firecracker exploded inches from his feet. With the Serbian-born

German international receiving treatment from the Red Star medical staff, the game stopped as whistles and insults from the terraces targeted Marin. The fans, although idiotic for throwing the pyrotechnic in the first place, were right in suspecting that the attacker was trying to use the incident to his advantage.

In comparison, eccentric Partizan goalkeeper Vladimir Stojković loved every minute of the increasingly tense atmosphere, attempting to orchestrate even more backing from the home fans. The 36-year-old had had two spells with Red Star in the early to mid-2000s, but on 23 October 2010 he celebrated a Partizan victory over their neighbours with a t-shirt reading 'please forgive my ugly past.'[64] He then had to apologise to the authorities for his actions, which were viewed as increasing tensions between the two sets of supporters.

The Zvezda fans were responding to the aggression of their counterparts, and Kirsten had become engrossed enough in the chants to have stopped checking on their phone how Aston Villa and Napoli were faring in their own respective domestic leagues. There did, however, appear to be some confusion over what they were reciting as loud as possible. Kirsten noted it began as a popular chant beginning with 'fuck your mother with a goat' and then evolved into more demands for Crvena Zvezda to attack the Partizan goal. The action on the pitch, though, was failing to match that in the stands and my attention again was drawn to the Partizan supporters, no longer hidden by the blankets of black and white smoke. Despite a vast gap between the rival fans, which spanned around 200 seats, the Partizan supporters had

---

64 Clapson, S., 'Former Nottingham Forest goalkeeper Vladimir Stojkovićon the time he was nearly attacked by fans "with torches in their hands"' (*Nottingham Post*, 2018)

thrown a flare into the Crvena Zvezda section to the obvious delight of the home crowd, who let out a tremendous cheer for the accomplishment of having a powerful arm.

Ahead of the game, as we were making our way inside, the Delije had invaded the empty area to get better access for throwing projectiles in the other direction, resulting in violent clashes with the armoured police. Now unable to break through a considerable wall of enforcement, I watched the two optimistic groups attempt to exchange more flares, although they were hitting their target fewer times than former Red Star striker Pančev scored goals at Milanese giants Inter.[65]

With an ill-tempered affair both on and off the pitch nearing the conclusion of the first half, I spotted half a dozen underwhelming red flares, given what had gone before, being held aloft across the pitch midway between the Grobari Ultras in the south stand and the Zabranjeni Ultras closest to the Delije. This was the Partizanovci Ultras, the third Partizan faction, fighting for more control. Given the averageness of the display, I supported Uroš's immediate assessment that they were never likely to have the 'numbers or energy' to dominate.

* * *

The Grobari took their name from the Archangel Gabriel church behind the north end of the Partizan Stadium, and remain a significant threat despite breaking into their various elements in 2011. When the Zabranjeni first broke away, the frequent clashes before games resulted in serious injuries and, eventually, tragedy. A member of the Zabranjeni, Ivan

---

65 Inter paid £7m for Pančev in the summer of 1992, to beat the likes of Real Madrid, Barcelona and AC Milan to his signing, but the Macedonian-born striker scored just three league goals in 18 months with the club

Perovic, was shot and killed on 22 October 2011. Six years later, the Partizanovci formed in the wake of the Vandal Boys group attempting, with the aid of several Croatian MMA fighters from Split, to take over the south stand from the Grobari. The brawls that day in 2017 were some of the most violent that Uroš had ever witnessed, and YouTube videos shared later that evening reinforced that claim, with hundreds leaving the scenes bloodied and bruised beyond anything I have ever experienced in person. Uroš also expressed surprise that the Vandal Boys had been 'helped, believe it or not, by Croatians'.

Physical violence inside the stadium has diminished massively in recent years but continues outside, with stabbing still the preferred method of inflicting pain upon a rival, I am told. It now appears that the only time the Partizan ultras put their differences aside is when they face their rivals, but bloody clashes do still exist away from the stadium across Belgrade. Even when both sets of fans played significant roles in ousting the president of the Federal Republic of Yugoslavia, Slobodan Milošević, in 2000, they could not put aside their differences. The first encounter between the pair after he lost power could have seen them celebrate the collective political movement many from both sides supported. Yet Partizan followers began destroying parts of the Marakana and thousands of Red Star fans stormed the pitch, causing a riot in which they fought with each other and the police, in one of the most intense clashes between the warring factions.

* * *

Partizan went close with a delicately flicked header just before the first period drew to a close, but the 22,000 in attendance had long lost hope that either side would break the deadlock. As expected, the off-pitch entertainment had surpassed anything the 22 players produced.

When the players re-entered the arena the sun had almost set and the dusky night sky provided the perfect backdrop as the Delije prepared their showpiece display. Within seconds of a first flare being held up, hundreds were being waved above the heads of the surrounding supporters, creating a wonderful sea of sputtering red flames among another ever-increasing blanket of smoke, which over time grew into a huge rosy pink plume that engulfed us as a handful of flags, being swayed by the few without pyrotechnics in hand, protruded from the clouds.

Rather than let the fires die out where they stood, though, they were then collectively hurled towards the pitch. All but one or two fell short and lay on the running track between us and the goal, surrounding the statuesque armed police and fire crew on hand with buckets, who eventually attempted to defuse the flaming projectiles. It all felt a little intentional as the Crvena Zvezda goalkeeper, Milan Borjan, could not see more than a few yards in front of him as the referee restarted the match.

The 31-year-old's concentration was already being tested with the home supporters to our right loudly suggesting that his wife was a whore, which the Zvezda fans disputed just as vigorously as the pair traded insults. As one flare tossed from the away section finally made a direct hit on their opposition, the crowd celebrated with an amended rendition of the hit country and western song 'Take Me Home, Country Roads' by John Denver. It felt like everyone was singing in unison, but Uroš stepped in to highlight that both sets of supporters had their own adaptations. Zvezda even had two themselves, one in which they sing to support their team and another insulting Partizan and their followers.

On 53 minutes, Borjan made a vital save to keep the game scoreless, but I nearly missed the opportunity as my eyes had once again focused on the Crvena Zvezda fans. About 20 yards to our left, flames flickered at the knees of a handful of supporters huddled around a small fire, just like the customary scene in every 1980s New York-set movie of homeless persons in a dark alley and warming themselves around a flaming oil drum. The stewards and police watching on, unfazed and unconcerned, that some seats set alight were burning intensely. The stench of the melting plastic cannot have been pleasant for anyone in closer proximity.

Then, with about 20 minutes remaining, it was the turn of the Grobari at the far end of the stadium to present their own mass pyrotechnic display. Just like the Delije, fans from corner flag to corner flag were waving flares in the air ignited with a distinct red spark. They soon took on an amber hue, and it looked as though an enormous white cloud had fallen from above, giving an alternative angle of the display we had been among as the half started. With visibility restricted by the dense fog, we were alerted to a Zvezda goal by their fans letting out a boisterous roar. Within seconds, though, the referee, who was unsighted himself, disallowed the effort. Later that night Uroš assured us there was nothing wrong with the goal, but he would say that.

What followed was widespread confusion as the official halted the match and everyone looking on exchanged confused shrugs. The stadium announcer then ordered the Partizan supporters to remove a banner insulting the current FSS president, Slaviša Kokeza.[66] The Grobari were convinced, Uroš noted, that everyone, from the government to the FSS

---

66 Slaviša Kokeza would eventually resign from office in March 2021 after being linked with organised crime

and 'even aliens', had conspired against them, which they felt was why the title had eluded them in recent seasons. The broadcast appeared somewhat counterproductive, considering few in attendance had noticed the sign, but all were now aware of its existence with smartphone cameras being raised to snap the offending banner and being circulated on social media.

With the game drifting to what had now become an all too frequent goalless conclusion, on 83 minutes Partizan midfielder Seydouba Soumah picked a loose ball up 25 yards from goal and skipped forward before hitting a ferocious strike from the edge of the box into the top corner, past a stationary Borjan. Without breaking stride, the Guinea international continued his run towards the shell-shocked away support and stood motionless in celebration. Rather than incite the Crvena Zvezda fans, though, it was those in red and white on the pitch who reacted to Soumah's provocation, in particular the Zvezda goalkeeper, who aggressively confronted the goalscorer as more and more of his team-mates arrived to celebrate. Significantly outnumbered, a handful of Crvena Zvezda players looked likely to spark a small brawl, but after a flurry of pushing and shoving they seemed more interested in pulling Borjan away from the skirmish, such was the absurdity of the Canadian international's reaction. The visiting supporters were themselves stunned into silence for a minute or two, although the drummers at the front of their terrace, to their credit, continued pounding a steady beat as the officials attempted to restore order. The Crvena Zvezda fans were now displaying a mix of nervous agitation, anger and even disbelief that their neighbours were looking set to emerge victorious.

Then, a minute before full time, they were dealt another emotional blow.

With the opportunity to avoid an embarrassing loss to their bitter rivals, the usually dependable Marin drifted into the opposition box but sliced a shot high and wide just six yards from the goal, crumpling to his knees in acknowledgment of the missed opportunity. To make matters even worse, almost immediately, Partizan substitute Rajko Brežančić broke down the right wing and sent over a defence-splitting pass, converted by the outstretched leg of former Manchester United flop Zoran Tošić. The veteran winger was well aware of the visiting supporters' location, sliding on his knees in celebration in our direction and prompted a mass exodus of supporters from our terrace. They still faced enduring seven minutes of injury time because of the fracas that followed the opening goal.

I got the feeling that Kirsten and Uroš were seeing out the final few moments more for my benefit than out of any sense of loyalty to Zvezda. However, a combative encounter – the game seeing eight yellow cards waved – ended for us with Zvezda's Miloš Vulić seeing red in the dying moments. Uroš immediately turned and nudged me towards the exit gate before the referee could blow the final whistle.

With the area surrounding the stadium visible mainly from the glare of the floodlights, security diverted us and our fellow supporters away from the city centre and towards the Museum of Yugoslavia, where the tomb of revolutionary president Josip Broz Tito can be located. Before we ventured too far out of our way, Uroš attempted to call another 'fake Uber', but was discouraged by the estimated pick--up time. Despite my eagerness to walk (as I walk everywhere), it was clear my companions for the evening were less than thrilled at the prospect, to the point that we resorted to knocking on the window of a parked bus, hoping the driver would tell us it would soon be departing. Whatever their response, it resulted in us finally setting off along the route now well trodden by thousands of other supporters. Had we not deliberated over our method of transport to our next drinking spot, the Tri Kralja Beer Bar, we might have encountered fewer safety concerns on our journey back.

Having mentioned earlier that I purchased a Crvena Zvezda scarf during my first visit in 2016, that I could have worn, Kirsten had joked, I thought, that 'in Belgrade you don't wear your colours, because you don't want to die!' However, as we ambled through a motorway underpass, we stumbled upon a handful of Zvezda-supporting teenagers harassing a lone Partizan fan of a similar age. They demanded that he remove a t-shirt listing Partizan's title successes and, as provocation turned to violence, landed several punches on the young man. As us and a few others walked past, I felt uncomfortable at how passive we were, not even crying out in his defence. Even with my lack of Serbian, something might have frightened them off or allowed their victim to escape.

Uroš and Kirsten insisted his attackers were probably carrying knives and losing your shirt in that scenario, and having an embarrassing walk home, was the lesser of two evils. After relieving him of his top they disappeared quickly, sprinting past us as they headed off into the Belgrade night.

It was at this point that both myself and Uroš noticed a group of older men behind us, significantly more menacing than a group of teenage boys. The men, probably around 30 years of age, had approached us at speed and overtaken, but noticeably slowed their pace as we approached another underpass, spreading themselves across the footpath to limit our bypassing them. We stopped walking momentarily, effectively to allow another group to encounter our would-be attackers.

Wanting to return unscathed from our trip, we climbed a flight of stairs alongside the subway and took our chances, avoiding the traffic as we crossed the carriageway. Uroš and Kirsten were certainly more concerned for their safety than about the defeat a few hours earlier, and we reached our destination unharmed. As we sat enjoying a drink and the mild Belgrade night, Uroš highlighted that the lack of despair at such defeats was partially because of the increased importance of European competition, rather than domestic spoils, for both clubs now, particularly financially. Later in the campaign, points totals are halved in the Serbia SuperLiga when the championship round begins, certainly diminishing the importance and impact of the result until spring time.

Maybe that justification was just a coping mechanism when losing to your most hated rival. Unfortunately for Serbian football and many smaller European championships, I fear that the importance of continental involvement is becoming an unhealthy norm now that the revenue these clubs can make from domestic competition continues to diminish. These fixtures provide a wonderful snapshot of the vibrancy and historic relevance of the teams and their fans, but now have minimal importance within the wider context of football across the county, other than bringing a seasonal payday to smaller clubs – whereas their success on a continental and world level is unlikely to ever be repeated in the modern era.

10

El Gran Derbi – Seville, Spain

AFTER SIX UEFA Europa League successes since 2006, Sevilla Fútbol Club has become almost as famous across the world as the city with which it shares its name, famed for intense hot summers and the orange trees that are scattered across it. I witnessed one of those triumphs in person as they came from behind to defeat Liverpool 3-1 in Basel, Switzerland, in 2016, and got to experience their passionate Estadio Ramón Sánchez-Pizjuán home first-hand 18 months later as they overturned a three goal half-time deficit to draw with the Merseyside giants in a UEFA Champions League group-stage tie.

It was their city neighbours, Real Betis Balompié, who I encountered first, a decade earlier. Surprise qualification for Europe's premier club competition paired them with Liverpool in 2005. Despite Sevilla's recent European pedigree, though, the rivalry between the two Sevillian clubs can get overlooked against the rivalries of Spanish sides within the same region (not city), such as Athletic Club de Bilbao and Real Sociedad, or those that have dominated sports pages worldwide as with *El Clásico* between Barcelona and Real Madrid, which can attract some 100 million viewers worldwide. *Los Blancos* (The Whites) also have a fiery rivalry with crosstown rivals, Atlético de Madrid, but it is the Andalusian derby which is regarded as the greatest same-city conflict in Spain. Tickets are some of the most sought-after in La Liga.

* * *

There is some contention around whether Sevilla are the oldest club in Spain,[67] but they are the older of these city neighbours. Edward Farquharson Johnston, Hugh 'Hugo' MacColl and Isaías White Junior established Sevilla FC in 1890 for the growing British expatriate population arriving in Andalusia because of mining companies around the Rio Tinto river and eventual surge of the exporting of oranges from the region. Sevilla appeared in the first known football match in the country when facing Recreativo de Huelva.

The trio did not register the club until 1905 and, until the discovery in 2012 of the documentation requesting that first meeting with Recreativo, that remained the date of formation. The incorrect year even appeared on early club crests and a centenary celebration was held in 2005. Supporters still sing the 'Himno Centenario' (Centennial Anthem) before each game, based on the original version 'El Arrebato', written by Francisco Javier Labandón which was also released that year.

Founding Real Betis was far more complex. As has often been the case during the birth of clubs over a century ago, there was a disagreement between directors, resulting in those who left Sevilla FC setting up Betis Football Club in

---

67 Recreativo de Huelva were formed in December 1889 and Sevilla in 1890, but Sevilla are certainly the first club specifically created purely to play football

response. Several of the directors refused to sign working-class players, but I was later told that this was overused as the basis for the animosity between the clubs. Betis FC would then merge with Sevilla Balompié in 1914, a club formed in 1907 by a group of local students and which had received royal patronage. The new entity kept the latter institution's formation date and club colours, inspired by Glasgow Celtic, and became Real Betis Balompié.

Betis comes from Baetis, referring to the Roman name for the Guadalquivir River, and Balompié is the literal translation of foot-ball. There is often a misconception that attachment of 'Real' (Royal in Spanish) means some form of imperial support or favouritism, whereas clubs got granted approval of its use upon request.

Early meetings were a sign that there was no love lost between the pair at the start of their long association. The first match between Real Betis and Sevilla in 1915 was abandoned due to rival supporters invading the pitch and, when they met on 10 March 1918 in the Andalucia Cup, a pro-Sevilla army general prevented several *Los Verdiblancos* (The Green and Whites) players on national service from playing. This left a team composed of youth players to lose 22-0. Betis would take revenge, defeating the *Rojiblancos* (Red and Whites) when they opened their Estadio de Nervión home in 1928 and then repeating that feat in 1958 with a 4-2 victory when they inaugurated the existing Estadio Ramón Sánchez-Pizjuán.

Their first top-flight clash in 1935 witnessed Betis winning 3-0 at Sevilla, during *Los Verdiblancos*' one and only title success. All were incidents early in the fixture's history which found their place within the narrative of a catalyst for long-standing feuds between clubs, increasing in significance as their infamy aged. While Betis would celebrate winning that maiden Primera Division fixture between the pair, the second encounter would have an even bigger impact. With just two league games remaining, Betis faced the *Rojiblancos* and fought back twice from behind to rescue a 2-2 draw, allowing them to edge past Real Madrid and lift the trophy. However, the Civil War in 1936 would have a significant and lasting impact on Real Betis, with crucial members of the side forced to flee the country and money struggles made worse by bombs destroying their club offices.

It was that moment when Sevilla pulled away from their neighbours, although a solitary La Liga title in 1945/46 and three Copa del Rey successes – in 1935, 1939 and 1948 – were a scant reward for almost two decades of regional domination. *Los Verdiblancos* had accepted the role of poor relations, adopting the club motto 'Viva el Betis manque pierda!' (Long Live Betis, even when they lose!) and by the 1950s they had spent more seasons in the third tier than the first.

The *Rojiblancos* would taste relegation from La Liga at the end of the 1967/68 campaign. Betis supporters could take little pleasure from their misfortune, though, with *Los Verdiblancos* demoted to the Segunda División on the same day. Sevilla would make an immediate return and Betis joined them in 1974, but the next two decades were mediocre at best for both clubs.

That all changed during the 1994/95 season, at least for a while. Real Betis finished above Sevilla in La Liga for the first time in eight years, but their neighbours also qualified for European competition. It was also the first time the duo had both finished inside the top five places in 60 years. The following season, a 3-0 victory for Betis over Sevilla at the Ramon Sánchez-Pizjuán appeared to signal a power shift in the city, with the *Rojiblancos* descending into chaos and several poor decisions taken by the club eventually resulting in their relegation in 1997.

Rather than take advantage of their newfound dominance, the world-record signing of Denílson was a disaster and *Los Verdiblancos* headed back to the Segunda themselves in 2000. By then, Sevilla had returned to La Liga and courted controversy by putting up minimal resistance when losing 3-2 to Real Oviedo and helping relegate Betis.

Over the last 20 years, the fixture has evolved a great deal, and transforming Sevilla into a team challenging both at home and abroad was a large part of that development. The club remained without a trophy for 57 years, but since winning the 2006 Europa League they have won ten major honours and lost a further ten finals. Real Betis still usurped their rivals during this period, finishing six points better off in La Liga in 2012/13 and coming from three goals behind to draw through an 88th-minute Nosa Igiebor strike.

The fixtures that captured the imagination throughout Europe, though, came during the 2013/14 season, when they met three times in a month after being paired in the Europa League last 16. Both would register memorable away victories in that competition, but Sevilla would triumph 4-3 on penalties, as they did when winning the final against Benfica in Turin, Italy, that same year.

* * *

With most tickets distributed among club members, the author of the wonderful *The Frying Pan of Spain: Spain's Hottest Football Rivalry*, Colin Millar, advised me that any still remaining would go on sale within two weeks of the match. Therefore, as 15 March 2020 approached, I spent days refreshing the Sevilla website, until just ten days before the game, tickets became available for general sale. They sold out within an hour of me purchasing for €100.

Disappointment then replaced the excitement of attending the game and completing my last planned trip, as the Covid-19 pandemic spread across Europe and they announced that the match would take place without spectators, behind closed doors. I refused to be defeated, though, and insisted on travelling to write about the experience alongside local supporters, even if from a local bar. However, the evening before I was due to fly, my wife Stacey convinced me not to travel. That proved an important intervention as, within hours, Spain locked down bars, restaurants, supermarkets and football. A friend flew to Benidorm that same weekend and was forced to spend four days locked in a hotel room, only allowed out for essential items.

The match at the Ramón Sánchez-Pizjuán would eventually take place on 11 June 2020, in an empty stadium, and Millar told *The Totally Football Show* a few days before that it was 'definitely going to be a bit strange, because it is the best game in Spain. Particularly as it is such a spectacle, and not having any fans will have a profound effect on the game itself, because the energy the supporters transmit to the pitch is very evident.'[68] It would be 20 months before they would play *El Gran Derbi* (The Great Derby) in front of supporters once more. I was adamant that I would be in attendance, this time at Betis's Estadio Benito Villamarín.

With certain pandemic restrictions in place, I secured a ticket at another eye-watering €105 and nine days before kick-off, easier than before, but without flights booked. Despite stadiums in Spain being almost back at full capacity, the eventual attendance came in at 50,534, just over 10,000

---

68 Richardson, J., 'Let's just use Teletext' (Muddy Knees Media, 2020)

below the 60,721 capacity of the Villamarín. That it was in November rather than prime tourist season helped with costs and La Liga had already confirmed the broadcast schedule, which allowed me to combine my visit with a city break with Stacey.

It is easy for the city of Seville to capture your affections whatever time of year you choose to visit, whether you are seeking to experience its hot steamy summers, the ridiculously mild winter months, or the individual charm of districts like the bohemian Tirana, the birthplace of flamenco. Even in November, we would perch ourselves on stools at a high table and enjoy the sights and sounds of late-night street performers, marvelling at the grandeur of its many monuments, gothic architecture, and Neo-Mudéjar plazas during the day.

With around 700,000 inhabitants, Seville is Spain's fourth-largest city and benefited from its port becoming the country's major gateway to colonies in the Americas in the 1500s, despite having to navigate through the Guadalquivir to reach it. Seville fell soon after the start of the Spanish Civil War, under the rule of Francisco Franco and remained neutral throughout the Second World War. Isolated from the outside world, both economically and culturally, which adds to the city's charm. Seville retains local customs that other large cities struggle to do through globalisation, even after the hosting of the 1992 Seville Expo brought a significant investment and improvement in infrastructure, connecting others to this intriguing city.

Despite spending our first 48 hours wandering the streets of Seville on foot, there was a noticeable lack of Betis or Sevilla shirts being worn around the city. With temperatures still hitting 24°C in southern Spain, though, most of those we encountered while sightseeing were unlikely to be locals. It was Stacey who noticed the first signs of either fan group making their presence felt as we enjoyed a drink in the sunshine opposite the former Real Fábrica de Tabacos building, which now hosts the University of Seville. Slapped across a wall of a neighbouring bar were the words 'ULTRA NORTE SFC' in black spray paint, prompting her to enquire what 'SFC' stood for.

Sometimes known under the monikers Biri Biri Norte or Biris Norte ultras, the left-leaning group have occupied the Gol Norte end of the Sánchez-Pizjuán since forming in 1975 and taking their name from the first black player in the club's history. A year before their creation, Gambian attacker Alhaji Momodo Njie, known as Biri Biri, arrived at Sevilla and became something of a cult hero during five years in Spain. Like the *Rojiblancos* themselves, there are suggestions they are the oldest such group in the country and claim to have over 1,000 members.

In recent years, the ultras have had several well-publicised clashes with fans of European opponents. In 2016/17 alone, they stabbed a Juventus fan and two members of the Biris Norte were arrested after altercations with Leicester City, having ended the previous campaign fighting with Liverpool supporters in the stands at the 2016 Europa League Final. Fights between Sevilla and Betis fans have always been part of the backdrop to the contests on the pitch, and 24 supporters were arrested in the wake of a mass brawl as recently as 2018.

Considering the level of violence associated with the group, it was comical that the Spanish Football Federation attempted to penalise the Biris Norte just for insults aimed at their neighbours in 2015, wanting to close a section of the Gol Norte for four games just for chanting 'verdiblancos hijos de puta' (Green and white sons of bitches). However, as a seasoned traveller at matches across the world and an away supporter with Liverpool, avoiding physical clashes can be done if you don't go looking for conflict and remain aware of your surroundings in unknown territory.

It was 24 hours later, on the day on which the two sides were due to meet, that we saw our first club jersey, as a middle-aged *Béticos* came walking towards us alongside Casa Consistorial de Sevilla wearing a vintage Kappa home shirt from their late 1990s heyday, when the club signed Brazilian forward Denílson for a world-record £21.5m fee.

Before flying out to Seville, I had asked a friend working for Spanish publication *Marca*, Conor Clancy, whether he had any contacts who could point me toward where *Béticos* fans might congregate ahead of games. Yet he went above and beyond for this last leg of my journey. One colleague at *Marca* suggested to him that I should head to Bar Uruguay around two hours before kick-off as 'it's a cool atmosphere', despite warning me to 'be careful if he wants to talk to them [Betis Ultras]. They are assholes. Especially if he is not white and Spanish.'

Another journalist contact, Alan Feehely, did provide Conor with contact details for a *Los Verdiblancos* supporter by the name of Enrique Roldán, who seemed happy to give me the full *Béticos* experience. Enrique invited me to Calle Tajo in the Heliópolis neighbourhood, 'where the ultras will be with flares, smoke [bombs] and firecrackers. There he will have his chaos.' I'm not sure I requested that, but I could then not wait to experience it. Rather than the two hours suggested before, though, Enrique requested I meet him around 4pm (five hours before kick-off) and forwarded his mobile number via Conor.

Failing to convince Stacey to come and see the chaos they had promised me, because she did not fancy a lonely

45-minute walk back to our accommodation, I headed south towards Heliópolis just before 4pm. Passing the famous Catedral de Santa María de la Sede provided another brief sign that kick-off was approaching. A Betis supporter wearing the current home shirt and a bright-green club hoodie stood in the doorway of a bar in animated discussion with another gentleman, who appeared to be looking past his frantic waving of arms. Whatever point they were attempting to make, it had lost all sense of purpose.

Some believe that Real Betis have the largest fanbase outside of Barcelona and the two Madrid clubs, and their large numbers at away fixtures have become known as the Green March, aided by the thousands who migrated north during the Spanish Civil War. That conflict also had a major impact on the club, with membership falling from the thousands into the hundreds. However, the rise of the Betis Socios was already being felt at the start of the early 1930s and linked to the team's success during that period, winning the La Liga within three years of being promoted to the top flight as 1931/32 Segunda División champions.

For the next 30 minutes I strolled along with the beating setting sun, making me regret the choice of jeans and a light jacket as I passed the crowds swirling around the Plaza de Espana and posing for selfies, receiving some strange looks from the families dressed for summer and making the most of the wide open spaces of the Parque de María Luisa. When I exited the park on to Avenida de la Palmera, another family greeted me crossing the road, this time dressed in near-matching Sevilla shirts. Approaching from the other side was a Betis fan and, as they had signalled to each other, I slowed my pace to witness the interaction. I was slightly surprised that they shared a quick joke and an affectionate embrace in the middle of the road, with little concern that traffic could head in their direction. It turned out that they were heading to a bar not quite visible from the main road, already hosting a significant number of Sevilla fans in high spirits. The odd song being sung squeezing its way through the dense perimeter bushes. A few yards on, a young Betis supporter was standing alone between two parked cars, regretting his collection point, but soon departed in a car full of fellow *Béticos*.

With my right side burning from the lack of shade, I envisioned switching places with them as an electronic sign confirmed that it was still a balmy 23°C and showing no sign of relenting. Before I questioned whether walking was the right decision, the north-east corner of the Estadio Benito Villamarín came into view between the palm trees and associated greenery lining the street.

The imposing structure was renamed in tribute to one of the most influential of the club's former presidents, after stabilising Real Betis's finances during the late 1950s and the purchase of the stadium now bearing his name in 1961, which helped improve their economic standing. This was also the case at Sevilla, who gave the same honour to Ramón Sánchez-Pizjuán for how he steered them towards the elite end of Spanish football during the 1930s, using his political power to ensure that Sevilla lost none of their key players to the front line of the Civil War. The Estadio Benito Villamarín was the Estadio Manuel Ruiz de Lopera between 1997 and 2010, though, when Betis's self-obsessed president gave the honour to himself. He had, after all, spent that world-record fee on Denílson!

Within touching distance of the stadium, I was waiting patiently at a traffic crossing. A large group of Betis supporters descended on the intersection almost from nowhere to join me, all carrying multiple plastic bags with refreshing-looking drinks which, with my head looking down, reminded me that my sweltering thighs were growing uncomfortable under a pair of tight-fitting jeans.

At that moment, the number two bus arrived across the road, packed full of home supporters chanting as they exited. So I followed them along one side of the ground to what I assumed would be even more supporters. However, despite a large vast parking area devoid of cars on the east side of the stadium, there were very few fans in attendance other than those entering and exiting a tiny club shop or visiting the few merchandise stalls that had already set out their products.

Yet I could still hear singing and did my best to identify which direction it was coming from. At one point it sounded like it was coming from within the Estadio Benito Villamarín and I wondered if fans from either club were already inside, as might often be the case in places like Belgrade or Buenos Aires. As they started testing the stadium sound system, with what I assumed was a current chart hit in Spain, a firecracker went off and echoed around the whole of the Heliópolis area just as Enrique sent a message to say he was running late.

I turned and walked down Calle Tajo, where I could see hundreds, if not thousands, congregating in the narrow streets, despite the expensive-looking villas around them, full of optimism. The further down the road I descended, the thicker the smoke consuming me became, while the vociferous chanting stopped only fleetingly when a firecracker startled the *Béticos* songsters. The lack of visibility and a tighter congestion of people forced me to stop, with the others more concerned with singing than progressing.

The *Béticos* had plenty of reason to be optimistic heading into this clash against their more decorated neighbours. Almost half the season had gone with *Los Verdiblancos* occupying one of the four automatic Champions League qualification places and looking all but assured of advancing from their Europa League group. Sevilla still had the upper hand domestically, sitting above Betis in third place and mounting a title challenge. Victory would see Betis overtake Sevilla, though, and there was a genuine sense it could or would be the hosts' night.

Opposite the corner of Calle Ecuador, where Enrique had asked me to meet him and the Supporters Gol Sur fans were selling merchandise, was a small convenience store, La Tienda De Rosi, and anyone who had not come prepared was queuing for refreshments. You could only just squeeze four people in at once, including staff, and a security guard was monitoring entry at the door, checking identification in front of multiple signs warning that they would not serve alcohol to those under 18. Having turned 40 years old a few months earlier, it was unsurprising that he chose not to request my credentials, but it was more laughable that some were exiting the store and handing drinks to those underage within yards of them. I stepped inside and ordered two one-litre bottles of Cruzcampo Especial for the bargain price of €4, but then realised I had no way of opening them. The authorities at Madrid–Barajas Airport had confiscated my Wallet Ninja[69] when returning from Atlético de Madrid the previous month.

I set about seeking some help, looking for anyone also drinking from bottles who looked approachable, and a few yards to my left stood the tall, imposing presence of a man in his late 20s, alone and sipping from a smaller bottle of Cruzcampo.

---

69 A credit card-sized piece of alloy steel with 18 everyday tools, such as Hex wrenches, can opener, fruit peeler, bottle opener, box opener

We embarked on a game of charades – mimicking opening a bottle – and he ushered me over with a hand gesture and a big positive smile that looked out of place alongside his rugby-player physique and rough appearance. Holding out a bottle opener that was hanging from a lanyard around his neck, I raised my beer towards him and an instant bond formed. Having just enough Spanish language skills not to offend the locals, breaking into a fluent discussion with my new friend was always going to be difficult, but it became apparent that he might have some learning difficulties and struggled with his speech. That did not stop me from discovering his name was Adrian, though, and he was a Betis fanatic.

A willingness on both sides allowed for pleasant, if broken, communication between us. Adrian found enjoyment in how quickly I finished the first of my two beers, chuckling as he presented his bottle opener once more. At that moment one resident attempted to squeeze their car through the crowds, stunning us both into silence. Watching the car edge along Calle Tajo, it became apparent that more and more people had joined the pre-match festivities.

With the setting sun and smoke flares being held aloft in the distance, it was impossible to see an end to the mass of bodies. Trying to avoid another awkward silence, Adrian began showing me his selection of glossy A6 size pictures of Betis players, which, although I failed to uncover why he had brought them to the game (maybe to have them signed?), unearthed his love for the attacker Joaquín. Unable to conceal his admiration for the Spanish international, Adrian turned his back to point out that the name and number emblazoned across the back of the shirt he was wearing were Joaquín's.

The winger scored one of the most memorable goals in recent memory when the two sides met on 2 September 2018.

Arriving as a substitute with 15 minutes remaining, his first touch on 80 minutes was to head home the only goal of the game in front of 53,451 spectators at the Benito Villamarín. At 37 years old, Joaquín became the oldest player to score in the derby this century and equalled the record number of appearances in the fixture. I did not expect him to be in contention three years later.

While most of the packed street stood sipping drinks wearing green and white, or bearing Betis merchandise, on the corner, across from La Tienda De Rosi, was a growing group of individuals dressed in black. As their numbers increased they became louder, and it was noticeable that they held some sort of authority over others. Some stayed away, and others, who seemed to be young and impressionable fans, wanted to be seen with them. No doubt standing out among the regulars, each time one of the group approached the store I could feel them looking me up and down, almost waiting until I would make eye contact as they stood tall and puffed out their chest to suggest that outsiders were not welcome on their turf. As several of them looked useful in a pub brawl I had little intention of trying to penetrate their inner sanctum, not to mention joining the fascist salutes I witnessed during some of their energetic and raucous singing. With three hours until kick-off I wondered how volatile they could become, but also if the threatening appearance of some was just for show.

Incidents like former Supporters Gol Sur leader Manuel Herrera Perejón's brutal assault on an Athletic Club de Bilbao fan in 2017, which saw him jailed, had lessened. Despite regular reports of both sets of supporters clashing with European opponents in recent years, the reduction in violence between ultras had failed to soften the atmosphere. The last notable instances of trouble within either stadium had come in the early 2000s, fuelled by a personal feud between *Los Verdiblancos* president Lopera and José María del Nido of Sevilla. In October 2002, a *Rojiblancos* fan entered the pitch and tried to punch Real Betis goalkeeper Antonio Prats.

Then, in February 2007, among the projectiles raining down from the stands, a whisky bottle just missed Andrés Palop in the Sevilla goal. The home supporters were objecting to del Nido, refusing to acknowledge Betis's centenary celebrations. A month later, when misfortune paired the two teams in the Copa del Rey, fans set bins on fire, blocking the visitors' entrance, and also doing the same to rival flags inside the ground. This time, when Sevilla went ahead, a frozen (a strangely specific and widely repeated detail) Bacardi bottle struck coach Juande Ramos on the back of the head and knocked him unconscious.

Removing my phone from my pocket to see a text message from Stacey asking if I was still on my own, I realised Enrique had attempted to contact me, so I responded, asking his location. His group had settled midway down Calle Ecuador, ahead of me. So I said my goodbyes to Adrian, who was already in deep conversation with some other fans who had arrived a few minutes ago. Having a vague idea what Enrique looked like from his Twitter avatar, it did not take long to spot him among the jubilant *Béticos*. Wearing a dark jacket over an emerald-green hoodie, of medium build with short dark hair and facial hair somewhere between a full beard and a few days unshaven, a beaming youthful face was staring back at me behind a pair of dark-rimmed glasses. With no need to seek confirmation, we shook hands without hesitation, embraced warmly, and Enrique introduced some of his entourage. The most important of these was his partner, Jessica Rincón, who was just as friendly as Enrique and displayed another cheerful grin when we first met; unlike Carlos, who was standoffish when we were introduced.

It turned out that Enrique also worked in academia and was a doctor of law and professor at the Universidad de Sevilla, with an interest in historical football culture and politics. More important, in the context of Real Betis, was his involvement in setting up the Betis Bohemio group, a collective created to promote the culture of the club and bring together those who loved the club but did not feel a belonging to the hardcore ultra elements, instead attempting to provide a place where everyone could feel represented and connected by nothing more than their passion for *Los Verdiblancos*. Betis Bohemio had also turned Enrique into something of a local celebrity and he was soon approached by a small group of Béticos, who had recognised him while passing. It was something that Jessica had become accustomed to, stepping to one side with me as we started one of the few non-football conversations of the afternoon.

I still maintained a focus on Enrique, though, watching him extract multiple packs of Betis Bohemio stickers from his jacket pocket and sending his adoring followers on their way. On his return to us he continued explaining the emphasis of what they had created the project for, while furnishing me with some stickers to take on my future travels. This also seemed the ideal time to question Enrique about the menacing-looking supporters from earlier, who were selling merchandise with ULTRAS 86 emblazoned across them.

While I waited for tickets to go on sale I had investigated where the ultras gathered in the Benito Villamarín, so I knew they named themselves the Supporters Gol Sur in honour of the stand which they occupied. Enrique explained that 86 was a reference to the year they formed, and they had not always been as right wing as their earlier actions suggested.

The group was left-leaning until another division, Skin Betis, arrived in 1991 and joined forces, resulting in a switch to a right-wing ideology that remains to this day. A willingness to share these views during fixtures has resulted in regular sanctions from La Liga.

With the sun disappearing from view shortly after I had met up with Enrique, I hadn't realised, while engrossed in conversation with him and Jessica, that it was growing ever darker and the temperature had plummeted. I was now actually dressed for the conditions. The atmosphere was heating up while the conditions were cooling. We were almost standing shoulder to shoulder with *Béticos*, and reaching the store for more alcohol would be difficult given the numbers. Everything and anything was being consumed. At the foot of an orange tree where we stood were several bags containing spirits and mixers. Coming well prepared for the hours of celebration ahead, a couple of people were acting as bartenders. Alongside us, a car was now acting as seating with two or three individuals sitting on the bonnet and the roof covered in drink containers (full or empty), in its capacity as a temporary table. An amazing act of confidence and bravery, or stupidity, by the owner that they would return to find their vehicle in the same condition they left it.

At that point I thought I would try to engage Carlos in conversation again as Enrique had described him as a 'massive Betis fan' and he had been circling the surrounding area, meeting and greeting fellow supporters. Carlos was not imposing from a physical presence. Just short of 6ft and of medium build, it was the regard in which the others greeted him that showed how his peers held him in high esteem. He looked the part, strutting around in a bright-green Betis Kappa jacket over a white t-shirt and scarf draped around his neck. Clean-shaven with fresh-cut short dark hair, the sunglasses hanging from his t-shirt neckline gave off an air of overconfidence.

When introduced, Carlos showed little interest in who I was or why I was there, and now thrust together through circumstance, I at least attempted to make small talk. However, after explaining the reason for my attendance and how I had contacted Enrique, the awkwardness continued and I was relieved when fortune ended our interaction as an orange from the tree beside us fell from above and hit Jessica on the head. With the firecrackers continuing to explode around us, there was a moment of concern that something more sinister had struck her, but this allowed myself and Carlos to break away to other endeavours.

With the sun having set for the evening, the firecrackers seemed to take a back seat, with flares and smoke bombs prioritised and ignited at an amazing rate. Looking back down the road at La Tienda De Rosi, the glowing pyrotechnics resembled the light at the end of a tunnel with the sparks from the flares providing the perfect back light for the green, and, on occasion blue, thick smoke plumes rising skywards. Within what felt like minutes, flares were being lit all along Calle Ecuador and the smoke clouds surrounded us. The sharp white flames made me squint and the smoke irritated my contact lenses. It was an amazing spectacle accentuated by the police helicopter hovering overhead, adding an element of illegality to a harmless street party.

Colin Millar highlighted the lack of tourists sanitising the fixture when speaking to the *Outside Write* podcast, and the closeness of the fans partying together certainly supported that statement. However, there was a number of smartphones, with 75 per cent of the crowd, myself included, filming the spectacle.

Having consumed six litres of Cruzcampo, any sense of disconnection from the group was disappearing fast and I was bouncing along with the songs being sung. Despite minimal understanding, multiple rounds of 'punta Sevilla, punta Sevilla' were as easy to join in with as they were to follow. The crowd had formed circles around a handful of individuals planting smoke bombs on the concrete floor while those around us waved flares and the dancing felt like it never stopped. Excitement from the last three and a half hours had made me forget that, from the moment at which I had reached the stadium, I had been seeking some toilet facilities to relieve myself. I soon realised that, unless I knocked on the front door of a local residence, I had to hold on. Therefore, when Enrique revealed he needed to take Jessica away for a toilet break, I jumped at the chance to be shown the facilities.

A few quickly taken corners and we were in a less-populated street, and Jessica found a position between two parked cars as Enrique and I made a human screen. We then broke away to a metal fence in front of a dense and leafy hedge. Mid-stream, a young man came and joined me at the fence, paused, but then ran away at speed. Was I urinating with such force (it had been several hours) that I scared him off? If he had spotted something on the other side, I was too drunk to notice and too desperate to stop.

After taking a less-urgent stroll back to our spot along Calle Ecuador, we soon said goodbye to Jessica. Unlike me, she was unwilling to pay the inflated prices, even for this fixture, and was watching the match back at their apartment a few blocks from the ground. We made our way to the stadium and Enrique checked I still had my mask to enter under Covid-19 protocols, but noted that 'once you're inside they do not care'. Having visited the Estadio Metropolitano, home of Atlético de Madrid a few weeks earlier, that came as no surprise.

Positioned in the lower section of the Gol Sur, at this point we said our goodbyes and I thanked Enrique for his hospitality and making me feel welcome and almost a Betis Bohemian myself. Despite the additional checks, entry was straightforward and I soon found myself walking along a large undecorated concourse and feeling the effects of the significant amount of alcohol consumed. I saddled over to the food and drink kiosk, seeking sustenance and, from what I remember, I attempted to order another beer and a baguette but ended up instead with two heated baguettes. This could have been because of my lack of Spanish or that I was slurring my words, but I took it as a sign that food in double the quantity was a good idea. I then walked to the end of the open concourse, placed the baguettes on the edge of a wide concrete wall and looked down at the tiny figures pouring into the stadium in increasing numbers. Our departure from the chaos outside was proving justified.

When I first looked at the playing surface, from high up on the third tier. I could see both teams were already on the pitch, going through their warm-up routines, and a sense of anticipation was filling the crowd even without either set of fans yet going through their collection of chants.

On the same level, above the corner flag opposite was the visiting section, which Enrique later delightfully described as a piece of cheese, although it was more like half a triangular slice as it ended with a flat horizontal edge. Only half of the allocated space was filled with *Rojiblancos* supporters, though, with the bottom half empty except for a few riot police spaced apart. On one side were Betis fans, but on the other, two further 'cheese pieces' were left totally empty. Enrique confirmed that this was standard for *El Gran*

Derbi. That seemed wasteful, unnecessarily cautious and unbalanced. There was no standard allocation of tickets for the derby, with distribution somewhere between 300 and 1,000 tickets. Enrique believed that Betis supplied Sevilla with around 400 in this instance. He thought this could have been because of the Covid-19 restrictions, but La Liga stadiums had returned to full capacity, so it was most likely a crowd-control measure.

When the players returned to the dressing room, I noticed that most of the *Béticos* had taken their places in the bottom tier, with flags and banners being waved. A few pockets of supporters started the occasional Betis chant, but it wasn't until hundreds of children with flags began lining the perimeter of the pitch that the crowd came to life. Once they were in position, the floodlights were switched off, allowing a handful of spotlights, accompanied by those on smartphones, to perform a lightshow as 2009 dance track 'Stereo Love' by Romanian DJ Edward Maya was booming in the background. The fans, with little care for the vocals of Moldovan-Romanian singer Vika Jigulina, were shouting along to the accordion instrumental chorus.

The song ended, the lights came back on in full, the referee led the two teams out on to the pitch and the Betis supporters broke into an emotionally charged *a capella* rendition of 'Himno del Betis'. The whole of the Gol Sur tossed bags of green and white ticker tape left on our seats into the night sky. It was an amazing sight, lit up by the floodlights and somehow hanging in the air for an age. Huge clusters of the pieces of material mimicked the starling murmurations often seen over Rome between October and February. They appeared to float in the air long after the game had begun and, once they had settled, there were large piles on the stairs to my side that you noticed the trainers wading through them as supporters came and went.

Given the ferocity of the pre-match scenes in the streets of Heliópolis and the atmosphere created inside the Benito Villamarín for the players' emergence on to the playing surface, the opening minutes of the game were subdued with few bone-shaking tackles or attempts from the home supporters to urge their heroes towards the opposition goal, seeking to strike an early blow on their neighbours.

On seven minutes, Real Betis attacker Nabil Fekir tried his luck with a soft effort from long range that Sevilla goalkeeper Yassine Bounou, aka 'Bono', saved with ease. But where the faintest opportunity would sometimes incite the crowd, the *Béticos* were not budging from their conservative approach. That was until a cross-shot midway through the first period almost caught Bono unprepared and sparked the home supporters into life, with the 'punta Sevilla' chants reverberating around the stadium. Then, on 26 minutes, everyone, even the Sevilla fans from what I could gather, rose to their feet and applauded as the name of Miguel 'Miki' Roqué Farrero displayed on the giant screens at either end of the stadium.

In March 2011, the then 22-year-old was diagnosed with pelvic cancer. Despite the fundraising of fans and a €30,000 contribution from Barcelona captain Carles Puyol to finance specialist treatment, the former Liverpool defender lost his battle with the illness just over a year later, in June 2012.

The moment of alliance between the bitter rivals, albeit brief, was understandable given the heartache suffered by the Sevilla fans when losing promising full-back Antonio Puerta. On 25 August 2007, just 35 minutes into the opening game of the 2007/08 La Liga campaign against Getafe CF, Puerta suffered a cardiac arrest, at the Ramón Sánchez-

Pizjuán Stadium. The defender had lost consciousness and was substituted, but collapsed again while in the dressing room and died three days later in the hospital.

The first incident of an on-pitch tragedy in Spain and for Sevilla came on 7 January 1973 when striker Pedro Berruezo Martín died of a heart attack during a league match against Pontevedra. He is now honoured with a bronze carving at the Sánchez-Pizjuán. Fresh in the minds of Sevilla fans, though, was former captain José Antonio Reyes. The striker had left the club to sign for Arsenal in January 2004, but returned in 2012 and won a hat-trick of Europa League trophies with them. Tragedy struck Reyes on 1 June 2019 when the 35-year-old died in a car accident just outside Seville.

The clubs have not always displayed a united front in the aftermath of tragedy, though, with the Real Betis board members refusing to hold a minute's silence for Francisco Antúnez after his death in 1994. The midfielder controversially left Betis for Sevilla in 1945, and the ensuing 50 years had done little to soften the ill feeling towards him.

Our moment of solidarity was brief as a Sevilla player clattered into an opponent, heading for the corner flag, in an act intended to intimidate rather than stop any imminent threat on their goal. That incited many around me, who rose from their seats and screamed obscenities (I assumed from the gestures) and instigated another round of 'punta Sevilla' chants. Rather than stemming from the outrage of the unpunished tackle from the Sevilla defender, it felt they were attempting to deflect their displeasure at the home side being dominated by the visitors.

Croatian midfielder Ivan Rakitić became the latest to go close with a header just over the crossbar, before Sevilla should have taken the lead on 38 minutes. Full-back Gonzalo Montiel broke at pace down the right wing and fizzed a low cross along the six-yard box, but despite Claudio Bravo diving past the ball it struck the heel of a Sevilla attacker and rolled back in the direction it came from to another Betis defender. Former Barcelona goalkeeper Bravo was screaming with rage at his team-mates and, while several of them were no doubt at fault, it was a classic case of a stopper refusing to take some share of the blame.

The Betis defence held firm until the break but not without suffering a minor setback. In injury time, Sevilla striker Rafael Mir Vicente looked to have created space to break through on goal only to be stopped illegally by defensive midfielder Guido Rodríguez. The foul brought the Argentine a second yellow card of the match and left his team to spend the interval contemplating another 45 minutes a player light.

My only thought was to locate the nearest toilet. The volume of alcohol consumed and continually dropping temperature was increasing the frequency with which I needed to relieve myself. It was an issue being experienced by hundreds of others judging by the queue and, if unable to contain themselves, using the bathroom basins. Even the water fountain was used as a makeshift toilet.

Within minutes of the restart, Sevilla asserted themselves once more and nearly opened the scoring when Marcos Acuña – who appeared for Sporting CP when I visited Lisbon in 2018 – saw a shot fly just wide of the post. The Argentine left-back had better luck on 55 minutes, arriving at a ball cut back to the edge of the box and firing a rasping drive through a crowd of players beyond a helpless Bravo. The goal sent the congregation of Sevilla fans in the distance into wild celebration.

The Betis supporters attempted to remain upbeat and rally those around us, but with little success. Each time the visitors regained possession, a chorus of whistles reverberated around the stadium and the occasional pro-Betis song could be heard in the background. Their encouragement was more in hope than expectation that a comeback was imminent.

I had shrunk into my seat by that point as the bitter Andalusian night consumed me, and I started regretting my earlier decision of a lightweight jacket rather than a more substantial coat. Substitute Cristian Tello provided some fresh attacking impetus and the ex-Barcelona man sliced a shot on 71 minutes that could, had it at least tested Bono, have whipped the crowd back into a frenzy. After that brief sign of hope, though, Betis were the creators of their own downfall and handed the points to their neighbours.

With less than ten minutes remaining, Betis conceded possession in midfield once more and Montiel was released down the right wing. The defender drove towards the byline and crossed low, just as he had done late in the first half, and on-loan defender Héctor Bellerín stumbled clumsily towards the ball. Caught somewhere between controlling the ball and kicking it out of touch, the ball struck his shin with such force that it looked from the other end of the stadium as if he had intentioned on firing an unstoppable effort past Bravo. The only thing moving quicker as the Betis net rippled was the stream of supporters heading for the exits.

I noticed the Sevilla fans had organised a handful of white banners across their section's lower rows, and I could just make out from my position 'NO CONQUISTAS GOL SUR, VAS A CONQUISTAR SEVILLA' (You don't conquer Gol Sur, [how] are you going to conquer Seville). There had been a recent power struggle and battles within the Gol Sur section of the Villamarín, Enrique explained. The United Family group, who formed around 2012, were challenging the Supporters Gol Sur. Four days earlier the groups had clashed in Germany Ahead of *Los Verdiblancos'* match with Bayer Leverkusen in some of the most violent fighting he had witnessed first-hand.

Given how high hopes were ahead of the match, it was understandable that disappointed Betis supporters were leaving, so I expected the greater outpouring of anger to be aimed towards the team, not them. As they walked out, a middle-aged man rose from his position a couple of seats to my right and was aggressively pointing and screaming at them, questioning their decision to leave. He had a point. With nine minutes plus injury time remaining, recovering a two-goal deficit at home was not impossible. Even if the previous 81 minutes didn't convince many, it could happen.

Just before normal time ended, Tello sent a curling free kick from 25 yards sailing just past the post and had those remaining gasping. The tormented Real Betis supporters got something to celebrate just after that, with Joaquín rising from the substitutes' bench to extend the all-time appearance record in the fixture. Even during a painful defeat to your bitter rivals, fans will find the energy to stand and applaud one of their legendary players.

Walking the few steps to the exit gate, I turned for one last look at the Benito Villamarín and was drawn to the Sevilla fans at the other end of the stadium, holding their scarves aloft in unison and singing joyfully. The sounds of the visiting supporters provided the background noise as thousands of silent Betis fans shuffled down the concrete stairwells.

After emerging on to the street outside, a quick look at my watch to see that it was well past 11pm reminded me how late the Spanish enjoy many activities. That would be difficult to adjust to should we ever move there. With the roads now full of cars heading home, the night sky had a tint of red from the many brake lights showing the way back to the city centre.

I weaved between the vehicles with care and reached for my smartphone to make one last voice note (which on several listens suggested my alcohol consumption had taken its toll). As I left the stadium, I developed a case of the hiccups, which accompanied me throughout my journey back to my accommodation. With a distinct lack of fans following me north, despite several residential areas at that end of the city, maybe the Betis supporters knew a better or quicker way than I.

As well as the hiccups, my throat was sore from the constant smoke plumes surrounding us earlier in the evening. So when a branch of Burger King came into view, an ice-cold milkshake seemed like the perfect remedy to both soothe my hoarse throat and attempt to resolve the hiccups. I just made it in time to order, but they kicked me out soon afterwards. As one day ended and another began, I found a bench to take a moment to reflect on a wonderful night (result excluded), and completing the last leg of my travels. Or so I thought.

11

Merseyside Derby – Liverpool, England

WHEN VARIOUS publications have listed the greatest ever derby fixtures, they had always placed the Merseyside derby between Liverpool and Everton near the top of the rankings, even including Premier League rivalries outside of a single city. As an Anfield regular since childhood, though, that my impartiality might transfer itself to these pages, provided the perfect excuse to exclude the encounters from this book.

That was before the opportunity arose to attend the encounter, deep within the confines of the home supporters, at Goodison Park in late 2021. Undercover, of course. Presenting a rare chance to witness the contest from a previously unseen perspective than my usual place on the Kop at Anfield.

On 24 November 2021, as I made my way back from the Reds beating FC Porto in the UEFA Champions League group stage, I received a call from a close friend, Paul McDonald, asking if I would still consider using his son's Everton season ticket as work commitments meant he could not attend, and the Toffeemen's[70] recent form – winless in seven games and languishing in 14th place – had left few Blues fans eager to attend. Under Jürgen Klopp, Liverpool were challenging for the league title and had breezed through to the knockout rounds in Europe with a 100 per cent record. I had half joked a few weeks earlier that, if either Paul or his son could not make it, it might be quite nice to get back to Goodison Park.

The rivalry between the two clubs is as old as Liverpool Football Club itself. In 1878, when John Houlding helped establish Everton Football Club, they quickly began playing fixtures at Anfield, the Reds' current home. The local businessman then had a row with other members. Houlding wanting the club to purchase the land they had been renting, but they refused his proposal. With payments set to increase, Everton moved less than a mile across Stanley Park to Goodison Park, leaving Houlding with a problem to fix. He did that by creating Liverpool Football Club in 1892.

For the next 130 years, you could describe their clashes as passionate and often aggressive, and, until the late 1970s, evenly matched on the pitch.[71] An unspoken transfer embargo has always appeared to exist on both sides, Liverpool not purchasing from Everton between 1959 and 2000 and no players heading in the opposite direction from 1961 until 1982. The fixture became labelled as the 'friendly derby', though, as supporters from opposite sides of the divide would regularly sit together at matches, and loyalties often were split

---

70 Mother Nobletts Toffee Shop was located near Goodison Park and, after the success of sweets sales at fixtures, invented the 'Everton Mint'. These became an instant favourite of the crowd, and the Everton Toffee Lady distributing these before games became tradition

71 In 1973 Liverpool won the UEFA Cup and began a period of European success, with six major continental trophies captured in 11 years, and then became the dominant domestic force of the 1980s

across families. I rarely heard or witnessed violent clashes between the two fanbases.

Any animosity often presents itself through the teasing or ridiculing of the other side, during a period of dominance or after emerging from an encounter victorious, similarly to how some had described the rivalry between the two Genoese clubs. The closeness of the two sets of supporters and competitiveness of both teams in the 1980s was emphasised by the four (one a replay) domestic cup finals that decade, including the emotionally charged 1989 FA Cup Final in the wake of the Hillsborough tragedy which caused the unlawful killings of 97 Liverpool fans who attended the semi-final against Nottingham Forest. The city came together in collective mourning and solidarity, with the Reds prevailing 3-2 after extra time at Wembley Stadium, arguably the best outcome of a horrifying couple of months for Merseyside.

I grew up in that environment, but Paul, 12 years my senior, remembers those times more vividly and even attended the derby at Anfield on 3 April 1999 alongside me, with his Everton shirt on full display in the Main Stand when rising from his seat to celebrate Olivier Dacourt giving the Toffees the lead within 41 seconds. It prompted actress Sue Johnston in the row in front to give a cry of, 'Sit down, blue nose!' and resulted in much laughter and chuckling from the surrounding spectators, almost all cheering for the red half.

Paul would struggle to go unnoticed, even if he was not an imposing 6ft 2in tall, and like me he has no trouble striking up conversations with strangers and quickly becomes the life and soul of most social gatherings while his wife Debbie often watches on through her fingers. Paul is what you would call a diehard Everton fan, refusing to drink from Liverpool mugs while visiting, and he asks for our branded merchandise to be moved out of his way, such as a handful of cushions scattered across our sofa.

He could not even bear to stay until the end of my wedding because he knew the 'You'll Never Walk Alone' anthem, performed ahead of every Liverpool home fixture, would get played last. That was mainly for my benefit, but also a nod to those of the blue faith in attendance.

When we first visited Paul and Debbie, after his career took them to California, United States, I knew both he and son Cameron 'Everton' McDonald would wear Everton shirts when we arrived at Los Angeles International Airport. That forced me to wear Liverpool colours for the flight out. When we reached their home, an Everton flag was hanging from the garage door and branded towels were provided for us!

In recent years the atmosphere between some within the two fanbases has soured, something I find prominent in those under 30 years of age.

Everton won the FA Cup against Manchester United on 20 May 1995. As their last major trophy to date, though, it has contributed to the increased rancour. Liverpool supporters take great pleasure in pointing out the accumulating years since that success, but what may have been playful mocking now incites Toffees followers and has led to more aggressive confrontations. Should the Blues ever meet either Manchester club in a domestic final again, I'm no longer sure which of their hated rivals Reds fans would prefer to triumph.

There had been signs on the pitch of the increasing tensions after the Premier League began in 1992/93. Lots of the early encounters were a war of attrition, more often than not low on quality and resulting in the fixture holding the record for the most red cards since the championship rebranded.

With little to get excited about from a 250-mile journey made hundreds of times over 30-plus years, it seemed fitting that the day would involve a traffic jam on the M6 motorway. On this occasion it was no minor delay, as it brought us to an abrupt stop within 30 miles of Liverpool and did not move for just over two hours.

We eventually started moving and were diverted around the motorway – a 48-tonne lorry having come off the road – through a variety of country roads, which left us reaching our intended destination less than an hour before kick-off. The Premier League scheduling a fixture on a Wednesday night would usually add to our travel difficulties, but it also denied us time to enjoy the famous city.

Unlike the other locations visited, it is difficult to describe what I or others fall in love with about Liverpool, having spent so much time there since a youngster. The Albert Dock wows first-time visitors these days, since it was fully refurbished and reopened in the late 1980s, and the wide-ranging activities make it a major tourist hotspot. The night life within the city centre still holds a certain amount of charm through the vast number of places playing live music and an abundance of places to drink and be merry most, if not all, days of the week, while Liverpool never seems to run out of fresh places to enjoy a wonderful and diverse dining experience.

I think it is the people who keep visitors coming back, though. The collectiveness of the locals is often displayed during the most difficult periods, but also that distinctive Scouse humour continues to shine through, although some newcomers take time to get used to it. Myself and Stacey have few doubts that when we eventually stop travelling so much and get a little closer to retirement, or maybe sooner, Liverpool is where we will settle down.

After parking in a side street off Queens Drive, we set off at pace attempting to reach the Taxi Club on Walton Hall Avenue in time for Paul's traditional pre-match pint with friends and to gauge the feeling among the Goodison regulars considering their lowly league position and almost certain fight against relegation for the rest of the campaign, with former Liverpool manager Rafael Benítez enduring a tough start to life in the Everton hot seat and their rivals from across the park challenging for trophies, both domestically and abroad. The mood around the club was less than positive, but I saw room for optimism.

The Toffees were unbeaten during the last three meetings between the pair and the last of those, on 20 February 2021, had seen them defeat Liverpool 2-1 with goals from Richarlison and Gylfi Sigurðsson for their first win at Anfield in 21 years. Both fixtures were played behind closed doors, though, in the wake of the Covid-19 pandemic, which was another incentive to attend, despite knowing I would have to hide my emotions for 90 minutes.

I had not realised quite how demoralised and toxic things had become within the Everton fanbase, but I soon understood why Paul had warned me to sit on my hands and not look too out of place. With a crowd of 39,641, there must have been some hope that they could somehow achieve an unlikely victory.

Arriving at the Taxi Club, an imposing, if maturing, security guard politely advised us that, with the venue packed out, there was little chance that we would have time to purchase refreshments and drink them before the match started. That sent us turning back into the lightly falling rain and icy winds towards an equally ageing Goodison Park, the stadium lighting up the bitter December night.

Moving quickly through the turnstiles into the Howard Kendall[72] Gwladys Street End, I wondered whether an obvious unfamiliarity with the surroundings would expose me as a Liverpool supporter in hiding. With overseas fans a constant and increasing presence at every Premier League ground up and down the United Kingdom, I probably just looked like your average football tourist who blurs into the background through the general acceptance from most match-going regulars.

The last significant development work on the stadium came in 1994, coincidentally the last season in which they added silverware to their trophy cabinet. After such a long period, though, it was unsurprising that walking into the narrow concourse felt a little like stepping back in time with an excess of steel supports propping up the old stand and steel girders running horizontally from one end to the other.

Although it had undergone a refresh while closed to supporters during the pandemic, the royal blue and sunshine yellow colour scheme burst out against the grey concrete walls, with a hint of the 21st century through modern refreshment windows. The amount of concrete on display contradicted the 'Woodison Park' reference used by Liverpool supporters.[73]

As with most current stadia, Everton also littered the concourses with television screens which showed rolling sports news or displayed a wide range of merchandise, and alerted me to the food counters. As it had been seven hours

---

72 Howard Kendall was one of the most successful players and managers in Everton's history, appearing 276 times as a player and winning four major honours during his first spell as manager between 1981 and 1987

73 The two-tier Bullens Road Stand which houses away supporters at Goodison Park was designed by Archibald Leitch and completed in 1926, but retains the original wooden floors and distinctive balcony trusses

since Paul and I had enjoyed a leisurely breakfast just off the M40, it was only right that I rewarded him for an exhausting nine hours in the driver's seat, albeit if not always driving, with the delay.

I'm not sure I even saw him devouring a pie. As I shovelled a foot-long hotdog down my throat, my attention was also being drawn to the malicious songs being spouted by younger supporters filling the congested space.

With Paul having recently returned from over a decade living in America, it was nice for the chance to enjoy the fixture with Paul again. Supporting clubs on opposite sides of the divide, though, meant it was so much more difficult than our last joint experience 22 years before. It is unthinkable now that either of us could enter the other's regular drinking establishment wearing our own team's colours (not that I purchase shirts these days) or sit among home supporters without reprisal.

The signs that things were changing appeared back in 1999 when Liverpool striker and local hero Robbie Fowler responded to the ongoing speculation relating to recreational drug use and chants from the Everton away support with a controversial winning-goal celebration, using the pitch markings to mimic the snorting of a line of cocaine in front of the Toffee's fans. It eventually resulted in a short suspension by the Football Association. In contrast to what I was witnessing now, though, the outrage back then spilling down on to the England international as he lapped up the abuse seemed almost insignificant.

As I stood with a drink in hand, watching the bustling crowd passing through, the chant of 'murderers, murderers' rang out across the concourse, and was soon accompanied by the singing of 'you haven't killed Italians since 1985'. Plenty of the supporters remained tight-lipped, though.

That was a recent phenomenon, referencing the Heysel Stadium disaster at the European Cup Final between Liverpool and Juventus that year, when 39 spectators died and around 600 were injured after a wall collapsed on them as they tried to escape Liverpool fans, storming the terrace during widespread fighting around the Belgian arena. As English league champions, Everton would have been contesting the prize the following season but a five-year ban (six for Liverpool) by UEFA on British clubs competing in Europe ended the Toffees' hopes of lifting the famous trophy.

Despite the obvious difficulties and unpredictability of knockout competitions, many Blues supporters have been insistent that they would have won the competition. Some Liverpool fans also now use that as another thing to tease them with, pointing out that, from a similar position of strength, since the ban has been lifted they have won two further European Cups.

Having witnessed opposition supporters of other teams, both home and away, continuing to use the 'murderers' chant in reference to Hillsborough, I felt uncomfortable witnessing those with a passion for a club within the city of Liverpool uttering those words. As mentioned, the majority revelling in these derogatory songs were young, ranging from 18 to 35 years old, and simply following the flock.

Those at the latter end of that spectrum, old enough to have lived through years of the city fighting for justice, should know better. They would also know that the British government had already requested that the FA withdraw English sides from European competition. Had UEFA not acted, there could have been a much longer wait to rejoin continental club competition.

While the togetherness post-Hillsborough helped maintain relations between supporters across the city,

Everton's subsequent lack of success and flirtations with relegation to the second tier as Liverpool started challenging for silverware again has now severed most, if not all, of the goodwill left between them.

An older gentleman then emerged from a pocket of individuals and approached Paul, and immediately asked where Cameron was. With Paul explaining that he had felt uneasy asking for time off after starting a new job, I, somewhat nervously, blurted out, 'Good thing for me, as I got his ticket!' My delight at securing a ticket was no doubt obvious, and genuine, but probably seemed a little unusual before Paul had introduced us. I was trying too hard to fit in among the bubbling atmosphere.

The man was a season ticket holder who sat near Paul and, after years of disappointment and false dawns, seemed content with the likelihood that he had left the comfort and warmth of his home to do little more than watch a defeat for his team, proclaiming, 'It's a free hit, isn't it?' A feeling many supporters of all teams have had at one time, and it suggested that, while technically and tactically inferior, Everton had nothing to lose. He was at least expecting a performance full of desire and determination.

Keen to get to my seat and fade into the crowd, I headed up the few steps to see that the Liverpool fans had already filled most of the away section in the far corner to the left of me. With the rest of Goodison Park in a state of nervous anticipation, you could hear them loud and proud, singing joyful songs to support their team. It was at that point that I realised I was yet to catch any songs celebrating the Everton team or players, directed either at those currently pulling on the famous blue shirt or who had graced the famous turf. If they were not yelling anti-Liverpool chants or calling for the board to be sacked, I could only see most of the crowd standing in quiet contemplation, concerned about how bad a result they might be about to witness.

I took my place in the latter group, swaying a little in silence but along with the singing of the visiting fans and displaying little more than eyes and nose through a mix of scarf and woollen hat. The surrounding seats eventually filled up. A few empty spaces suggested to me that some had avoided a potential night of embarrassment or were standing elsewhere with friends, which happens when reasonable self-policing of safety allows movement around a terrace.

Liverpool fans still sing about the biggest victory in recent (at least my lifetime) memory in a Merseyside derby when their all-time top scorer, Ian Rush, netted four times at Goodison Park during a 5-0 triumph on 6 November 1982. The Reds had recorded four-goal winning margins three times in the last decade alone and with the most recent in the league during the successful 2019/20 Premier League campaign, Everton supporters would have feared the record being beaten as much as the travelling Liverpool supporters could have had confidence in it happening. When one side is dominant, these little details can liven up a local derby.

After a vociferous roar from the crowd when the Everton players emerged from the tunnel, the mood quickly became one of nervous excitement, if not anxiety. Liverpool controlled possession and started attacking the goal at our end of the stadium time after time. The home supporters appeared unable to cheer for their own players still, instead hurling insults at whichever visiting player was on the ball or at the opposing fans. This time, a chorus of 'show us your iPads, show us your iPads, you dirty tourist cunts' rang out around me.

When a Liverpool player required treatment after being fouled, it prompted several supporters to start aggressively articulating their desire to see the onrushing physios break their legs as they ran across the Goodison turf. It was all quite bizarre, but perhaps this was the disadvantage of speaking the language this time. Similar levels of vitriol were no doubt present during my foreign trips. An unhealthy level of hatred had consumed the stand, just as Paul had warned.

On nine minutes the inevitable happened as Liverpool captain Jordan Henderson opened the scoring with a curling left-footed effort from the edge of the box before wheeling away in celebration and halting his run at the Everton supporters in front of me. I rolled my eyes to the sky in apparent dissatisfaction at going behind, but I was smiling inside.

As his team-mates joined the England international, someone hurled a bottle of Beck's lager from the crowd, just missing left-back Andrew Robertson's head. That the Scottish defender's only reaction was to aim a mischievous grin towards his aggressors angered them even more than if he had reacted with fury. One row in front of me was a couple in their mid-30s, equally incensed. They had clearly been expecting the worst since their arrival and also only attended out of a sense of duty.

Ten minutes later, when Mohamed Salah sprinted past Lucas Digne on to a Henderson through ball and curled a delightful shot around Jordan Pickford to make it 2-0, they left without consulting each other as if agreed pre-match that they would exit at that very scoreline. They were not alone, with a widespread exodus from around the stadium, despite 70 minutes remaining. Suddenly there were 30 to 40 previously occupied seats now empty.

The Reds continued to dominate but could not extend their lead any further, and the Toffees took advantage. Demarai Gray raced through on goal on 38 minutes and fired a powerful shot that Alisson Becker could not stop, despite getting part of his body on the strike.

The remaining people jumping around me were enjoying the moment too much to notice that I had remained virtually frozen, apart from contorting my body in disappointment. I had been hoping that Everton's lifeless attack would save me the distress of having to celebrate a goal, but ultimately, my love for the visitors had rendered me motionless.

The goal brought a change in approach from the home supporters as it sparked a change of direction towards pro-Everton songs and, for a moment, I wondered how amusing it would be (providing Liverpool won, of course) if they equalised. All those who surged out of the stadium and heading home would have been fearing they might have missed the chance to celebrate a rare victory of their neighbours.

It remained 2-1 as the match reached half-time and, rather than face potential questions regarding my allegiance, I decided that a pint back in the concourse was the better option, discovering when I reached the bar that, although plenty of those who left on 20 minutes had exited the stadium, a significant number had been drowning their sorrows rather than watching on from the stands.

The late first-half goal had a galvanising effect on the Everton players, with visible signs of improvement when the second period got under way. Liverpool were still dictating play, though, and the hosts soon imploded in stunning fashion.

With 30 minutes to go, midfielder Andros Townsend saw a free kick just outside the Liverpool box deflected wide of goal. The 30-year-old then sent the resulting corner straight towards the first player between him and the goal, and the ball was cleared downfield. Blues captain

Seamus Coleman looked in control of the situation but stumbled in possession, allowing Salah to stride forward and make it 3-1.

The home crowd's toxicity returned to the surface and with an increased intensity, and the fans in our stand were given the perfect excuse to raise the level of rage already consuming the stadium with Alisson accidentally kicking the ball into the crowd when attempting to strike the advertising hoarding, in frustration at missing a routine catch.

An apologetic hand raised from the Brazilian international was invisible behind the anger of the supporters in close by, and a host of projectiles rained down on the South American. The police identified the culprit of one object and attempted to remove him from the stadium, but a scuffle broke out between several officers and supporters. Those around me then directed their fury at the officers aiming blows at their fellow fans, which they deemed an overzealous response.

Many were no longer interested in what was going on out on the pitch, other than ferociously screaming 'hit him, hit him' any time a Liverpool player took possession of the ball, reminding me why such games have a significant physical edge. As had been the case with plenty of the games I had witnessed, the vitriol from the terraces rolls down to the pitch and sometimes consumes the players.

The Liverpool supporters had long been singing the name of their former manager Benítez at this point and were taking great pleasure in the misfortune that had befallen their neighbours. When Diogo Jota added an impressive fourth goal on 79 minutes, those inside the stadium who stuck around stood in disbelief.

The Everton fans could no longer summon the energy to hurl insults at either side. One man in his 20s to my right, though, started sharing his displeasure so loud that a few of us became transfixed on his outburst. 'How are we sitting here and taking this?' he screamed, his voice crackling a little more each time he repeated the sentence and became angrier and more upset. He added a second line of 'I've gotta go to work with these tomorrow. Look at them! They're laughing at us!' In the background, a more collective chant of 'sack the board' became the backing track of his desperate pleas for others to take some sort of action.

I struggled to feel sorry for his plight, and not because of my support for the other side, but asking myself how someone so young could be in such distress at where Everton found themselves. They were too young to have been born, or at least remember, the last time they won a trophy. The Blues reaching the Champions League qualification places in 2005 was a rare occasion and a long-forgotten achievement, just like victories over Liverpool. The mediocrity, despite hundreds of millions of pounds spent, was an obvious disappointment I could at least understand.

When referee Paul Tierney blew the final whistle, several young Liverpool supporters ran on the pitch to goad the home supporters and were chased around the turf by stewards, eventually returning from where they emerged, while an Everton fan in his 40s also joined them.

In a peculiar interaction, he took around 20 paces towards the team benches, gesturing towards Benítez, the board in the seats above him and a couple of players still on the pitch. The stewards seemed to plead for him to return to the stand rather than force his removal, as did the police. He apparently got so far and then realised he didn't quite know what he was going to do should he reach a player, coach or director so he turned around, stepping back on to the terrace and walking away unchallenged.

Paul could not hide his disappointment as we headed out of Goodison. Despite expecting defeat, he wanted to see more desire from those in blue. As we emerged on to Walton Hall Avenue, two supporters started having a slanging match as they weaved in and out of slow-moving traffic. One foolishly suggested that Liverpool were too good for Everton to have had a chance of victory, which the other would not accept. It is the sort of conversation that is unproblematic if facing a high-flying Manchester City or Chelsea team, but not your local rivals, regardless of how good they might be.

Given the result, travel problems and the emotionally charged atmosphere, we no longer had any interest in squeezing in a beer and hearing more misery, and embarked on the short drive to the Holiday Inn in Runcorn, thankful that we didn't have another five hours or more driving ahead of us.

Luckily for Paul, we took long enough leaving the city to miss the start of *Match of the Day*, so we settled down with a couple of beers at the hotel having saved him having to relive the trauma of the last few hours.

12

That Frequently Asked Question

THE ONE constant throughout this process and while on my travels was the same question asked countless times. It could be straight after returning from a trip, while explaining to friends, family or colleagues what I had been doing, or meeting supporters at the matches the preceding pages have detailed. It was almost always guaranteed to arrive, though.

Which fixture was or is the best? Or the slight variation, which game did you enjoy the most?

They are difficult, near-impossible questions to answer, more so when asked on the spot by the supporters I met in the process of writing this book. At that moment, I would feel my lips shape to deliver my response as the fans often looked at me similarly, waiting to pounce on my reply with sense of anticipation in their eyes or an open-mouthed air of expectancy staring back at me.

I would get the hint of a wry smile breaking in the corner of their mouths, almost acknowledging they knew just how difficult a task they had set me to answer. I found it was better not responding, saying 'this one, of course', or just diverting their attention elsewhere. An unexciting, yet predictable, response, you might think.

The honest answer is that I do not know which one I have enjoyed most. There were some things that I favoured or remember more fondly, whether that was the intensity of the atmosphere inside the stadium; a difficult yet satisfying journey to reach my destination; fun with supporters at games; and even, if rarely, the action on the pitch.

The most pleasing aspect without doubt, though, and touched upon in the acknowledgments, is the friendships formed over the last five years, and the willingness of others to help me in my quest. I have spoken to them all, via WhatsApp, social media channels or email, within the last 12 months, and not just to confirm quotes and details for this book. As I sat down to revise this chapter, Enrique from Seville messaged, inviting me to watch some football together in the wake of favourable UEFA Champions League and Europa League draws for our teams.

Guillermo, from Lisbon, contacted me in April 2022 to invite me along to watch his hometown club GD Estoril Praia when visiting his city to watch Liverpool in the Champions League. Then he thanked me the week after, when I was back on Merseyside, for the Reds knocking Benfica out, while we had also celebrated together (virtually at least) the respective 2019/20 title triumphs of Liverpool and Sporting CP.

The bond made with others while experiencing their most intense fixture of a season left me no choice but to follow the fortunes of the team I supported on the day because I want those friends and acquaintances to experience the footballing highs, and I can picture in my mind their ecstatic faces if clinching an unexpected trophy, as with Real Betis's Copa del Rey success on penalties in April 2022.

The one exception is Buenos Aires. While Sam Kelly, Tom Nash and others made the trip so enjoyable, so generous with their time and knowledge, I could not warm to River Plate as a team or club. Maybe a deep admiration for Diego Maradona or growing up in an underappreciated area brought more affection for the club of the social underclass, Boca Juniors. Walking around their La Bombonera home just for a tour made me desperate to return and experience a fixture at the famous stadium, and I will go back as soon as possible.

Cities like Buenos Aires are another contributing factor to any ranking I could try to assign. I fell in love with the Argentine capital but the Covid-19 pandemic foiled an attempt to celebrate a milestone birthday (you can probably guess which) there in 2021. While it was difficult to immerse myself in the people and the culture during such fleeting visits, they still have a massive impact, even within the first 24 hours, because of the weather, ambience, people or the food, as is almost certainly the case with me.

The locations and rivalries also displayed so many similarities that are hard to ignore. Many cities were major ports at one time, helping turn them into significant parts of their country's history, and bring a financial dominance that helped fuel a deep hatred and often long-term success of one side. The rich/poor narrative was present in most, but only in Budapest, Lisbon, Liverpool, Rio and Seville had there been a recent long period of dominance of one club.

Then there are the visual similarities between the teams. As someone who grew up with the off-the-shelf blue and red Subbuteo teams of the 1980s, that colour scheme had filled my subconscious as a must for traditional battles. Therefore, I found it a strange coincidence that four sides played in green and white stripes or hoops, witnessing the green and white of Sporting CP, Celtic and Ferencváros in consecutive trips, and then Real Betis at the end. It still feels weird considering how few teams my mind wants me to think exist competing in those colours. That three, yes three, clubs had a live eagle swooping down ahead of fixtures was odd.

Each game had a special moment or two. The *Derby della Lanterna* saw Sampdoria all but mathematically relegate Genoa, which had been a historical element of the fixtures and the penalty save from Emil Audero is now being immortalised on flags and banners. There were many additional fixtures I got to undertake in Istanbul, Buenos Aires, Belgrade and Rio de Janeiro, where I had to navigate one of the most deprived areas to watch Vasco da Gama. In the Serbian capital I made a significant dent in their craft ale stocks, which is a fast-growing hobby of mine. Access to the ultras in Budapest, Lisbon and Seville continued to outdo each other, while the fun alongside the Real Betis supporters around the streets of Heliópolis was a perfect ending (kind of) that will live long in the memory. I could not squeeze others in.

By the time you have finished reading this, the preparation will have already started on identifying another set of same-city derbies to further expand my footballing knowledge and experience.

Bibliography

Books

Anderson, Chris and Sally, David, *The Numbers Game: Why Everything You Know About Football is Wrong* (Penguin, 2014)

Bellos, Alex, *Futebol: The Brazilian Way of Life* (Bloomsbury Publishing, 2014)

Downie, Andrew, *Doctor Sócrates: Footballer, Philosopher, Legend* (Simon & Schuster UK, 2018)

Foer, Franklin, *How Football Explains the World* (Cornerstone, 2006)

Inglis, Simon, *The Football Grounds of Britain* (CollinsWillow, 2016)

Jones, Tobias, *Ultra: The Underworld of Italian Football* (Head of Zeus, 2020)

Kennedy, David, *The Man Who Created Merseyside Football: John Houlding, Founding Father of Liverpool and Everton* (Rowman & Littlefield Publishers, 2020)

Kuper, Simon, *Football Against the Enemy* (Orion Publishing, 1996)

McAteer, Jason, *Blood, Sweat and McAteer: A Footballer's Story by Jason McAteer* (Hachette Books Ireland, 2017)

McManus, John, *Welcome to Hell?: In Search of the Real Turkish Football* (Orion Publishing, 2018)

Millar, Colin, *The Frying Pan of Spain: Sevilla v Real Betis: Spain's Hottest Football Rivalry* (Pitch Publishing, 2019)

Smyth, Rob, *Kaiser: The Greatest Footballer Never To Play Football* (Yellow Jersey, 2018)

Souness, Graeme, *Football: My Life, My Passion* (Headline Book Publishing, 2017)

Wilson, Jonathan, *Angels With Dirty Faces: The Footballing History of Argentina* (Orion Publishing, 2017)

Wilson, Jonathan, *Behind the Curtain: Football in Eastern Europe* (Orion Publishing, 2006)

Wilson, Jonathan, *Inverting the pyramid: The History of Football Tactics* (Weidenfeld & Nicolson, 2018)

Wilson, Jonathan, *The Names Heard Long Ago: How the Golden Age of Hungarian Football Shaped the Modern Game* (Blink Publishing, 2019)

Wilson, Jonathan, *The Outsider: A History of the Goalkeeper* (Orion Publishing, 2013)

Newspapers and magazines
Ahval News
AS
Bloomberg UK
Daily Record
El Mundo
El Pais
FourFourTwo
Hirado
Nemzeti Sport
Nottingham Post
Ripost
Telegraf
The Guardian
The Independent
The New York Times
The Telegraph
The Times
The Scotsman
World Soccer

Websites

https://abouthungary.hu
https://betisbohemio.es
https://dialectik-football.info
https://football-italia.net
https://gencfb.org
https://hungaryultras.blogspot.com
https://mymodernmet.com
https://news.bbc.co.uk
https://thesefootballtimes.co
https://weloveyoueverton.blogspot.com
https://www.besoccer.com
https://www.espn.co.uk
https://www.fedelissimi61.it
https://www.fluminense.com
https://www.footballfancast.com
https://www.footballhistory.org
https://www.haber61.net
https://www.hungarianfootball.com
https://www.insideworldfootball.com
https://www.kurir.rs
https://www.maccabi-tlv.co.il
https://www.marca.com
https://www.mirror.co.uk
https://www.sportskeeda.com
https://www.theplayerstribune.com
https://www.toffeeweb.com
https://www.ultras-tifo.net
https://www.worlddata.info